Table of Contents

Contributors

This book is the product of years of study, work and effort from not only myself, but from the team at Devslopes.

This particular version could not have been released without the help of Jason Brewer and Nathan Brewer. Jason is a full time software engineer and technical writer. He is responsible for all of the editing and formatting of the book. Nathan is a full time iOS developer who spent many hours reviewing each project in the book and ensuring that they met best practices.

I would also like to give a special thanks to the 350,000+ students who have learned from Devslopes and who have gone on to do great things. We couldn't do this without your support!

Mark

Welcome to the world of programming and iOS development. Learning to code can be tough. I taught myself how to write code in 2007 completely on my own. It was one of the most difficult experiences of my life. Resources were few, and support was non-existent.

Today is a lot different. Learning to code is now a *"thing"* and resources are everywhere. You have been set on a path for success. That doesn't mean that learning how to code is going to be easy. It probably won't be. You are going to get discouraged. You are going to tell yourself, *"I don't have the brain for this"* and you're going to want to give up. You will run into cyber-coder bullies who will belittle your skills and tell you that unless you have a degree in computer science, you aren't a *real* programmer.

I want to give you some advice to keep you on the straight and narrow when discouragement sets in:

1. Don't **ever** compare yourself to other programmers. Compete against yourself. Someone will always be more skilled than you.
2. You do belong here in the world of programming – no matter what anyone says. You have unique talents as a programmer and human being that others will not have.
3. If the learning is painful and your brain feels broken, then you are doing it right. Pain brings growth.

Programmers can live rewarding lives. I have spent over half of my programming career working from home. That meant more time with my family and also meant I could go to the movie theater whenever the heck I wanted.

Become a good programmer and you will have the chance to live whatever lifestyle you want. Whether that be a lifestyle with more personal time and freedom or whether that means receiving a big fat paycheck working for top companies – or perhaps both!

The last and most important thing I could ever tell you as you are learning how to code is this - Learn **every** single day and do some hands-on coding **every** single day.

Ready. Set. Go.

Mark Wahlbeck

Chapter 1: Installing Xcode

Canvas is to the artist as Xcode is to the iOS Developer. It serves as our workspace, creative outlet, source of frustration and more.

What you will learn

- How to install Xcode
- Opening Xcode

Key Terms

- `Xcode`: an integrated development environment created by Apple to allow for the creation of software and apps.

Xcode is an amazing application. It is a fully-loaded suite of tools that empowers developers to build apps for iOS, tvOS, WatchOS, macOS and more. As you will see, it is simple to install and get started with minimal fuss.

Going to the macOS App Store

To begin, open the macOS App Store and in the search bar in the top right, type `Xcode` and press `Enter` to search for it.

Once the results load, Xcode will be the first result. Next, click `GET` and enter your Apple ID information to begin downloading it. Bear in mind that it is a massive application (>4.5 GB) and after installation takes up nearly 12 GB.

Opening Xcode

To open Xcode, all you need to do is go into your Applications folder and click `Xcode`. It's that simple, really.

Once Xcode opens up, you will be presented with the 'Welcome to Xcode' screen which gives you several options to select. This will be our launchpad for all projects in this book. You will open Xcode and create projects from here. Once you understand the Xcode interface, you will see just how powerful it can be as you build your apps.

Wrapping up

This chapter was ridiculously short and for good reason – Apple has made our job easy by creating such a streamlined experience. The barriers to beginning iOS development are so few nowadays that we can get started with just a few clicks.

Chapter 2: Intro to Swift

Apple has always been on the cusp of new technologies. When they released Swift, (some of) the world cheered.

What you will learn

- What is Swift?
- What makes Swift different
- The future of Swift
- Variables
- Constants
- Types
- Collection Types
- Control Flow
- Conditionals
- Functions

Key Terms

- `Syntax:` the specific structure and order of a programming language.
- `Safe:` a characteristic of Swift which means that it is less prone to syntax errors or other compile-time errors.
- `Fast:` a characteristic of Swift which means that it is performs quickly and is efficient in nature.
- `Expressive:` a characteristic of Swift which means that it's syntax is easily readable.

Swift is Apple's baby. According to Swift.org:

> *Swift is a general-purpose programming language built using a modern approach to safety, performance, and software design patterns.*

If you don't come from a computer science or programming background you may be thinking, "That's neat. BUT WHAT DOES IT MEAN?"

Trust us when we say that it means that your learning-to-code life will be much easier than it could be.

Swift is an excellent first programming language to learn as it's syntax is generally easy to follow. There are also a ton of resources online (i.e. tutorials, YouTube videos, blogs, forums, etc.) to help you learn Swift.

Swift Foundations

Variables

Every programming language uses variables. They are like a container which allows you store data of many different types.

To declare a variable you must use the keyword `var`:

```
var message: String = "Hello, World!"
```

What we've just written tells our computer that we want to create a container (variable) with the name `message` of type `String` which contains the text "Hello, World!"

Something amazing about Swift is that it includes a feature called Type Inference. This means that Swift can analyze the data inside a variable is (text, number, true/false, etc.) and infer it's type.

To test this, simply remove `String` after declaring the variable `message`:

```
var message = "Hello, World!" //Type-Inferred String
```

As you can see above, we never explicitly told our computer that we wanted `message` to be a `String` but because of the quotes around `Hello, World!`, Swift can infer it's type.

Variables are called variables because, well, they are variable - their value can be changed.

For example, if we wanted to change the value of our `message` variable we would need to write the name of our variable and change it's value like so:

```
var message = "Hello, World!"

message = "Hello, Swift!"
```

Now **message** is equal to "Hello, Swift!".

Constants

Sometimes, there are values where you don't want a certain value to ever change. A date like your birthday, the version number of your application, or the name of your hometown for instance.

In Swift, we call these values constants.

To declare a constant, you must use the keyword `let`.

If we were to change the keyword **var** to the keyword `let` in our example above we would be presented with an error because we cannot modify a constant.

```
let greeting = "Hello, World!"

greeting = "Hello, Swift!" // Error
```

Types

String

So far, in the code above we've only referred to values of type `String`. A `String` can be used to hold textual data.

Strings are also powerful in how they can be modified or even convert and hold other types of values.

For example we can use String Concatenation to combine several `String` values together using the + operator.

```
let album = "Nevermind"

let artist = "Nirvana"

let review = " is amazing!"

let description = "The album " album + " by " + artist +
review
```

```
//description = "The album Nevermind by Nirvana is
amazing!"
```

Another neat thing we can do is use String Interpolation to encapsulate other variables and pass them into a `String` value when we want.

```
let birthday = "April 1, 1976"

let bio = "My birthday is \(birthday)."

// bio = "My birthday is April 1, 1976."
```

You can even pass in values that are not of type `String` and Swift can convert them.

Int
The keyword `Int` is short for Integer. In math, an integer is most basically defined as a whole number.
    We can use an `Int` value in a variable or a constant:

```
var age: Int = 43 // Explicitly declared Int

var salary = 920000 // Type-inferred Int

let birthYear = 1976

let daysInAYear = 365
```

Bool
The keyword `Bool` is short for Boolean. Booleans are simply true and false values. Just like all the above types, you can explicitly declare a variable of type `Bool` or let Swift infer it's type by setting the value of a variable to be either `true` or `false`.

```
var isFinishedLoading = true // Type-inferred

var dataLoaded: Bool = false // Explicit
```

Double / Float
A `Double` is a number value similar to the type beneath it - `Float`. The difference between the two is how precise you can be.

A `Double` is a 64-bit floating point number value which can be as precise as 15 decimal digits.

A `Float` is a 32-bit floating point number value which can be precise to 6 decimal places.

As you can see, a `Double` is more precise than a `Float`.

```
var intersectVersion = 2.0  // Type-inferred Double
```

Something to note: Swift defaults to type-infer decimal values as a `Double`, not `Float`. To declare a variable of type `Float`, be explicit:

```
var intersectVersion: Float = 2.0
```

Most of the time, you will be using `Double` values in Swift (and in this book).

Collection Types

In Swift, there are two different ways to store collections of values - `Array` and `Dictionary`.

Array

An array is a collection of values which are organized by index. The index is the count of how many objects there are inside of the array.

In Swift, zero-indexing is used meaning that the first item in the array actually has an index of 0. From then on, the number increases by one.

Defining an Array

Arrays are always written inside of brackets. Each value is separated by a comma.

```
var unoCards: [String] = ["Skip", "Wild", "Wild + Draw
Four"] // Explicitly-declared Array of Strings
```

```
var unoCards = ["Skip", "Wild", "Wild + Draw Four"] //
Type-inferred as [String]
```

Arrays can contain values of a single type like the one above, but you also can include multiple types in an array.

To get the value for a single item from our array, we need to do the following:

. . .

```
print(unoCards[0]) // Prints
```

Using `print`, we can print the value of the first item (at index 0) in our `unoCards` array - "Skip".

Modifying an Array

I am going to create an array with a grocery list.

```
var groceryList = ["Milk", "Eggs", "Cheese"]
```

To add an item to our list, we simple use the `.append()` function in Swift:

```
var groceryList = ["Milk", "Eggs", "Cheese"]


groceryList.append("Marshmallows")


//groceryList = ["Milk", "Eggs", "Cheese",
"Marshmallows"]
```

This will add the value "Marshmallows" to the end our `groceryList` array.

To add multiple items to our array, we can use the `.extend([])` function in Swift:

```
var groceryList = ["Milk", "Eggs", "Cheese"]


groceryList.append("Marshmallows")
groceryList.extend(["Oreos", "Quinoa"])
```

```
//groceryList = ["Milk", "Eggs", "Cheese",
"Marshmallows", "Oreos", "Quinoa"]
```

To insert an item at a certain point in an array, use the `.insert(_:atIndex:)` function in Swift:

```
var groceryList = ["Milk", "Eggs", "Cheese"]


groceryList.append("Marshmallows")

groceryList.extend(["Oreos", "Quinoa"])

groceryList.insert("Potatoes", atIndex: 2)


//groceryList = ["Milk", "Eggs", "Potatoes", "Cheese",
"Marshmallows", "Oreos", "Quinoa"]
```

The value "Potatoes" get added and has an index of 2. Remember, that Swift uses zero-indexing.

To change a single item in an array, subscript the item you want to change and give it a shiny new value.

. . .

```
groceryList[0] = "Bread"


//groceryList = ["Bread", "Eggs", "Potatoes", "Cheese",
"Marshmallows", "Oreos", "Quinoa"]
```

Dictionary

A `Dictionary` allows you to store data in pairs containing a key and a value. Just like a dictionary in a spoken/written language, each word has a definition. Comparing the two, in a Swift `Dictionary`, the key = word and the value = definition.

Look at the dictionary I have declared below:

```
var screenSizeInInches = ["iPhone X" : 5.8, "iPhone
XR" : 6.1, "iPad Pro" : 12.9]
```

To access the value of an item in a `Dictionary`, you could do the following:

```
print(screenSizeInInches["iPhone X"]) // Prints 5.8
```

Notice how I called the `Dictionary`, then inside of the brackets subscript, I included the `String` value for the key? After putting that inside the `print` function, it prints the value.

Modifying a Dictionary

Now, I want to add an iPad Air 2 to my array of screen sizes. To do this, we need to type the name of our array, add brackets as a subscript, and add a value inside the brackets to add the key. To add the value, we add an equals sign (=) and set the value we want.

```
screenSizeInInches["iPad Air"] = 10.5


//screenSizeInInches = ["iPhone X" : 5.8, "iPhone XR" :
6.1, "iPad Pro" : 12.9, "iPad Air" : 10.5]
```

Control Flow

Loops

There may be times where you'll want to loop through a collection of data and perform a certain task or do something while a certain condition is met.

There are 3 main loop types in Swift: `while`, `repeat-while`, and `for-in`.

The `while` loop

This, in my opinion, is the easiest loop to understand. It essentially states that while something is true, that it executes a block of code until it is false. Then it stops looping.

Here is an example:

```
var finished = false


while !finished {

    print("Loading...")

}
```

The code above means that while the variable `finished` is false, our code should print "Loading..." to the console. Note that the exclamation mark (!) before `finished` means the logical *not* and read as "not complete".

The `repeat-while` loop

The `repeat-while` loop operates very similarly to a regular `while` loop, with one key difference.

In a `repeat-while` loop, the code to be repeated is executed first, then the condition is checked to see whether or not the loop continues.

A `while` loop, the condition is checked first and that determines whether or not the code runs.

Here is an example:

```
var sum = 10


repeat {

    size = size + 1

} while size < 15
```

This loop will continue increasing the size by adding the value of `size` plus one until it reaches 15. The thing to remember here is that the condition is checked after the code loops.

There are opportunities where you need to run code before checking if a condition is met. The `repeat-while` loop is the way to make it happen.

The `for-in` **loop**

Another type of loop is `for-in`. It is used to iterate through a collection of data and perform an action to each item in that collection.

For example:

```
var unoCards = ["Skip", "Wild", "Wild + Draw Four"]


for unoCard in unoCards {

    print(unoCard)

}
```

The code above would iterate through each item in the **unoCards** array and print the name of each item until it reaches the end. Then, our loop terminates.

You also can loop through a range of values. In Swift, a range is denoted by two or three dots.

1...5 is an inclusive range of the numbers from 1 until 5. The three dots means that values will be 1, 2, 3, 4, and 5.

1..< 5 is a non-inclusive range of numbers from 1 until 4. The two dots and less-than sign indicates that the values considered will be 1, 2, 3, and 4.

Conditionals

If Statements

Sometimes you might want to create conditional code that only will execute under certain conditions. That is where the `if` statement becomes very useful.

Basically, they work like this: if `x` is true, then perform `y`.

For example:

```
let carModel = "Delorean"


if carModel == "Delorean" {

    print("Great Scott!")
```

```
} else if carModel == "Geo Metro" {

    print("It drives, right?")

} else {

    print("If it's got wheels and drives, it's a car!")

}
```

In the above statement, we've said that if the **carModel** is equal to "Delorean", that it should print a message to the console.

If it is equal to "Geo Metro", it should print a message specific to that model. Finally, if it is neither a Delorean or a Geo Metro (thank goodness), then we should print a generic message.

The **if** statement combined with **else   if** or **else** is frequently used.

If you have more than a few conditions to be met, then the next section will shed some light on what to do.

Switch Statements

The **switch** statement in Swift 3 is really useful for scenarios with multiple cases. Usually most decisions in code can be run through an "if/else" block, but for those that can't we can use a **switch** statement.

For example:

```
var unoCardValue = "Skip"


switch unoCardValue {
case "Skip":
    print("Skip") // "Skip" will be printed
case "Draw-Four":
    print("Draw-Four")
case "Reverse":
    print("Seven")
case "Wild":
```

```
    print("Wild")
default:
    print("No card selected!")
}
```

In the above example, we have set the value of `unoCardValue` to "Skip". We have created a `switch` statement and named it the same name as our variable.

Now when our value changes, it will be passed into our `switch` statement and if it meets one of our 5 conditions, it will run the code written for that case.

When creating a `switch` statement, you must be exhaustive and write a case for every possible scenario. If you don't need or want to do that, you can declare a `default` case at the bottom of the `switch` statement to handle any case that is not one of the cases you have written. Since the only value we're checking is a `String` which could be *anything*, we need to declare a `default` case since there are endless possibilities outside of our defined cases.

Functions

In Swift 3, we can write functions which are like a set of directions or code that can be written once and used in multiple places.

Basic Function

To create the most basic function we need to use the keyword `func` and give it a descriptive name to describe *what* it does.

For example:

```
func printName() {
    print("Devslopes")
}
```

Function With Parameter

The function above is great and all, but what if we want to print a name other than Devslopes?

We can pass in a parameter so that it can say any name by naming a parameter and giving it a type within the parentheses of our function.

Like so:

```
func printName(name: String) {

    print(name)

}
```

Now when we call our function, we can pass in a `String` value with the parameter `name` containing any name we want!

Function With Parameter and Return Value

Sometimes, you want to perform a function and return a value to a variable of some kind. To do this, you simply add the return type you want to return and ask the function to return the relevant value.

Here's an example:

```
var fullName = buildName(firstName: "Mark", lastName:
"Wahlbeck")
```

```
func buildName(firstName: String, lastName: String) ->
String {

    return "\(firstName) \(lastName)"

    // Returns "Mark Wahlbeck" to our variable above.

}
```

The function above requires two parameters - `firstName` and `last-Name`. When we pass in those values, we return a `String` to the variable `fullName` returning the full name.

Wrapping up

This chapter has been a flyover of the Swift programming language. I hope you can see how great it is, just by looking at it briefly. If you're completely new to programming, don't worry. If this is confusing or overwhelming, you're not alone. But, the most important thing at this moment is that you push through, remember that truly anyone can learn to code, and that you need to compete against yourself at this point to get better.

Chapter 3: Programming & Variables

In this chapter, we are going to talk about variables, operators, and a little bit about how computers work. This is not a theoretical book, but I do want you to understand some of the basic principles that are happening underneath the hood so that you can have a foundation to build upon.

What you will learn

- Creating your first variable
- Unary, Binary, and Ternary Operators
- Another variable example

Key Terms

- `Variable`: A container used in programming to store a value of some type.
- `String`: A stored value consisting of characters or words.
- `Boolean`: A stored value consisting of a true or false property.

`Variables` are used in programming to store information which can be referenced and manipulated in a computer program. They also provide a way of labeling data with a descriptive name so that our programs can be understood more clearly by other programmers and ourselves.

If it's helpful, think of a `variable` as a container that holds information, their sole purpose is to label and store data in memory which can later be used in your program.

This is a basic flyover of what a `variable` is and how it works, but now you will create some `variables` in Xcode to help you understand how they work in the context of software development.

Creating your first variable

First, open Xcode if you haven't already and click `Get started with a playground`. Choose a "Blank" playground and click `Next`.

Give it a name like *Variables*, and choose somewhere to save this .playground file and click **Create** to save it. You should see a screen like the one in Figure 1.3.1.

Figure 3.0

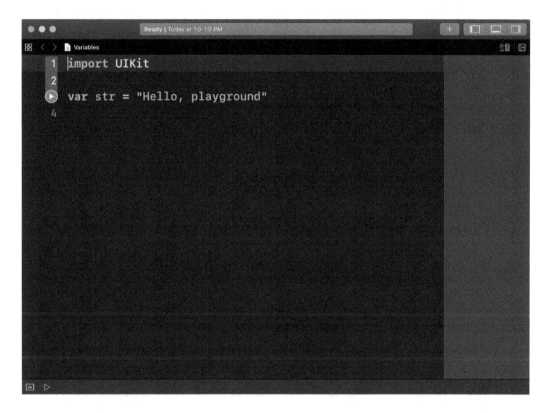

Playgrounds in Xcode are an amazing way to test code snippets to see if and how your code works. It's also a great way for me as an instructor to teach you basic coding principles in Swift.

By default, the Playground we just created already contains a **variable**. Figure 1.3.1 shows the code below:

```
var str = "Hello, playground"
```

Wherever you see **var**, that's short for **variable**. You're telling your computer that you want to create a **variable** (a container that you want to put data into). We can name it whatever we want for the most part, but some names are not allowed. For instance, we can't put numbers in front of a `variable` name (i.e. "2WeeksPay"), but you can use words first and then numbers (i.e. "day1").

```
var
```

In this case, let's use *message* as our `variable`'s name. `Variables` should always be descriptive and should tell you what's being stored in them.

```
var message
```

To give our `variable` a value, we need to use an equals sign just like in any math equation to show that our `variable` is equal to *something*.

```
var message =
```

We are storing some words in our `variable`, and the name for this is a `String`. To declare a `String`, you must use double quotes like so:

```
var message = "Insert String information here..."
```

The key term for what we have written in code here is `String Literal` because we have given our `String` an inherent value.

Later on, we will see how a `String` can be created with an empty value or no value at all.

Let's change the value of our `variable` **message** to be "Hello, playground".

This is your first `variable`. The data type is a `String`, made up of characters and words. That information will be stored in the `variable`.

Under the hood, this program is running on our mac, so it's actually being stored in the memory on the computer somewhere which is pretty cool! All of this is happening for us automatically.

So, in review we created a `variable` by specifying **var**, gave it a descriptive name, and then we gave it a `String` value of, "Hello, playground".

`Variables` can be changed as many times as you want. The data stored inside of them can change as our app needs it to. We'll talk about this more later on when we compare it with a `Constant`.

Unary, Binary, and Ternary Operators

For a moment, let's talk about Operators. There are 3 types of Operators in Swift - unary, binary, and ternary. But what the heck do these words mean?

Unary operators only only affect one target.

For example, you can create a `Boolean` (true/false value) which is called "amICool":

```
var amICool = true
```

Based on the code above, I am definitely cool.

Then say a new fad or trend comes out that I haven't started yet... So now I'm "uncool". Well, now we can use a unary prefix operator to change that:

```
var amICool = true

amICool = !amICool
```

A unary operator basically inverts the value of `amICool`, our `variable`. Now `amICool` is false because it is the opposite of `amICool`.

Sadly, I'm no longer cool because I didn't follow the new fad or trend.

Unary operators affect one target, but binary operates on two targets.

Binary operators operate on two targets.

They are seen regularly throughout code as most `variables` and constants rely on another value to do their work. Here are some examples:

```
var accountBalance = 9.00

var isBatmanAmazing = true

var officialJobDescription = "Mad Scientist & Rare
Cheese Connoisseur"
```

All of the above lines of code operate on two targets - the `variable` name (i.e. isBatmanAmazing) and the value following the equals sign (i.e. `true`).

Ternary operators affect three targets.

Now we are going to add another `variable` called *feelGoodAboutMyself* and set it's value to `true`:

```
var feelGoodAboutMyself = true
```

That's a `variable` and it's of type `Boolean`. We are storing the value `true` into this `variable`. Now let's use a ternary operator just for fun.

```
var feelGoodAboutMyself = true

feelGoodAboutMyself = amICool ? true : false
```

In a ternary operator, the question mark symbol (?) means "if" and the colon symbol (:) means "otherwise".

The code above means that if the value of `amICool` is `true`, then `feelGoodAboutMyself` should be set to `true`, otherwise it should be set to `false`.

It's a ternary operator because it works on 3 targets - `amICool`, `true`, and `false`.

`Helpful Tip:`
When you're programming, you're not going to use these terms, but if you're in an interview, they might ask you to define them, so they're good to know about!

Another variable example

In your Playground file, create a `variable` called *bankAccountBalance* and set it to equal 100.

```
var bankAccountBalance = 100
```

Next, create a `variable` named *cashRegisterMessage*. We want to have a message that will print out for someone who wants to buy something at a store.

```
var bankAccountBalance = 100

var cashRegisterMessage = "You are broke as a joke."
```

Now create a `variable` named *itemPrice* and set it's value to 60.

```
var bankAccountBalance = 100

var cashRegisterMessage = "You are broke as a joke."

var itemPrice = 60
```

We're also going to write a ternary operator to check if our bank account balance is greater than or equal to 50. If the operator returns `true`, then you are able to buy the item, otherwise, you can't buy the item because you are broke.

```
var bankAccountBalance = 100

var cashRegisterMessage = "You are broke as a joke."

var itemPrice = 60


bankAccountBalance >= itemPrice ? "Item purchased!" :
cashRegisterMessage
```

Now, change the price of the item to 150 and add in the following conditional if/else statement (more on these in a following chapter).

```
var bankAccountBalance = 100

var cashRegisterMessage = "You are broke as a joke."

var itemPrice = 150


if bankAccountBalance >= itemPrice {

    cashRegisterMessage = "Item purchased!"
```

```
    print(cashRegisterMessage)

} else {

    print(cashRegisterMessage)

}
```

What do you notice changed in the console output on the right-hand side of your Playground window? "You are now broke as a joke."

The if/else code above means that if the value of `bankAccount-Balance` is greater than or equal to the `itemPrice`, then `cashRegisterMessage` should be set to `"Item    purchased!"`, otherwise it should be set to the default message we set.

There are other operators that we'll learn about later such as math operators for adding, subtracting, multiplying, and dividing. There is even a remainder operator for doing division and getting only the remainder of the result. We will talk more about those later.

Wrapping up

This chapter was a flyover of how `variables` work and what a `variable` is. We talked about unary operators, binary operators, and ternary operators. You learned that you can create a container called a `variable` by starting with the keyword `var` and giving the container a descriptive name like *bankAccountBalance*.

You learned that you can store a value into that container such as a `string` (text), `boolean` (true/false), or even a number (integers/decimals). You can assign the value using the assignment operator (equals sign).

Finally, I want to encourage you to dig more into this! Search online for the three types of operators and look up what a `variable` is. It's important to know these things because you want to become a great programmer!

Exercise

Create 4 variables to hold these types of data:

- Your name (String)
- Your age (Int)
- The temperature in your location (Double)

- Something that is true about yourself (Bool)

Chapter 4: Functions

Functions are a core component in programming. They are building blocks in building functional applications. Functions help our code to be more readable, compartmentalized, and ultimately more efficient. We can write a function to perform a specific task and then reuse it at will throughout our application.

What you will learn

- Creating your first function
- Another function example
- Constants

Key Terms

- `Function`: a container for a block of code that performs a specific singular task.
- `Parameter`: a value passed into a function. Can be of any type.
- `Constant`: a value in code that cannot be changed.

Every day, most humans live their lives under a set of routines. Things they do often times without even thinking about or realizing that they're doing them.

Think about what you do when you first wake up. I know for myself, I slither out of bed and stumble across the room to my noisy phone and silence the alarm. That event alone contains several different steps that I follow in the same order every day (unless I forget to set my alarm).

1. Wake up to alarm sound
2. Slide out of bed, trying not to accidentally wake my wife.
3. Stagger my way over to my alarm.
4. Silence my alarm.

The steps above are a `function`. A set of steps that I complete over and over again (every morning). In pseudo code, this could look like:

```
var awake = false

var inBed = true

var walking = false

var alarmSilenced = false


func getUp() {

    awake = true

    inBed = false

    walking = true

    alarmSilenced = true

}
```

Functions run the code inside them *asynchronously*, or, in a top-to-bottom manner. How's that for a five-dollar word?

In other words, `awake` gets set to `true`, `inBed` gets set to `false`, `walking` gets set to `true`, and `alarmSilenced` gets set to `true` - in that order.

My waking up metaphor is imperfect however, because it takes me probably 10-15 seconds to fully wake up, walk over, and silence my alarm. Modern devices can process the code inside `functions` so quickly that it is almost as if it's running instantly, even though it is running asynchronously.

Most simply put, `functions` are a way to perform an operation over and over. You will use them throughout many of the advanced projects you will complete later on in this book.

But enough *talking* about `functions`... Let's write some!

Creating your first function

If you've taken any advanced math courses, you probably have some background knowledge regarding `functions`. You probably know them by another name: Formulas. You can use `L  x  W` (length multiplied by width) to calculate the area of a rectangle or a2 + b2 = c2 to determine the length of the hypotenuse of a right triangle.

We will create one of these formulas in Swift to illustrate how `functions` work.

First, open Xcode if you haven't already and click `Get started with a playground`. Choose a "Blank" playground and click `Next`.

Give it a name like *Functions*, and choose somewhere to save this .playground file and click `Create` to save it.

To declare a `function`, we need to:

1. Begin with the keyword `func`.
2. Give it a descriptive name, similarly to how we name variables.
3. Include a set of parentheses and inside that any parameters we want to pass in.

`4.)` Declare what value the `function` should return, if any.

In your Playground, type the following:

```
func calculateArea(length: Int, width: Int) -> Int {

//Code to calculate the area will go here.

}
```

As it currently exists, we have declared a `function` called `calculateArea(width:height:)`. There is no code inside our `function` and we are passing in a value for the length and width - both of type `Int`. We have also declared that we want to return a value of `Int` by typing `-> Int`. Let's add some code to calculate the area.

```
func calculateArea(length: Int, width: Int) -> Int {

    let area = length * width

    return area

}
```

Our `function` is now complete. We've created a `function` that calculates the area of a rectangle. We can pass in a value for the length and width (both are required) and the code inside the `function` multiplies them together to give us an area value.

We then `return` the value of `area` to our `function`. But in Playground, our `function` doesn't print to the console like it should.

That's because we haven't called it yet. We need to type the name of our `function` and pass in values for length and width so that Xcode knows to run the code inside.

At the bottom of your Playground window, call the `function` by typing it's name. Use Xcode's AutoComplete feature and press the **Enter** key when it pops up to make your life easier. Pass in a length of 10 and a width of 20.

```
func calculateArea(length: Int, width: Int) -> Int {

    let area = length * width

    return area

}


calculateArea(length: 10, width: 20)
```

To see the result of our `function`, look at the right-hand side of the Playground window (Figure 1.4.1) to see the value our `function` returns from our `area` variable.

Figure 4.0

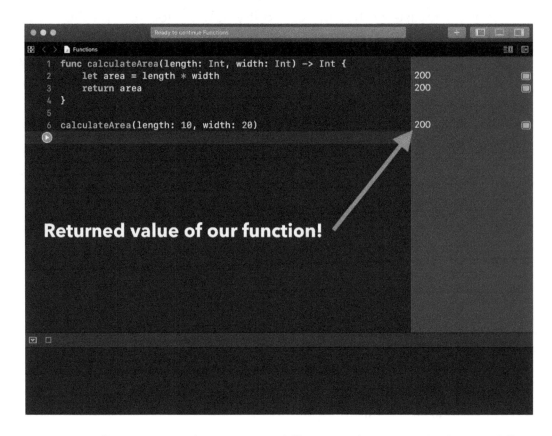

Let's try calling it again but pass in different values to calculate a different area (Figure 1.4.3).

```
func calculateArea(length: Int, width: Int) -> Int {

    let area = length * width

    return area

}


calculateArea(length: 10, width: 20)

calculateArea(length: 24, width: 15)
```

Figure 4.1

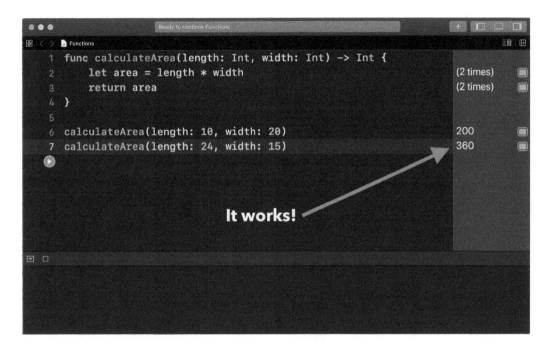

As you can see, the **function** works with a rectangle of any area with side lengths that are whole numbers.

Another function **example**

Functions can be used for anything! We used them above for a simple area calculation and now we will write one about our bank account.

At the bottom of your Playground file, type the following:

```
var bankAccountBalance = 500.00

var selfLacingNikes = 350.00
```

We created two variables – one to manage our bank account balance and one to declare the price of some cool self-lacing shoes. Great Scott! We could just write out the conditional code to say that if we have enough money, then we can buy the shoes but a **function** is an even better way to do this. This way, we can reuse the **function** and apply it to other item prices.

```swift
var bankAccountBalance = 500.00

var selfLacingNikes = 350.00


func purchaseItem(currentBalance: Double, itemPrice:
Double) -> Double {

    if itemPrice <= currentBalance {

        print("Purchased item for $\(itemPrice)")

        return currentBalance - itemPrice

    } else {

        print("You are broke. Balance still at $\
(currentBalance)")

        return currentBalance

    }

}
```

What just happened?

Alright, whoah...That was a lot of code to write without any explanation. Let's talk about that now.

We declare a function named `purchaseItem(currentBalance:itemPrice:)`.

We gave it two parameters to accept input values - `currentBalance` and `itemPrice`.

Next, we asked our `function` to return a value of type `Double` after it has finished running.

Inside our `function`, we wrote that if the `itemPrice` we pass in is less than or equal to our `currentBalance` value we passed in, then we should 1.) print `Purchased item for $\(itemPrice)` and 2.) return `currentBalance` minus our item's price.

If that condition cannot be met, or in our code: `else`, our function will 1.) print: *You are broke. Balance still at $(currentBalance)* and 2.) return the value of our current balance unchanged.

At the bottom of our Playground, let's call our `function` now.

```
var bankAccountBalance = 500.00

var selfLacingNikes = 350.00


func purchaseItem(currentBalance: Double, itemPrice:
Double) -> Double {

    if itemPrice <= currentBalance {

        print("Purchased item for $\(itemPrice)")

        return currentBalance - itemPrice

    } else {

        print("You are broke. Balance still at $\
(currentBalance)")

        return currentBalance

    }

}



//Pass in the values for "bankAccountBalance" and
"selfLacingNikes" below.


purchaseItem(currentBalance: bankAccountBalance,
itemPrice: selfLacingNikes)
```

As you can see on the right-hand side, the `function` works! Our item's price is less than our account balance, so the operation 500.00 - 350.00 takes place for the price of the shoes to be subtracted by our account balance. This gives us a **bankAccountBalance** value of 150.00.

To actually do something with that value, we can override our **bankAccountBalance** to update it after our `function` runs.

. . .

```
bankAccountBalance = purchaseItem(currentBalance:
bankAccountBalance, itemPrice: selfLacingNikes)
```

Now `bankAccountBalance` is equal to 150.00 instead of 500.00 because our `function` has modified it *AND* we printed a message to the Debug menu.

```
"Purchased item for $350.0"
```

We can create a new item to buy and pass it in through our `function`, too!
    Create a variable beneath `selfLacingNikes` named *stainlessSteelAppleWatch* and give it a price of 599.00 like so:

```
var bankAccountBalance = 500.00

var selfLacingNikes = 350.00

var stainlessSteelAppleWatch = 599.00
```

Now pass it in to our `purchaseItem(currentBalance:itemPrice:)` function:

```
...
```

```
bankAccountBalance = purchaseItem(currentBalance:
bankAccountBalance, itemPrice: stainlessSteelAppleWatch)
```

As you can see, our `function` prevents the purchase from being made and prints out an error message for us in the Debug menu.

```
"You are broke. Balance still at $150.0"
```

String Interpolation

As an aside, let's talk about why I used `\()` and placed `itemPrice` inside of it i.e. `\(itemPrice)`.
    In Swift, when you want to print a message or create a `String` value and include a value of a different type, we can pass it in and convert it using String Interpolation. Like so:

```
var price = 250

var message = "The item's price is $\(price)."
```

The message that will print to the console is: "The item's price is $250."

The variable `price` is of type `Int` (inferred by Swift) and it's passed in and interpolated by using the syntax `\()`. Pretty cool!

Return Values Are The End of the Road

Whenever you call a return in a `function`, that is the end of that `function`. Code written after a return will never run. So make sure that any code written goes before the return statement.

Here's a bad example:

```
var pizzaSlices = 8

var amountOfPizzaEaten = 2


func eatPizza(slicesEaten: Int, pizzaSlices: Int) -> Int
{
    if slicesEaten >= 1 {

        let updatedSlices = pizzaSlices - slicesEaten

        return updatedSlices

        print("\(updatedSlices) slices of pizza left!")
    } else {

        print("Meh, not hungry.")

        return pizzaSlices

    }

}


eatPizza(slicesEaten: amountOfPizzaEaten, pizzaSlices:
pizzaSlices)
```

Do you smell something funky? In programming, we actually call this a "code smell" - when something just ain't right.

The print `function` called after `return` will never run because it was called too late. In fact, Xcode will even warn us that the code written afterward will not run. Our `function` *SHOULD* look like this:

```
var pizzaSlices = 8

var amountOfPizzaEaten = 2


func eatPizza(slicesEaten: Int, pizzaSlices: Int) -> Int
{

    if slicesEaten >= 1 {

        let updatedSlices = pizzaSlices - slicesEaten

        print("\(updatedSlices) slices of pizza left!")

        return updatedSlices

    } else {

        print("Meh, not hungry.")

        return pizzaSlices

    }

}


eatPizza(slicesEaten: amountOfPizzaEaten, pizzaSlices:
pizzaSlices)
```

Choosing To Not Return Anything

What if we don't want to deal with return values? Well, thanks to `inout` parameters, we don't have to.

An `inout parameter` allows for us to directly modify variables outside our `function` instead of having to return a value to them in order to update their value.

You can use an `inout parameter` by modifying the pizza function we wrote above:

```
var pizzaSlices = 8

var amountOfPizzaEaten = 2


func eatPizza(slicesEaten: Int, pizzaSlices: inout Int)
{

    if slicesEaten >= 1 {

        pizzaSlices = pizzaSlices - slicesEaten

        print("\(pizzaSlices) slices of pizza left!")

    } else {

        print("Meh, not hungry.")

    }

}


eatPizza(slicesEaten: amountOfPizzaEaten, pizzaSlices:
&pizzaSlices)
```

Inside the *if* block of our `function`, we are able to directly modify the variable `pizzaSlices` which is super cool.

When we call the function `eatPizza(slicesEaten:pizza-Slices:)` we add an ampersand to the front of the `pizzaSlices` variable we pass in. This is the syntax to tell Xcode that we want to use an inout `parameter`.

By writing a `function` this way, we aren't required to return a value but we can still modify the variables we want. You want to use this sparingly, and you don't **need** to know about this yet, but it's good to have in your tool-belt.

Constants

Throughout this chapter, you have seen the keyword `let` used in a similar way to how we create variables. That keyword is actually incredibly important. It is used to declare a `Constant` in Swift.

A `constant` is exactly like a variable except for the fact that it can never change once it is given a value.

Some examples of data that could be `constants` are: your birthday, a city name, car model, etc. Things that never change and remain constant (hence the name!). The keyword `let` is used in a "let that value stay the same" kind of manner.

Here are some pseudo-code examples:

```
let birthYear = 1976

let mothersMaidenName = "Squillagree"

let jennysPhoneNumber = 8675309
```

These values are all unchanging and we won't need to change them. If we try to change them, Xcode will yell at us and give us an error asking us to change our `let` into a `var` so it can be modified as you can see on your screen.

To be honest, that is the only information you will need to know about `constants` as they are identical to variables except that they cannot be changed once given a value.

Wrapping up

We've learned a lot in this chapter about `functions` - reusable bits of code that perform specific tasks. 99.9% of coding is writing and using `functions`, so this is very important for you to know and understand well.

We talked about the anatomy of a `function` which contains the keyword `func`, a descriptive name of what the `function` does, a set of parentheses optionally including `parameters` to pass in, and a return type if needed.

In the following chapters, you will use `functions` frequently so if there are any parts of this chapter you don't fully understand read back through it again and make sure you really get it down.

Exercise

Write a function called `canDivideSlices` that takes in two values - `numberOfSlices` and `numberOfFriends` and returns a value of type `Bool`(true or false). This function will be used to determine whether or not a pizza can be divided evenly by your group of friends.

Chapter 5: Arrays

An array is a collection type. It stores collections of data of multiple types and orders them numerically.

What you will learn

-   Creating your first Array
-   Appending an item To an Array
-   Removing an item From an Array
-   Creating an empty Array
-   Other Neat things Arrays can do

Key Terms

-   `Zero-indexing`: a term to describe the starting point (0) at which a Swift Array begins counting.
-   `Array`: a collection type in Swift where values are collected and ordered numerically.
-   `Append`: to add a value to an `array`.
-   `Empty Array`: an `array` with no values stored inside - how sad.

The variables we learned about in the previous chapter are great for storing single values. In the real world, we need to keep track of multiple pieces of data that are all a part of the same category. For example - employee salaries, the value of each comic book in our collection, or the cost per item in a store inventory.

It is time and labor-intensive to create an individual variable for each of the above items and honestly it wouldn't be good code. This is where `arrays` come in *cue triumphant music*!

`Arrays` are a collection of values that allow us to store multiple values. In this chapter, we will see just how useful they can be.

Setting up a Playground

First, open Xcode if you haven't already and click `Get started with a playground`. Choose a "Blank" playground and click `Next`.

Give it a name like *Arrays*, and choose somewhere to save this .play-ground file and click **Create** to save it.

Creating your first array

Let's use one of the examples below: the value of each comic book in our collection. Imagine that you have a small collection that includes 5 comic books. They each have differing values. We *could* create a variable for each comic book and store the value like so:

```
var comicBook1 = 10.0

var comicBook2 = 27.50

var comicBook3 = 1015.0

var comicBook4 = 55.0

var comicBook5 = 2.0
```

What if someone stole one of your comic books? What if you sold one? You would need to manually remove that line of code and then re-number the variables that follow it because each variable has a specific number and order.

Instead, create an `Array` called **comicBooks** and place the values inside of it like so:

```
var comicBooks = [10.0, 27.50, 1015.0, 55.0, 2.0]
```

Now we have a single line of code to replace the five lines we wrote above. We've written an `array` of type `Int` and have filled the braces ([]) with data.

Appending an item to an array

When we foolishly wrote the 5 variables above, it was difficult to manage and change. If we wanted to add a new comic book, we'd have to add it at the end. Otherwise we'd have messed up the number order of each variable. With an `array`, it is easy to manage and modify our data.

For instance, let's pretend that you scored and found an ultra-rare comic book at a garage sale. After researching, you learn that it's value is $500.

To add is to our `array`, simply type:

```
var comicBooks = [10.0, 27.50, 1015.0, 55.0, 2.0]
```

```
comicBooks.append(500.0)
```

Run the code. On the right-hand side of the Playground window, you should see the `array` print out, this time with a new value at the end - 500.0!

Other things arrays can do

`Arrays` can do a couple cool things to help us manage a collection of data. For instance, we can calculate the total number of objects in our `array`. Just for explanation purposes, we are going to print the number of items in our `array` before we added our new $500 comic and after, too.
Try this:

```
var comicBooks = [10.0, 27.50, 1015.0, 55.0, 2.0]
```

```
print(comicBooks.count) // Prints 5 because of total
above.
```

```
comicBooks.append(500.0)
```

```
print(comicBooks.count) // Prints 6 because we added a
new value!
```

Pretty cool! What if you sold one of your comic books on eBay? How would we remove that item from the `array`?

Removing an item from an array

`Arrays` in Swift include a function called `.remove(at:)` which allow us to remove a certain item at a certain point in our `array`.

To remove the third value from our `array`, we need to add the following line of code:

```
var comicBooks = [10.0, 27.50, 1015.0, 55.0, 2.0]

print(comicBooks.count) // Prints 5 because of total
above.


comicBooks.append(500.0)

print(comicBooks.count) // Prints 6 because we added a
new value!


comicBooks.remove(at: 2)
```

Wait a minute... Didn't I just say to remove the third value from our array? Yes, and that is exactly what I did. You should see the third value (1015.0) printed out on the right-hand side of the Playground. So it worked, but if this is confusing it's okay because this is where I will talk about zero-indexing.

In most programming languages, `arrays` use what is called zero-indexing meaning that the first value in our `array` is given an identifier of 0 to indicate the first value. The second value has the identifier (or index) of 1, and so on. If you want the fourth value, you need to ask Swift for an index of 3. It may seem confusing, but that's just the way it is.

In the above code, we wanted to remove the third comic book from our `array`, so we asked to remove the item at index 2.

If we print **comicBooks.count** below **comicBooks.remove(at: 2)** you should see that the count is back down to 5.

```
comicBooks.remove(at: 2)


print(comicBooks.count) // Prints 5
```

Creating an empty array

Let's move on to another example - students in a classroom. Type the following beneath all the code you wrote above:

```
var students = [String]()
```

The above code is an empty `array`. We have declared a variable called **students** and have asked Xcode to make it an empty `array` containing String values. In regards to an `array`, "empty" means that it doesn't yet have any values - like an empty box or container would be with nothing inside.

To show that there is nothing inside, add the following:

```
var students = [String]()


print(students.count) // Prints 0 because our array is empty!
```

Now we can add students to our `Array`! Use the `.append()` function to do so:

```
var students = [String]()


print(students.count) // Prints 0 because our array is empty!


students.append("Jon")

students.append("Jacob")

students.append("Jose")

students.append("Jingle")

students.append("Heimer")

students.append("Schmidt")
```

In your Playground window, you should see the following:

```
["Jon"]
["Jon", "Jacob"]
["Jon", "Jacob", "Jose"]
["Jon", "Jacob", "Jose", "Jingle"]
["Jon", "Jacob", "Jose", "Jingle", "Heimer"]
["Jon", "Jacob", "Jose", "Jingle", "Heimer", "Schmidt"]
```

The pyramid-like print out of values on the right-hand side shows how each time we run `.append()` to add a value, the `Array` becomes longer and includes more values.

Wrapping up

There are many more cool things that `arrays` can do, but you have learned the essentials in this chapter. `Arrays` are collection type and as such, they are great for storing collections of values. Whatever you have a list of - teachers, hot wheel cars, Minecraft collectibles, you name it - `arrays` are a great way to store that data.

We are starting to get better at organizing and writing cleaner code and will continue to do so throughout this book. Nicely done on getting this far! You deserve a high-five!

Exercise

Create an Array called `favoriteAlbums` and fill it with the titles of four albums that you love. (Hint: They should all be values of type String). Add a new album title to your array by using the `.append()` feature in Swift. Print the total count of the items in the array using `.count`.

I'm going to make you be picky now... Use Swift's `remove(at:_)` feature to remove an album from your array.

Chapter 6: Loops

Loops are repeating blocks of code that we can use to perform one action to multiple pieces of data in Swift.

What you will learn

- Writing your first `repeat-while` loop
- Writing your first `for-in` loop
- Writing your first `for-each` loop

Key Terms

- `Loop:` a section of repeated code that repeats until a condition is met.
- `The DRY Principle:` a programming principle meaning "Don't Repeat Yourself", in an effort to remind programmers to use the most efficient coding practice.

The `DRY principle` states "Don't Repeat Yourself". It is a coding principle that has existed for a long time, but `loops` in Swift are blocks of repeating code.

How can using `loops` be a good practice? While a `loop` repeats the same code over and over, it does so within the confines of a single `loop`. We can pass in data from an array, for example, and the same operation can be performed on each item of that collection.

This is a very useful component of the Swift language. We will learn about the 3 popular types of Swift `loops` in this chapter. Let's get loopy!

Setting up a Playground

First, open Xcode if you haven't already and click `Get started with a playground`. Choose a "Blank" playground and click `Next`.

Give it a name like *Loops*, and choose somewhere to save this .playground file and click `Create` to save it.

Why you should use loops

Let's imagine that we have 4 employees working at our company. Each employee earns a different salary:

- Employee 1: $45,000
- Employee 2: $100,000
- Employee 3: $54,000
- Employee 4: $20,000 (Sorry, bro.)

Create 4 variables (one for each employee) and set the value of each variable to be the related salary above:

```
import UIKit


var employee1Salary = 45000.0

var employee1Salary = 100000.0

var employee1Salary = 54000.0

var employee1Salary = 20000.0
```

We just finished up Q4 of 2016 and we've had a very successful year. We want to give each employee a raise of 10%. In your Playground, type:

```
import UIKit


var employee1Salary = 45000.0

var employee2Salary = 100000.0

var employee3Salary = 54000.0

var employee4Salary = 20000.0


employee1Salary = employee1Salary + (employee1Salary *
0.10)
```

The above code performs the operation `45000.0 + (45000.0 * 0.10)` as it takes our variables value and adds it to 10% of itself.

Let's perform this operation for each employee:

```
employee1Salary = employee1Salary + (employee1Salary *
0.10) // prints 49500

employee2Salary = employee2Salary + (employee2Salary *
0.10) // prints 110000

employee3Salary = employee3Salary + (employee1Salary *
0.10) // prints 59400

employee4Salary = employee4Salary + (employee1Salary *
0.10) // prints 22000
```

I don't know about you, but I smell some stanky code. If you were thinking, "WAIT. We're repeating ourself... What if we had 100 employees?" Doing this operation for 100 employees would be very exhausting and likely would result in errors.

We are also violating the `DRY principle` (Don't Repeat Yourself).

There is no need for us to have 4 separate variables for storing employee salaries. Let's instead consolidate them into a single array named `salaries`:

```
var salaries = [45000.0, 100000.0, 54000.0, 20000.0]
```

How can we cycle through these and add 10% to each person's salary? Well, we could type:

```
salaries[0] = salaries[0 + (salaries[0] * 0.10)
```

But that would result in the same issue. We still need to write a line of code for each employee and repeat ourself. Yuck! Delete that line of code leaving only the array called `salaries`.

How do we solve this problem? This is where `loops` in Swift become very useful. For each employee, we've given them a salary and need to perform the same operation on each one - `salary + (salary * 10%)`. Let's write a `loop` to handle this.

Writing your first loop

The first `loop` we will write is called a `repeat-while` loop. There are a few different types of `loop`'s, but they all run code on repeat while or until a certain condition is met.

Writing a repeat-while loop

Below our salaries variable, type:

```
var salaries = [45000.0, 100000.0, 54000.0, 20000.0]


var x = 0

repeat {

    x += 1

} while (x < salaries.count)
```

You should see that on the right side of the Playground window our `loop` runs 4 times. But why?

`salaries` is array that stores all the employees salaries.

`x` is the variable that keeps track how many times the `loop` repeats.

The `.count` following an array will give you the value of how many items there are in that array. There are 4 salaries, so therefore, `salaries.count` = 4.

We ask our `loop` to repeat taking the value of our variable `x` and adding one to it.

Then our `loop` checks against the condition we declared: `x  < salaries.count`.

We ask it to see what the value of `x` is, and then see if it's less than the total number of items in the array `salaries`.

So under the hood, we are doing the following:

```
var salaries = [45000.0, 100000.0, 54000.0, 20000.0]


var x = 0

x + 1 // Now x = 1
```

```
// Check condition: 1 < 4 is true, continue to loop


x + 1 // Now x = 2
// Check condition: 2 < 4 is true, continue to loop


x + 1 // Now x = 3
// Check condition: 3 < 4 is true, continue to loop


x + 1 // Now x = 4
// Check condition: 4 < 4 is false, stop looping
```

Adding the 10% salary equation

Now all we need to do is add our salary equation but instead of using a number value to call a specific element of our array (i.e. `salaries[0]`), we will use our variable `x` (i.e. `salaries[x]`) because it's value iterates from 0 up until 3 when ran through our `loop`. Remember, in arrays in Swift use zero-indexing, meaning that the first element is numbered 0.

Add the following to your repeat-while `loop`:

```
var salaries = [45000.0, 100000.0, 54000.0, 20000.0]


var x = 0
repeat {
    salaries[x] = salaries[x] + (salaries[x] * 0.10)
    x += 1
} while (x < salaries.count)
```

The variable `x` could be named anything, but `x` is simply a common choice used in `loops`. A variable that is more wordy but also more descriptive is **index**. Remember that in an array, the index is the number used to identify each element in the array.

To be more descriptive, change the variable **x** to be **index** instead. Like so:

```
var salaries = [45000.0, 100000.0, 54000.0, 20000.0]


var index = 0

repeat {

    salaries[index] = salaries[index] + (salaries[index]
* 0.10)

    index += 1

} while (index < salaries.count)
```

So what is this doing? We begin with our **index** variable set to 0.

Then we declare a repeat-while **loop**. Inside the repeat block we add an equation which adds 10% of our salary to our current salary for the item at the index with the same value as our variable **index** (at this point, it's equal to 0).

Then we add 1 to our **index** variable making it equal to 1.

Finally, we check using our **while** condition to see if index is still less than the total number of elements in our **salaries** array.

Writing a `for-in` loop

Another type of **loop** that you may want to write at times is called a **for-in** **loop**. It enables you to **loop** through a range of values and perform an operation for each value.

Here is an example of a **for-in** **loop**:

```
for x in 1...5 {

    print("Index: \(x)")

}
```

If you type the above code into your Playground, you will see the result "(5 times)" meaning that we have **looped** 5 times. In the console at the bottom of the playground window, you should see this message:

```
Index: 1

Index: 2

Index: 3

Index: 4

Index: 5
```

The beginning of a **for-in** loop is indicated by the keyword **for**. Then we create a variable named **x**, but it could be named anything.

The value of **x** is being set to a value of 1, then we print the message **Index: 1** because **x** is equal to 1.

The **loop** then restarts but this time **x** is set to the next value in the range: 2.

The console prints **Index: 2** and the **loop** repeats. This continues until we hit a value of 5.

Next, we use the keyword **in** to indicate that we are about to declare a range of values. At the end we state which values the **loop** should operate within.

The use of **...** means "inclusive" and indicates that we should include every value from 1 until 5.

If we wanted to make it "exclusive" - so that our **loop** considers everything except the last value in the range - we would need to add a new "exclusive" **loop** as follows:

```
for x in 1...5 {

    print("Index: \(x)")

}


for x in 1..<5 {

    print("Exclusive Index: \(x)")

}
```

You should only see 4 lines print out for the second **loop**. This is because we have asked it to exclude the final value of 5 from being used.

To continue with our salaries example above, type the following `for-in` loop in your Playground window:

```
for i in 0..<salaries.count {

    salaries[i] = salaries[i] + (salaries[i] * 0.10)

    print(salaries[i])

}
```

This `loop` creates a variable named `i` and declares a range of 0 to "less-than" the value of `salaries.count`. Since `salaries.count` is equal to 4, our `loop` is exclusive and can only check values between 0 and 3 since 4 is not less than 4.

This is perfect, however, because the index of our salaries array begins at zero and ends at 3.

The flow of the above `loops` goes like this: the variable `i` gets set to 0 - the first value in our range.

Then `i` is passed in as the index for our `salaries` array.

Afterward, we do the math to add a 10% raise like before.

Finally, we print the raised salary to the console below.

Here is the key difference between a for-in `loop` and a repeat-while `loop`:

in a for-in `loop`, the value of our placeholder variable (in this case `i`) is modified by the range of values we set at the end.

In a repeat-while `loop`, we need to increment the variable `index` by writing `index += 1`.

Creating a `for-each` loop

The next `loop` is for when you may have a variable number of items to `loop` through. We've used predefined ranges or an array with static information inside of it.

What if all salary information was stored on a server which could change from day to day with new hires and fires? If we were to enter in everybody's salary information manually in a static array, it would be much harder to change or modify anyones salary. It also would be a troublesome task to locate a certain employee's salary if they were fired.

To write a **for-each** `loop`, type the following:

```
for salary in salaries {

    print("Salary: \(salary)")

}
```

As you can see in the console at the bottom of your Playgrounds window, every salary in our array is printed nicely.

The above code works by starting with the keyword **for** to indicate we are creating a loop.

Then, we create a variable called **salary** and ask it to loop through each item in the **salaries** array until we reach the end.

For each item loop through in the array we print it's value into a String like so: "Salary: 24200.0"

Personally, I find **for-each loops** the easiest for a beginner to understand as you can name the variable something specific related to the contents of your array.

Wrapping up

Loops are a foundational concept to understand when learning to code. If you feel confused about how they work, I encourage you to re-read this chapter. Try typing out the examples a few times.

It's also a great idea to do some research online. Find examples and real-life scenarios where people are using loops and learn from them.

We've learned about **repeat-while**, **for-in**, and **for-each** loops in Swift. Now you can loop through collections of data and write better, more efficient code. Whenever you need to perform the same operation over and over, instead of writing multiple lines of almost duplicate code use a loop!

Exercise

Create an Array that stores the names of all four members of the Beatles. Write a **for-each** loop that walks through the Array and prints the name of each Beatles member.

Create another Array that stores four countries populations. Write a **for-in** loop that walks through the array and prints a sentence with the population value passed into the sentence using String Interpolation. **The population is 12378932**, for example.

Chapter 7: Dictionaries

Similar to a Swift array, dictionaries are a convenient way of cataloging information. They are super useful if you need to store data with two related values (i.e. word and definition).

What you will learn

- Creating your first dictionary
- Adding an item to the dictionary
- Accessing the amount of items in a dictionary
- Checking to see if a dictionary is empty
- Overriding a dictionary value to modify it
- Iterating through a dictionary
- Clearing out a dictionary of all data

Key Terms

- `dictionary`: a collection type in Swift which allows for the storing of data in a key-value pair.
- `Key`: a unique identifier that is associated with a value.
- `Value`: a value which is identified and linked to a unique key.

When you were in school, you were probably asked at one point to look up the definition of a word to determine it's meaning. You knew that the words were sorted alphabetically, so you could efficiently track down the general location of the word, then fine-tune your search as you flipped through a couple pages as you got closer to your target word.

Once you had found your target word, you would read the definition and use that in whatever assignment you were working on.

In Swift, a dictionary (called hash tables or hash maps in other programming languages) is a collection type which associates a `key` with a value similarly to how a `dictionary` for a language associates words with their definition.

Swift `Dictionaries` operate just like a language `dictionary` does. You start with a `key` of some type (String, Int, Double, etc.) and a value of the same or a different type. While the `value` per `key` can vary, each `key` in a `dictionary` must be unique.

The thing that makes them unique is that they are much more efficient to search through than an Array and they are much easier to find particular items. An Array in Swift orders items numerically, which is great in some circumstances, but if you want to find a specific piece of information, a `dictionary` is better. You can associate a `key` with a `value` so you can track down the item by it's `key` - just like you would in a language `dictionary`.

Let's dive into creating a `dictionary` in Swift now.

Setting up

First, open Xcode if you haven't already and click `Get started with a playground`. Choose a "Blank" playground and click `Next`.

Give it a name like *Dictionaries*, and choose somewhere to save this .playground file and click `Create` to save it.

Creating your first dictionary

To create your first Swift `dictionary`, create a variable called **namesOfIntegers** like so:

```
var namesOfIntegers = [Int: String]()
```

What we have done above is declared a variable and called it *namesOfIntegers*. We've set it to be equal to a `Dictionary` as indicated by the square brackets. Inside, we have declared that the key type should be `Int` and the value type should be `String`.

This means that any data we try to add to this `dictionary` has to adhere to that rule. We also declared this as an empty `dictionary` as indicated by the parentheses following the `dictionary` brackets.

You should see the following print out in the console indicating that we successfully created an empty `dictionary` (there are no values, but brackets and a colon in the middle):

```
[:]
```

Adding an item to the dictionary

A `dictionary` is no use if it is empty! Let's add some data so that it is a bit more useful to us.

Type the following on a new line beneath the variable *namesOfIntegers*:

```
var namesOfIntegers = [Int: String]()
```

```
namesOfIntegers[3] = "Three"
```

You might be thinking, "Hey! That's just like an Array!

3 must be the index and "Three" must be the data that's stored!

While that is a fair assumption at the moment, you will soon see how a `dictionary` is quite different.

The number 3 is actually the name of the `key` (of type Int) in our dictionary and the `value` associated with it is a `String` with a value of `"Three"`.

We added a new `key` called 3 with a `value` of `"Three"`.

These `key-value` pairs are what make `Dictionaries` in Swift so powerful.

Let's add another `key` and `value` pair to our `dictionary`.

Add the following at the bottom of your Playground file:

```
var namesOfIntegers = [Int: String]()
```

```
namesOfIntegers[3] = "Three"
namesOfIntegers[44] = "Forty Four"
```

The thing to note here is that it does not matter at what order you add these `values`. We access the items in a `dictionary` by their `key` not their number order.

Another dictionary example

Let's pretend for a moment that we're building an app that monitors and keeps track of important flight data for all the world's airports. Each airport should definitely have it's own unique code separating if from the others.

If Stockholm, Los Angeles, and Dubai all shared the same airport code, LAX, it would cause a massive amount of confusion and headache all the time.

Luckily, each airport has a unique airport code so that they are all differentiated from one another. A few airports could actually have the same name as long as their code was unique.

The thing about `Dictionaries` in Swift is that every `key` must be unique. This is so that all of the data you want to save into it can be differentiated and easily accessed just like each airport code needs to be easily accessible and quickly understood.

Continuing with this example, let's create a `dictionary` for a list of airport codes. Add the following `dictionary` at the bottom of your Playground:

```
var airports: [String: String] = ["YYZ": "Toronto
Pearson", "LAX": "Los Angeles International"]
```

OK, cool. So what is happening here? We created a variable called *airports* and explicitly declared it as a `dictionary` of type `[String: String]`.

We used the assignment operator (=) and added a pair of square brackets. Inside, we created two `key-value` pairs.

For each pair, we added a `key` of type `String` for each airport code followed by a colon (:).

We then added a `value` of type `String` containing the airports name. Since we created two `key-value` pairs, we used a comma to separate the `values` just like we would in an Array.

Accessing the amount of items in a dictionary

In order to access the amount of items in our `dictionary`, we can use the same function we do with Arrays. Let's print out a `String` and pass in the `airports.count` to show how many airports we've added to our `dictionary`. Like so:

```
var airports: [String: String] = ["YYZ": "Toronto
Pearson", "LAX": "Los Angeles International"]
```

```
print("The airports dictionary has: \(airports.count)
items.")
```

In the console, you should see the following: "The airports dictionary has: 2 items."

This should seem familiar from our chapter on Arrays like I said above. Arrays and `Dictionaries` both share this ability – to count their total number of objects.

Checking to see if a dictionary is empty

We can also look to see if we have any `values` at all. Use the built in function `isEmpty` to check this:

```
if airports.isEmpty {

    print("The airports dictionary is empty!")

}
```

Since we have two items in our `dictionary` nothing will print. If you were to remove everything from the `dictionary`, this `String` would print out in the console.

Overriding a dictionary value to modify it

Let's add a new `value` to our *airports* dictionary. At the bottom of your Playground, add the following:

```
airports["PDX"] = "Portland"
```

We have now added a new `key-value` pair, but what if you want to update the `value` to something different. To override the `value` we just set all we need to do is change it like so:

```
airports["PDX"] = "Portland"
airports["PDX"] = "Portland International"
```

Now, the old `value` `"Portland"` is gone and the current `value` for the key `"PDX"` is `"Portland International"`. Easy as that!

Removing an item from our dictionary

Let's add a new imaginary airport with a `key` of `"DEV"` and a `value` of `"Devslopes International""`

```
airports["DEV"] = "Devslopes International"
```

To remove this item completely from our `dictionary`, all we need to do is the following:

```
airports["DEV"] = "Devslopes International"

airports["DEV"] = nil
```

Now our `key-value` pair of "DEV": "Devslopes International" is gone forever from our `dictionary`.

```
---
Helpful Hint:
nil is used to declare an empty value in Swift. We haven't used
nil yet at this point in the book, but know that it is used to set a value
to be empty and sometimes is used in removing values from collec-
tion types.
---
```

Iterating through a dictionary

We can use a `for-in` loop to do something with the `keys` and `values` in our `dictionary`. Let's make one now! Add the following loop at the bottom of the Playground window:

```
for (airportCode, airportName) in airports {



}
```

Now, before we write any code inside of our loop let's talk about what we're doing here.

Since a `dictionary` works under the condition of `key` and `value` together, we need to loop through both `values` simultaneously. Thus, we have the tuple.

Here is how Apple's Swift documentation defines a tuple: "Tuples group multiple values into a single compound value. The values within a tuple can be of any type and do not have to be of the same type as each other."

We are doing just what the definition describes when we loop through our `dictionary`. We combine the airport code and the airport name into a singular compound `value` and can modify it as we please.

Using both Key and Value

Let's put our tuple to use. Inside the `for-in` loop, add the following:

```
for (airportCode, airportName) in airports {

    print("\(airportCode): \(airportName)")

}
```

In the console below, you should see the following print out:

```
LAX: Los Angeles International

YYZ: Toronto Pearson

LHR: London Heathrow
```

Using only Keys from a dictionary

If we only wanted to print the airport codes (the keys in our `dictionary`), all we need to do is create another `for-in` loop and access the `keys` property of our `dictionary` like so:

```
for key in airports.keys {

    print("Key: \(key)")

}
```

After writing that code, you will see the following print out in the console:

```
Key: LAX
```

```
Key: YYZ

Key: LHR
```

Any `dictionary`'s keys can be accessed this way. Pretty cool! But so can the `values`. Check it out below!

Using only Values from a dictionary

We can do the same thing as above, but for the inverse - the `values` inside our `dictionary`.

Create another **for-in** loop to demonstrate this:

```
for value in airports.values {

    print("Value: \(value)")

}
```

The following will print out in the console:

```
Value: Los Angeles International

Value: Toronto Pearson

Value: London Heathrow
```

Clearing out a dictionary of all data

To clear out your `dictionary`, you can simply set it to be equal to an empty `dictionary`. Like so:

```
namesOfIntegers = [:]
```

This will reset and clear out all data from our `dictionary`.

Wrapping up

`Dictionaries` are powerful and can be used in a ton of different ways.

It is a much more orderly and efficient way to organize data when you want to be able to access that data by a `key` and `value` pair.

Arrays are great and have their place, but Dictionaries are much more versatile in their everyday use.

If you still feel confused, it's always a good idea to read Apple's documentation on Swift. Learning to read documentation is an important part of becoming a developer. Don't overlook that!

Nicely done on completing this chapter! Let's move on.

Exercise

Create a Dictionary called `movieReleaseYears` that stores the title and year of release for three movies you love. The title of the movie is the **key** and the release year is the **value**. Write a `for-in` loop to pass in the movie titles and release years together and print them both, IMDb-style (i.e. "Toy Story (1995)")

Chapter 8: Boolean Logic & Conditional Statements

In this chapter, we will discuss Booleans, Conditionals, and Comparison Operators. Booleans are a foundational piece of programming that you will use throughout your code. They are used to compare things or perform an action based on a condition.

What you will learn

- Creating your first Boolean
- Type Inference
- Conditional Statement Basics
- Comparison Operators

Key Terms

- `Boolean:` a binary variable, having two values – "true" and "false."
- `Conditional  Statement:` a block of code with one or two conditions that only runs when certain requirements are met.
- `Comparison  Operator:` a function used to determine equality, inequality, or difference between two.

When you were a kid, there may have been a time where your parents said, "if you clean your room", then _____ would be the reward. You can fill in the blank. A trip to Disneyland? A Japanese-imported Robby the Robot toy? Perhaps a near-mint copy of Action Comics No.1 "Superman"?

But if you failed to clean your room, then the consequence would be not getting that reward.

If **x** is true, then **y** happens. Otherwise, **z** happens. This "cause and effect" relationship is the foundation that `Booleans` rest on.

Simply put, a `Boolean` is true or false.

Creating your first Boolean

First, open Xcode if you haven't already and click `Get started with a playground`. Choose a "Blank" playground and click `Next`.

Give it a name like *BooleansConditionalsComparisonOperators*, and choose somewhere to save this .playground file and click `Create` to save it.

Type the following code:

```
var isThisTheBestBookEver = true
```

You should see on the right-hand side, that the variable is equal to `true`.

Since we have declared our variable `isThisTheBestBookEver` as `true`, we have actually used one of Swift's most helpful features - Type Inference!

Swift Magic: Type Inference

Remember in the chapter about `Variables` we learned that variables can be of many types: Characters or words (`String`), numbers (`Int`, `Float`, `Double`), or even of type `Bool` (short for `Boolean`).

Thanks to Swift, we don't need to tell Xcode that we are declaring a `Boolean` when we type `true` or `false` because those are the only two values that a `Boolean` can be. In the `Variables` chapter, when we wrote the following code, we used Type Inference as well:

```
var message = "Insert String information here..."
```

We used quotation marks (") to help Swift infer that the variable we wrote was of type String.

To explicitly declare a variable you can use the following syntax:

```
var message: String = "Insert String Information
here..."
```

```
//or
```

```
var isThisTheBestBookEver: Bool = true
```

Thanks to Swift, we don't *need* to explicitly declare these types, although at times it is necessary which I will explain later on.

Back To Bools

Alright, now that we understand Type Inference, let's journey back over to our Swift Playground in Xcode.

We left the following code in our Playground:

```
var isThisTheBestBookEver = true
```

Beneath that code, we're going to change the value of our variable to now be `false`.

```
var isThisTheBestBookEver = true

isThisTheBestBookEver = false
```

By writing the name of our variable and setting it to be equal to `false` it is now false!

Helpful Hint:

Only return a Boolean value for the sake of making a decision. It returns a true or false value, so it is perfect for making these kinds of decisions.

Conditional Statement Basics

`Conditional` statements help our code make decisions and run code depending on certain conditions. We can use conditionals to check against all kinds of values and conditions.

Write the following `if` statement and `if/else` statement at the bottom of your Playground:

```
var numberOfMinutes = 525600

var hasMedals = true


if numberOfMinutes == 525600 {

    print("Time to pay the rent.")

}
```

```
if hasMedals == true {

    print("You're amazing, Felix! Let's have a party!")

} else {

    print("Go away, Ralph!")

}
```

As you can see in the console, the first `if` statement prints out "Time to pay the rent."

And the second `if/else` statement prints out "You're amazing, Felix! Let's have a party!".

If you want to add a third condition, you can also use `else  if` like so:

```
let num = 9


if num < 0 {

    print("Number is negative.")

} else if num < 10 {

    print("Number is single-digit.")

} else {

    print("Number is multi-digit")

}
```

The above code will print "Number is single-digit." because `num` is less than 10. In the rest of this chapter, we will use conditionals and comparison operators together in new and exciting ways.

Comparison Operators

Declaring something as `true` or `false` is great and all, but what can we actually do with it? We can use `Comparison  Operators` to make our code compare things!

To begin, here are the six `Comparison  Operators` in Swift:

Equal to: ==

Not equal to: !=

Greater than: >

Greater than or equal to: >=

Less than: <

Less than or equal to: <=

Let's see how these work with a commonly-used example - a bank account.

Example 1: Bank Account

At the bottom of your Playground, add the following variables *bankBalance* and *itemToBuy*:

```
var bankBalance = 400

var itemToBuy = 100
```

So we have a bank account holding $400 and want to buy an item with a price of $100.

Let's use a conditional and a `comparison operator` to determine whether or not we can purchase the item we want.

```
var bankBalance = 400

var itemToBuy = 100


if bankBalance >= itemToBuy {

    print("Purchased item!")

}
```

On the right-hand side of the Playground, you should see "Purchased item!n" print out. Don't worry about the "n" part. That is only Xcode telling you that after our message is printed it will create a new line.

I'm sure you see how powerful and useful `comparison` operators are. Here is yet another example of using `comparison` operators. We will write some code to check if a download has completed or not.

Example 2: Download completion checker

At the bottom of your Playground, type:

```
var downloadHasFinished = false


if downloadHasFinished == true {

    print("Download complete!")

} else {

    print("Loading data...")

}
```

Or we could simply use the "Not Equal To" `comparison operator: !=`

```
var downloadHasFinished = false


if !downloadHasFinished {

    print("Download complete!")

} else {

    print("Loading data...")

}
```

It's okay if the code above is confusing and seems flipped from the example above it. That's because it is! But let me explain.

1. First, we declare `downloadHasFinished` and set it's value to `false`.
2. Then, inside of an `if/else` statement we type `!download-HasFinished` meaning whatever value `downloadHasFinished` currently has, in this case `false`, make it NOT equal to that (invert it to `true`).

3. Afterward, since the value of `downloadHasFinished` is now true, print "Download complete!"

The same principle can be applied to check or verify `String` values or any other values so long as they are of the same type.

Example 3: Book title verification

Imagine that you hired a new librarian who was always messing up the titles of books when entering them into the computer:

```
var officialBookTitle = "Harry Blotter and the Moppit of
Meyer"


var attemptedEntryBookTitle = "Harry Plotter and the
Muppet Mayor"


if officialBookTitle != attempedEntryBookTitle {

    print("Need to check spelling, try again.")

}
```

Closing thoughts

`Booleans`, `Conditional Statements`, and `Comparison Operators` are foundational components of programming in any language, but especially in Swift. You will use `Booleans` for all kinds of verification, completion handling, etc.

Wrapping up

We learned that a `Boolean` is a true or false value. We also learned that a `conditional statement` only runs code that meets a certain condition (hence the name!). Finally, we learned that the six `comparison operators` come in handy for comparing values of all kinds.

You rock! Way to complete another chapter!

Exercise

Create a variable of type Bool named **syncComplete** and set it to false. Write a conditional statement to check whether or not syncing is complete. If syncComplete is true, print "Sync complete!". If syncComplete is false, print "Syncing...".

Create a variable and write a conditional statement that will check the balance of arcade tokens. If the balance is equal to or greater than 500, print out "Gamer Supreme!". If the balance is less than 500, print out "Child's Play...".

Chapter 9: Math Operators

Math, being an integral part of programming, can be used easily in Swift with a bit of know-how and a basic understanding of arithmetic.

What you will learn

- Basics of Math in Swift
- The Assignment Operator
- Arithmetic Operators
- The Modulo Operator

Key Terms

- `Assignment Operator`: the equals sign used in Swift to show assignment to a certain value or equality to another value.
- `Arithmetic Operators`: the four basic math operations - addition, subtraction, division, and multiplication.
- `Modulo Operator`: a math operator in Swift that allows for calculating the remainder of a division problem.

Math is a necessary part of programming. There's no getting around it. Those who are learning to program who don't come from a math/science background; those of you who don't have a degree in engineering, can still learn to code, though!

The math needed in programming doesn't often go far beyond what a majority of the population knows.

In Swift, there are several operators that we can use to perform mathematical equations. In this brief chapter, we will discuss each one.

Setting up

First, open Xcode if you haven't already and click `Get started with a playground`. Choose a "Blank" playground and click `Next`.

Give it a name like *Math Operators*, and choose somewhere to save this .playground file and click `Create` to save it.

The Assignment Operator

The `assignment operator` (=) is used just like the equals sign is used in math - to declare equality. Type out the example below in your Playground to see how this works:

```
var three = 3
```

When we create the above variable and name it *three*. We set it to literally equal three. The name of the variable is actually irrelevant. We could have named it anything and it still would serve as a way to use the value 3 throughout our code.

Arithmetic Operators

The four basic `arithmetic operators` (+, -, * , /) are used in Swift just as you would in a math class or in a graphing calculator. Here are some examples to show you how they can be used in Swift. Add the following to your Playground:

```
var product = 10 * 20 // Multiplication operator = *

var sum = 5 + 6 // Addition Operator = +

var difference = 10 - 3 // Subtraction Operator = -

var quotient = 30 / 3 // Division Operator = /
```

Helpful Hint:
The division operator performs division and rounds to the nearest whole number.
If we wrote 12 / 5, we would get a return value of 2.

The Modulo Operator

There is an amazing operator in Swift (and other languages, too) called the Modulo (sometimes referred to the remainder operator).

It's purpose is to show the remainder left over when dividing two numbers. Here is an example of it in use for you to try in your Playground:

```
var remainder = 13 % 5 // Prints 3 because 10 / 5 is the
nearest whole number division that is possible. Three is
left over as a remainder.
```

Here is another way you could look at the modulo operator to help it make sense:

```
var quotient = 13 / 5 // Prints 2 because Swift rounds
up when it divides.
```

```
var remainder = 13 % 5 // Prints 3 because that is the
remainder.
```

```
var result = "The result of 13 / 5 is \(quotient) with a
remainder of \(remainder)"
```

```
// Prints "The result of 13 / 5 is 2 with a remainder of
3"
```

Wrapping up

That wasn't so bad was it? Using math in Swift is basic and easy. There's not much to it. Remember these operators and they will get you far as you go deeper into learning Swift.

Exercise

Create a variable that stores the result of 4 x 7. Create another variable that stores the result of 4 * (5 - 6) - 5. Use the modulo operator (%) to calculate the remainder of 123 / 7.

Chapter 10: Classes

Classes have been a part of society for as long as humans have been around. Each class has specific traits unique to itself. In Swift, this is no different. Classes are the cornerstone of Object-Oriented Programming.

What you will learn

- Creating your first Class
- Adding Variables and Functions
- Understanding OOP
- Reference Types

Key Terms

- Class
- Object-Oriented Programming
- Reference Type

If you just starting your learn-to-code journey, you may have heard of Object-Oriented Programming.

It's a widely popular and highly revered model for programming that has stood the test of time. It is starting to get to a point where it may be replaced by other more modern models like *Protocol-Oriented Programming*, but it's still very important to understand.

Classes are a key component of OOP (Object-Oriented Programming) which allow us to create a blueprint of sorts and then copy it and modify it as needed.

An example could be a car in a car factory. Imagine an engineer created a blueprint for a car. In the factory, you can use that blueprint to create multiple copies of the same car by following the plans laid out in the blueprint.

Let's create our first class and use the car example from above.

Setting up

First, open Xcode if you haven't already and click Get started with a playground. Choose a "Blank" playground and click Next.

Give it a name like *Classes*, and choose somewhere to save this .playground file and click **Create** to save it.

Creating your first Class

Declaring a Class

In your Playground window, create a `class` by typing the following:

```
class Vehicle {



}
```

We used the keyword `class` followed by the name of our `class Vehicle`.

```
---
Helpful Hint:
```

It is best practice to start your class names with a capital letter (i.e. Vehicle, Motorcycle, Scooter).

```
---
```

Adding Variables And Functions

Now, we need to add in variables for properties that we want all of our cars to have. Like so:

```
class Vehicle {

    var tires = 4

    var headlights = 2

    var horsepower = 468

    var model = ""


    func drive() {

        //Accelerate the vehicle

    }
```

```
func brake() {

    //Stop the vehicle

}

}
```

As you can see, a `class` can have properties (i.e. *tires, headlights, horsepower, model*) and functions (i.e. *drive(), brake()*) to describe it.

Understanding OOP

To understand OOP, you really need to try to visualize the world around you. This concept is usually pretty easy to understand for people who are more artistic and have a designer brain because you can easily visualize things as objects.

If your brain operates more on the numbers and logic side, this can be difficult to understand because you may want to turn it all into numbers or algorithms of some kind.

Here's another example, I hope this helps to explain OOP a little more.

Instagram has users who can like other photos, so you may have a `User` object which contains a user id, account, password, amongst other properties.

This user may also have functions like: `resetPassword()` or `deleteAccount`. Even the photos on Instagram could be objects.

If we have a `Photo class`, it may have properties for: `selectedFilter, numberOfLikes, numberOfComments`.

Some functions a `Photo` may have could be: `addLike()`, `removeLike()` - kind of actions to perform on that object.

Start trying to look at objects in the real world in regards to their properties and functions (what they're like and what they do).

Everything around you can be put into an object in code.

Creating an Instance of a Class

Let's create an instance of our `Vehicle class` by adding the following at the bottom of our Playground:

```
let delorean = Vehicle()
```

We created a constant called *delorean* and initialized it as an instance (or copy) of our `Vehicle class` by typing `Vehicle` and following it with parentheses.

The *model* property from above is initialized as an empty `String` above, so let's give our car a model name.

```
let delorean = Vehicle()

delorean.model = "DMC-12"
```

Create a few more instances of our `class` at the bottom of the Playground:

```
let delorean = Vehicle()

delorean.model = "DMC-12"


let bmw = Vehicle()

bmw.model = "328i"


let ford = Vehicle()

ford.model = "F150"
```

Can you see what's happening? We wrote the code for a Vehicle once, but we created multiple instances of that code and setting the properties of it.

We can also call the functions for `Vehicle` as well. Just so you're aware, once we create an instance of a `class`, we call it an object.

Just like when the car leaves the factory it's then considered an object.

Try this out by adding the following to your Playground:

```
let delorean = Vehicle()

delorean.model = "DMC-12"
```

```
delorean.drive()


let bmw = Vehicle()

bmw.model = "328i"


let ford = Vehicle()

ford.model = "F150"

ford.brake()
```

We called **drive()** on our **delorean** object and **brake()** on our **ford** object.

We've told these objects to do something.

Again, think of a **class** like a blueprint – does it have any properties I should note? Are there any abilities it has or things it can do? In most cases, the answer will be yes.

Classes Are Reference Types

In Swift, there are **reference types** and value types. They are different, but we only need to know about reference types today.

I won't be going in depth into what it means, only what it means for you as the reader right now.

To demonstrate how **classes** are **reference types**, add the following function and print **ford.model** at the bottom of your Playground:

```
func passByReference(vehicle: Vehicle) {

    vehicle.model = "Cheese"

}


print(ford.model) // Prints "F150"
```

Next, call **passByReference(vehicle:)** and pass in the *ford* model:

```
func passByReference(vehicle: Vehicle) {

    vehicle.model = "Cheese"

}
```

```
print(ford.model) // Prints "F150"
```

```
passByReference(vehicle: ford) // Pass the ford class by
reference
```

```
print(ford.model) // Prints "Cheese"
```

I thought when we declared **ford** we made it a constant by using `let`?!

How is it that the model value can be changed? Well, to put it simply an object has a reference in memory.

You can't copy an object. Things like *Integers* and *Doubles* can be copied because they are value types, but not objects.

Here's another example to show how passing by reference works. Add the following variable and function to the bottom of your Playground:

```
var someonesAge = 20
```

```
func passByValue(age: Int) {

    age = 10

}
```

You probably notice that Xcode displays an error saying that **age** is a `let` constant.

Because an *Integer* is a value type, we can't modify it in the same way we can a reference type. Let's try calling our function and passing in **someonesAge**:

```
var someonesAge = 20
```

```
func passByValue(age: Int) {

    age = 10

}


passByValue(age: someonesAge)
```

Xcode won't allow for this to work. `Reference types` can be modified and they are stored in a specific place in memory, but value types (i.e. Integer, Double, Float, etc.) cannot be modified, but can be copied.

Wrapping up

This chapter covers the basics of `Classes` in `Object-Oriented Programming`. A `class` can contain properties that describe it and actions (functions) that it can perform.

We can create a copy of a `class` by instantiating it as well. While this may still be confusing, you will continue to use it in context throughout this book which will help you rapidly gain understanding.

Continue to do your research and always stay curious about learning to code. Don't ever settle with doing enough or knowing enough. There are always ways for us to improve and become better programmers.

Exercise

Create another instance of the `Vehicle` class for a car of your choice. Be sure to set a value of type String for the `model` property. Create a separate class named `Smartphone` and include some properties and/or functions that all smartphones need. Create an instance of the `Smartphone` class called `iphone` and another called `android` and set the properties to be unique to those devices. Create another instance of the `Smartphone` class for another type of smartphone.

Chapter 11: Inheritance

In programming, inheritance isn't at all about randomly gaining a large sum of money from a long-lost relative. But understanding what it means is worth much more... Possibly.

What you will learn

- What is Inheritance?
- Creating a Parent Class
- Creating a Child Class
- Overriding functions from a Parent Class

Key Terms

- `Inheritance:` a term to describe when a class is based on another class and inherits its default variables and function implementations.
- `Parent Class:` a code template with default values for variables and default implementations for functions.
- `Child Class:` a copy of a parent class with the ability to override or modify default parent class implementations and values.

In this chapter, you will read about inheritance. No, not the kind where a wealthy relative passes away leaving you with a huge lump of cash and you quit your job and run away to Bali for a permanent vacation. We're talking about `inheritance` as in inheriting features or traits as in genetics.

We will talk more about this in a moment, but let's dive into the code first.

Creating a Parent Class

First, open Xcode if you haven't already and click `Get started with a playground`. Choose a "Blank" playground and click `Next`.

Give it a name like *Inheritance*, and choose somewhere to save this .playground file and click `Create` to save it.

What is Inheritance, really?

In iOS development, `inheritance` is a feature of Object-Oriented Programming which you learned about in the previous chapter on Classes. Classes can inherit traits from other classes which makes it very useful.

Think of all this in regards to a family. In every family, there are parents and children. The parents have certain traits which get passed down to the children.

For instance, my hair is brown and my dad's hair is brown. I received that trait from him. There are a number of other traits that are the same between the two of us, but I am different from my dad in a number of ways.

While much of me is similar, I have certain skills and traits that are not like my dad.

In Swift, we will create a class to act as a `parent class`. It will contain many general traits. Then we will create a `child class` which will inherit traits from the `parent class`.

The `child class` will have the same traits as it's parent but we can add in special traits unique to the `child class` alone. But let's start by building our `parent class`.

Building a Parent Class

While we could create a class about our actual parents and make this a sort of code-based genetics experiment, let's roll with the `Vehicle` example we used in the previous chapter.

Writing a Parent Class

In your Playground window, add the following `Vehicle` class and create a few variables for things that all vehicles have in common:

```
class Vehicle {

    var wheels = 4

    var make: String?

    var model: String?

    var currentSpeed: Double = 0
```

```
}
```

Every car has 4 wheels, which is why we created that variable. But why have we not given a value for the make or model of our car?

Well, every car has a make and model of some kind, so we actually don't need to specify these properties in our `parent class`.

Adding some functions

Inside of our `Vehicle` class, we can actually create some functions that all cars will do also:

```
class Vehicle {

    var wheels = 4

    var make: String?

    var model: String?

    var currentSpeed: Double = 0


    func drive(speedIncrease: Double) {

        currentSpeed += speedIncrease

    }


    func brake() {

        currentSpeed = 0

    }

}
```

The functions above may not be the best way to actually perform the driving and braking of a car, but you get the idea - you can add functions to a `parent class`.

Now let's see `inheritance` in action - with a `child class`.

Creating a Child Class

We will create a child class (or subclass) called *SportsCar* that inherits from `Vehicle`. This means that it will inherit all the properties and functions inside the `Vehicle` class unless we change them.

Writing A Child Class

Add the following code beneath the `Vehicle` class:

```
class SportsCar: Vehicle {


}
```

What we're doing above is declaring a class called `SportsCar` and using a colon : to identify that we want to inherit from another class (in this case - Vehicle).

As our class currently stands, it is a clone of the class `Vehicle`. Everything will be implemented exactly the same way as `Vehicle`, unless we tell it to do otherwise. That is exactly what we will do now!

Before we can do anything with our `SportsCar` class we actually need to go back and add an initializer function to our `Vehicle` class.

Adding an Initializer function in the `Vehicle` Class

Inside of the `Vehicle` class, add the following `init()` function:

```
class Vehicle {
    var wheels = 4

    var make: String?

    var model: String?

    var currentSpeed: Double = 0


    init() {


    }
```

```
func drive(speedIncrease: Double) {

    currentSpeed += speedIncrease * 2

}


func brake() {

    currentSpeed = 0

}

}
```

This will give us access to the properties in `Vehicle` later on when we want to specify them in our `SportsCar` class.

We can actually do that now by overriding the `init()` function in the class `SportsCar`.

Overriding functions from `Vehicle`

Add the following code to `SportsCar`:

```
class SportsCar: Vehicle {

    override init() {

        super.init()

        make = "Lotus"

        model = "Elise"

    }

}
```

By overriding `init()` from the `Vehicle` class, we are able to change how we use it in our `SportsCar` class.

By using `super.init()` we actually are calling the function from within `Vehicle`.

Because of this we are able to initialize **make** and **model** giving them a combined value of "Lotus Elise".

Great, so our fancy-pants sports car has a name now, but we should also think about how it drives.

A sports car drives differently than, say, a minivan, right? So we should override the `drive(speedIncrease:)` function, too. Try this out in the `SportsCar` class:

```
class SportsCar: Vehicle {

    override init() {

        super.init()

        make = "Lotus"

        model = "Elise"

    }


    override func drive(speedIncrease: Double) {

        currentSpeed += speedIncrease * 4

    }

}
```

We have overridden the function `drive(speedIncrease:)` so that the amount `currentSpeed` is increased by, is much faster since a sports car should drive faster than a regular car.

Creating a Sibling Class

If we continue with the example of classes being like a family, creating another class from the `parent class` results in another `child class` and we can actually call it a sibling class in relation to the other `child classes`.

Let's create a `child class` for another type of car - the minivan. I'm fairly certain that anyone without children reading this just shuddered at the sight of that word - minivan. Sorry about that.

Aside from being an icon of the classical American family, the minivan is very different from a sports car and therefore will need to have different information inside it's class. Let's make it.

Writing another Child Class

In your Playground, add a `Minivan` class, inheriting from `Vehicle` beneath the `SportsCar` class:

```
class Minivan: Vehicle {


}
```

Overriding functions from the Parent Class

If we want to add in a custom make and model value, we need to override the `init()` function from `Vehicle` just like before. Add the following code to `Minivan`:

```
class Minivan: Vehicle {

    override init() {

        super.init()

        make = "Chevrolet"

        model = "Astro"

    }

}
```

We've now initialized the variables `make` and `model` and given them the values for a Chevrolet Astro (ah, childhood).

What we should do now is override the `drive(speedIncrease:)` function to change how our minivan drives. Anyone who's ever driven in or driven behind a minivan knows that they aren't the quickest vehicles in the world – especially if loaded up with all the kids.

Inside of the `Minivan` class, override `drive(speedIncrease:)` like so:

```
class Minivan: Vehicle {

    override init() {

        super.init()
```

```
        make = "Chevrolet"

        model = "Astro"

    }


    override func drive(speedIncrease: Double) {

        currentSpeed += speedIncrease

    }

}
```

Wrapping up

Why does this matter? It allows us to compartmentalize our code and adapt it to meet specific needs.

In closing, here's a real-life example from Instagram.

For creating their filters, Instagram may have used a `parent class` including a generic filter. But each individual filter (i.e. Valencia, Inkwell, Nashville, etc.) could have been made into a `child class` containing a unique algorithm for filtering a photo a certain way.

Rather than putting all filters in one gigantic class, `child classes` could have been used to make a much more readable and compact code base.

`Inheritance` is a foundational principle of Object-Oriented Programming and is super important to understand if you want to be a professional programmer.

Remember that this chapter is not exhaustive. There are endless resources online to help in understanding this. Never stop learning and seeking understanding.

Exercise

Create a class for a Pickup Truck that inherits from `Vehicle`. Override the initializer and set the `make` and `model` properties to fit the truck. Override the `drive(speedIncrease:_)` function so that the car can drive half as fast as the SportsCar.

In the `Vehicle` class, add a property of type `Bool` called `hasStor-ageSpace` but don't initialize it yet. Initialize that property in the classes which do or don't have storage space using `true` or `false`.

Chapter 12: Polymorphism

If you're expecting this chapter to be about a band of teenagers with "attitude" that transform into superhuman heroes, you're bound to be gravely disappointed, but don't worry. Polymorphism is just as cool as any 90's TV show.

What you will learn

- What is Polymorphism?
- Creating a base Class with requirements
- Creating a Subclass
- Implementing base Class requirements in a Subclass

Key Terms

- `Polymorphism:` being able to assign a different usage to something (like a class) in different contexts - specifically, to allow something like a variable, a function, or an object to have more than one form.

In this chapter, you will end your voyage into the basics of Object-Oriented Programming by reading about Polymorphism.

Other than being a really cool word, polymorphism is a very important concept to understand when becoming a programmer.

It is common in a developer job interview to be asked, "Can you please define 'polymorphism'?" Instead of looking like a deer in the headlights, we are going to break down what polymorphism is, what it means, and how it actually plays out in code.

What is Polymorphism?

A long-winded programming definition for polymorphism is: "Polymorphism allows the expression of some sort of contract, with potentially many types implementing that contract in different ways, each according to their own purpose."

That may be a bit of a textbook definition, but the basic concept here is that our code can occur in many different forms and its functions can be implemented in different ways.

This may still be confusing and that is okay. Let's build a code example as it is much easier to understand polymorphism this way.

Creating a new project

First, open Xcode if you haven't already and click `Get started with a playground`. Choose a "Blank" playground and click `Next`.

Give it a name like *Polymorphism*, and choose somewhere to save this .playground file and click `Create` to save it.

Creating a base Class with default functions

To begin, we will create a class called *Shape* with an area property and a function to calculate the area of our shape. Add the following to your Playground:

```
class Shape {

    var area: Double?


    func calculateArea(valueA: Double, valueB: Double) {


    }
}
```

Our base class `Shape` contains everything we need - a variable to store the area and a function to calculate an area with two input values.

Let's create a child class to inherit from our `Shape` class. What we need to do to demonstrate polymorphism is to obey the "contract" set in `Shape`, which is to have a `calculateArea` function.

Creating a Triangle Subclass

Add the following class and override the function `calculate-Area(valueA:valueB:)` at the bottom of your Playground:

```
class Shape {

    var area: Double?


    func calculateArea(valueA: Double, valueB: Double) {


    }
}


class Triangle: Shape {
    override func calculateArea(valueA: Double, valueB:
Double) {

        area = (valueA * valueB) / 2

    }
}
```

We now have created a subclass called `Triangle` and have overridden the function to calculate the area.

We're calling the same function, but the code inside is relevant to a triangle only.

This is `polymorphism` in action. The class `Shape` has a contract that all subclasses must follow which is to use the function `calculate-Area(valueA:valueB:)`.

We used it and wrote custom code inside to calculate a triangle's area.

Let's now create a Rectangle subclass and override `calculate-Area(valueA:valueB:)`.

Creating a Rectangle Subclass

Add the following code beneath the `Triangle` class:

```
class Rectangle: Shape {
    override func calculateArea(valueA: Double, valueB:
Double) {
```

```
        area = valueA * valueB

    }

}
```

Now we have two separate classes implementing the same exact function, but the logic inside is different - this is `polymorphism`.

One object (`Shape`) taking different forms (`Triangle` & `Rectangle`).

We are obeying the contract set by `Shape` by implementing `calculateArea(valueA:valueB:)` but in different ways.

Wrapping up

If you're in a job interview and are asked to define polymorphism, you can instead give them an example to explain that you understand the concept.

For instance:

Imagine that you have a Shape class and you need to calculate the area of a shape, but you don't know which shape will be passed in at runtime.

So, we create a calculateArea function and we also create two more classes for Triangle and Rectangle that inherit from Shape and at runtime they can each perform their own area calculation independent of each other and assign it into the area value.

It doesn't need to know beforehand what type of shape to pick because we have a different implementation set for each shape.

`Polymorphism` is a simple concept with a really technical definition but I hope you can see how easy it is to implement in code.

In summary, we created a base class called `Shape` which had a variable called `area` and a function called `calculateArea(valueA:valueB:)`.

Then, we created two subclasses called `Triangle` and `Rectangle`. They each inherited from `Shape`.

We obeyed the requirements from `Shape` and implemented and overrode the function `calculateArea(valueA:valueB:)`.

Inside each individual subclass, we added custom logic to calculate the areas for those particular shapes.

`Polymorphism` is what makes this possible.

Exercise

Create an subclass of `Shape` for a parallelogram. Override the area function so that it can calculate it's area. The formula for the area of a parallelogram is `A = b x h`. You're welcome.

Student Project - 1

Woohoo! You made it through section 1 and now have a good understanding of the fundamentals of Swift! That wasn't so bad, right? Now let's put your skills to the test.

Requirements:

1. Create a new Swift Playground.
2. Declares a few variables to your Playground of the following types and assign them any valid values:
3. `String`
4. `Int`
5. `Double`
6. `Float`
7. `Bool`
8. Write a function which calculates the volume of a cube. It should accept one parameter (side length) and return a value of type `Double` for the volume. The formula to determine the area of a cube is: `V = a^3^`
9. Create an array containing the names of your 4 favorite Pokémon. The values should be of type `String`.
10. Write a `for-in` loop that loops through the Pokémon array and prints "`[Pokémon name goes here], I choose you!`"
11. Create a Dictionary that contains the make and model of 4 different cars you like. If you don't like cars, you can use something else.
12. Create a Boolean variable called `downloadFinished` and write a conditional statement (`if/else`) which checks to see if it is true or not and then prints a relevant message.
13. Create a class called `Shoe` and give it properties for `hasLaces` of type Bool, `color` of type String, and `releaseDate` of type Int.

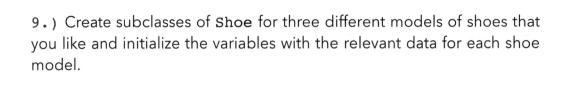

9.) Create subclasses of `Shoe` for three different models of shoes that you like and initialize the variables with the relevant data for each shoe model.

Chapter 13: Your First iOS App

Believe it or not, you're about to build your very first iOS app! I feel all bubbly inside too. From this moment on it is all projects, app building and practical application. At Devslopes we teach by doing and you learn by doing. So do it! It is going to get tough but stick with it and never give up.

What you will learn

- How to create a project in Xcode.
- How to navigate through key elements and features of Xcode.
- How to add objects such as buttons and images so the user can interact with the app.

Key Terms

- View Controller
- Utilities
- File
- Group
- Assets
- Assistant Editor
- View
- UIButton
- UIImageView
- @IBOutlet
- @IBAction
- Aspect Fill
- Aspect Fit

Resources

Download here: https://github.com/devslopes/iOS13-book-assets/wiki/iOS13-Book

Get ready, because we are about to build our very first iOS app. It will be called "Hello, World!" but it isn't the "Hello, World!" you're thinking of if you're already a programmer. Ours is going to be exciting!

Creating a new Xcode Project

First, open Xcode if you haven't already and click `Create a new Xcode project`.

Click `Single View Application`.

Click `Next`.

You should see a screen like the one in Figure 13.0.

Figure 13.0

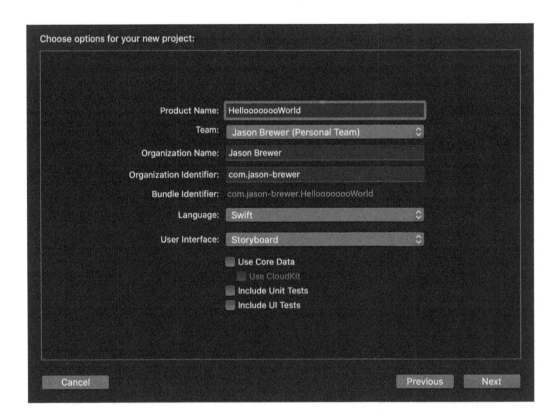

Give your project a name like *HelloooooWorld*.

Below the name field, there are a few drop down menus.

On the "User Interface" dropdown, change it from `SwiftUI` to `Storyboard`.

For the sake of this chapter, you won't need to change any of the other dropdown's. Click **Next**. Choose somewhere to save this project file and click **Create** to save it.

The next screen displayed contains your main dashboard. You will see your project settings in the center panel of the Xcode window, your project files on the left-hand side, and some document-related information on the right-hand side (Figure 13.1). We're not actually going to mess with any of this at first, but it's good for you to know where it is for later.

Figure 13.1

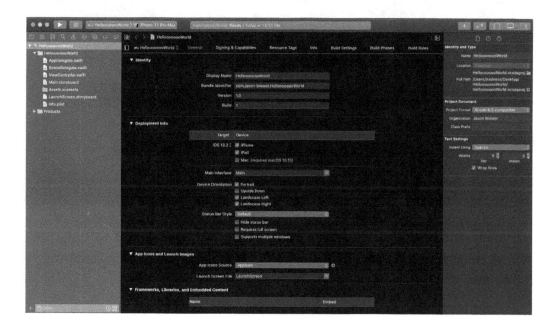

—

On the left-hand side of the Xcode window, you should see a list of files including:

- *AppDelegate.swift*
- *ViewController.swift*
- *Main.storyboard*
- *Assets.xcassets*
- *etc.*

These are the base files made by Xcode when you create a new project. Click `ViewController.swift` to open it. You will see that the center panel changes to a code editor showing the *ViewController.swift* file (Figure 13.2)

Figure 13.2

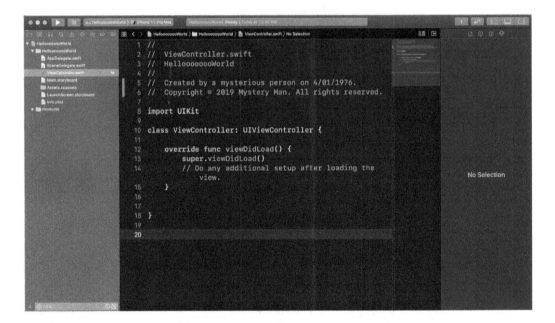

Here we will write the code for our "Hello, World!" app in this chapter. Before we write any code, however, let's go back to the `Main.story-board` by clicking on it. This should be your starting point.

Figure 13.3

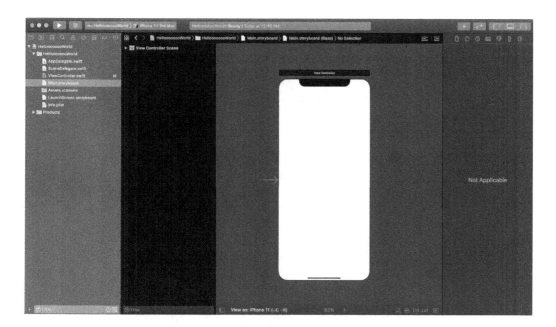

What you are seeing is called the `View Controller`. Inside the rectangle is a `View` that holds all of the objects the user is going to see and interact with. We'll go further into detail later in this chapter.

On the right you will notice a column with several icons at the top (Figure 13.4).

This is the `Utilities` column, or sometimes referred to as the `Inspector` column. This is where you will modify your objects.

Figure 13.4

To the left of the `View Controller` you will see a column titled `View Controller Scene`. (Figure 13.5)

Figure 13.5

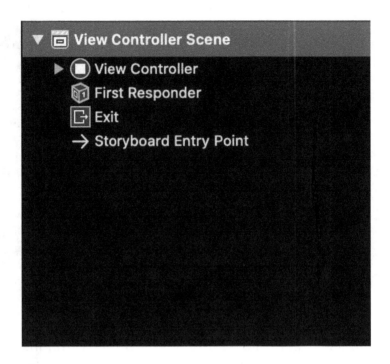

This is the `Document   Outline`. Here you will see the hierarchy of all your objects. When you want to modify an object as we mentioned above, such as a `View`, you will select it here then choose an inspector from the `Utilities` column on the right.

Just above the `Inspector` column, there is a (+) button. This is where we can access our `Object   Library`. Here you can search for objects you want to drag onto the Storyboard `View   Controller`. (Figure 13.6)

Figure 13.6

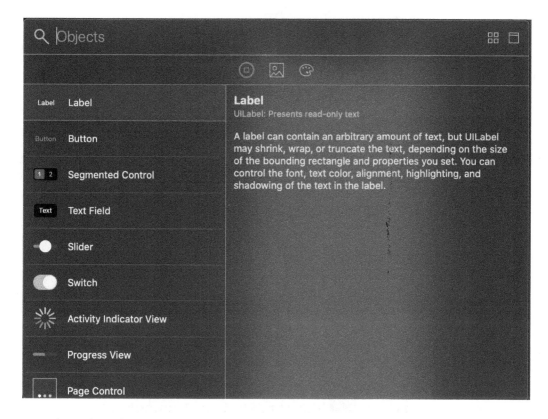

Go ahead and type the word *button* into the search bar.

To select the `Button` object simply click and drag it to the `View Controller` and let go. The `Button` will then populate the `View`.

Figure 13.7

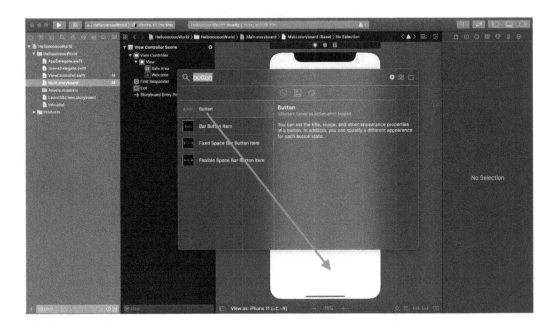

Notice in our `View Controller Scene` the `Button` now resides within the `View`.

In the `Utilities` column on the right, click the icon that looks like an arrow pointing down (the `Attributes Inspector`).

In this inspector find the "Title" dropdown. Beneath it you will see where it says *Button*. Rename it to *Welcome*.

On the Storyboard, make the button space wider by dragging the white boxes surrounding the *Welcome* so the entire word will display.

Now go into the `Assets.xcassets` folder on the left column. Drag and drop both the `HelloLogo.png` and the background image from your computer into Xcode, beneath the `AppIcon`. *These images are found in the "Resource download" link at the start of this chapter.* (Figure 13.8).

Figure 13.8

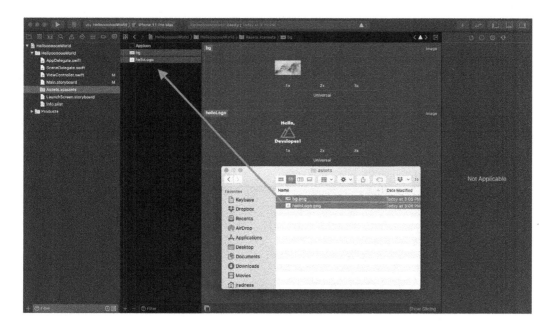

Open the Object Library again by clicking the (+) above the `Utilities` column. Type `uiimageview` into the search. Drag the image view to the top left corner of the view.

Then increase the size to touch all edges. To do this pull on the white boxes around the image view. Then put the button on top of the image view by switching their places in the `Document  Outline` column on the left. (Figure 13.9)

Figure 13.9

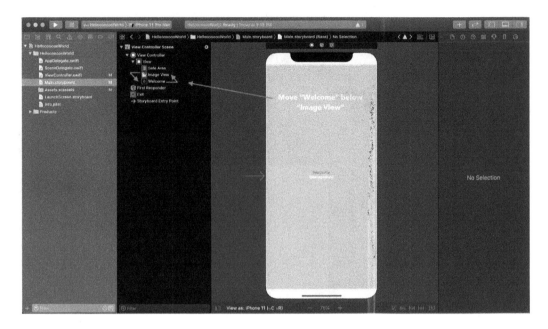

Now we need to set the image of the ImageView. To do so select the ImageView and select the `Attributes Inspector` in the `Utilities` column on the right. Find the `Image` dropdown menu and select the the background image (bg). Then find the `Content Mode` dropdown menu and change it to `Aspect Fill`. This setting basically tells the image to maintain it's aspect ratio and for it to fill the entire ImageView.

Lets repeat what we just did for the background except we are going to change the `Content Mode` to `Aspect Fit` for the logo (HelloLogo) and we are only going to extend it to the top instead of the whole view. This setting tells the image to maintain it's aspect ratio and simultaneously fit the entire image inside the ImageView. (Figure 13.10)

Figure 13.10

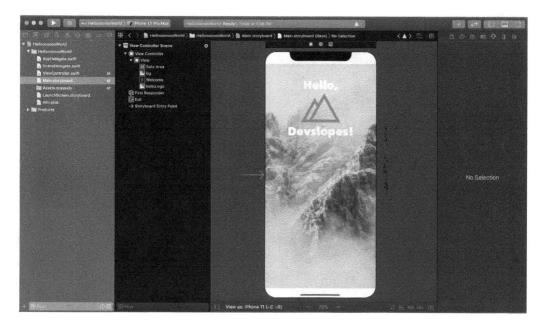

Now we need to hide the images when the app starts so that when we click the Welcome button they appear. To do so select both images by holding down the command key and click on each. Find the word `Hidden` in the `Attributes  Inspector` and click the white box next to it (Figure 13.11). The images should not be visible when you run the app.

Figure 13.11

At the top left of Xcode you will see a triangular button looking similarly to a Play button. To the right of it you can select a device to "run" the project on (Figure 13.12).

Figure 13.12

Now click the triangular "Play" button. The app you built is now being built and copied over to an app called Simulator. Simulator allows you to test your app on a virtual iPhone or iPad. When the app builds and runs, you should only see the welcome button which you can click but will have no functionality yet.

Good going so far! Isn't this awesome? Now stop the running project by clicking the square "Stop" button icon next to the "Play" button.

Next we need to tell the Welcome button to make our images visible again. To do so we need to create a couple of @IBOutlets and an

@IBAction. If we want to change anything about the current state of an object, such as the images, we need to tell the view controller to do so. We connect the objects with @IBOutlets and we give it functionality with the @IBAction.

At the top of the storyboard there is an icon to "Adjust Editor Options". From here we will select the Assistant.

Figure 13.13

You will now have a split screen with the storyboard on the left and a code editor containing ViewController.swift on the right.

As you can tell it is a bit cramped. Lets make some room by closing the two columns on the outside by clicking the blue highlighted icons at the top right of Xcode (Figure 13.14).

Figure 13.14

To connect the objects as we discussed hold the `control` button on your keyboard then click and drag from the objects , one at a time, to the `ViewController` file inside the `class` and above the `viewDid-Load()` function (Figure 13.15). Do this first with the background image.

Figure 13.15

A small gray box will box up. In the `Name` field type in `backgroundIm-age` then press `Connect`. Do the same process of adding an @IBOutlet for the other ImageView by control-dragging from the ImageView to `ViewController.swift`. Name this one: `titleImage`.

Figure 13.16

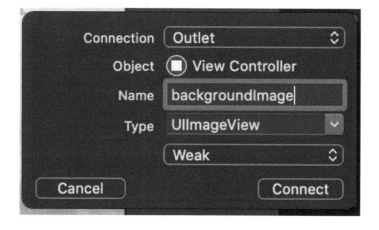

Then do the same for the welcome button because we need to hide it once we click it. Name it `welcomeBtn`. The code in your `ViewCon-`

troller.swift file should now look like the code below. Note - be sure you control_DRAG_ the images and button so they are *connected* to the ViewController. Do not copy/paste the code below.

```swift
import UIKit


class ViewController: UIViewController {


    @IBOutlet weak var backgroundImage: UIImageView!

    @IBOutlet weak var titleImage: UIImageView!

    @IBOutlet weak var welcomeBtn: UIButton!


    override func viewDidLoad() {

        super.viewDidLoad()

        // Do any additional setup after loading the
view.

    }



}
```

Now let's create an @IBAction for our welcomeBtn. Control-drag it _again_from the button to right under the viewDidLoad() function. The same box will pop up - but this time change Connection from an Outlet to an Action and name it "showImages". Then click Connect (Figure 13.17).

Figure 13.17

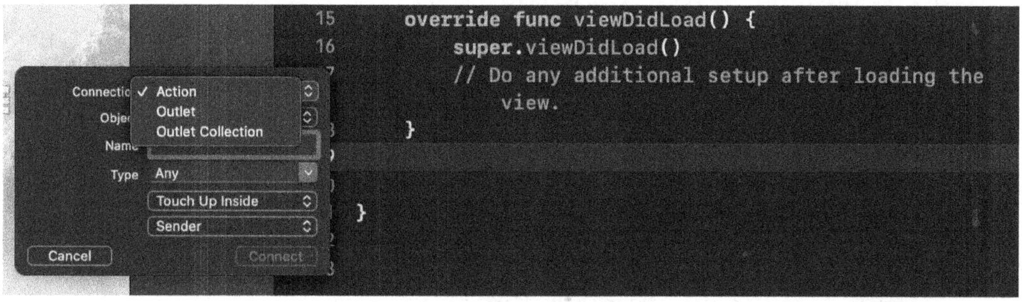

Your file should now have an @IBAction.

```
@IBAction func showImages(_ sender: Any) {

    //TO DO

}
```

In this example, an @IBAction runs the code that we put in it's brackets whenever our button is pressed. Remember earlier in this chapter, I said that inside the @IBAction is where we tell the ViewController to show the images and hide the button? Lets do it!

```
@IBAction func showImages(_ sender: Any) {

        backgroundImage.isHidden = false

        titleImage.isHidden = false

        weclomeBtn.isHidden = true

    }
```

Now, an ImageView has a handy little property called isHidden which is a Boolean. We set both images to false and the button to true. What this code does is when our button is pressed, the code inside of the @IBAction we wrote is run, making the "Welcome" button hide and both ImageViews unhide.

Click the triangular "play" button at the top left to run your app and push the "Welcome" button.

Wrapping UP

Success! Wow, you just built your very first app using Storyboards and the Swift language. You found out it is not as intimidating as you thought it was going to be and it was actually fun! Lets test those new skills with the following exercise.

Exercise

- Create a new project
- Find an image on the INTERNET of your choosing
- Have it visible when you first open the app.
- Create two buttons. One that makes the image disappear and one that makes it reappear.

Chapter 14: UIStackView

Interface Builder and Storyboards make creating app interfaces super easy and straight-forward. UIStackView is a way we can optimize and organize views in our interface in amazing, scalable ways.

What you will learn

- Use UIStackView to align your objects equally within the View Controller.

Key Terms

- UIStackView (Stack View)
- Content Mode
- Aspect Fit
- Distribution
- Axis
- Alignment

Resources

Download here: https://github.com/devslopes/iOS13-book-assets/wiki/iOS13-Book

Imagine you have added a bunch of objects into a View Controller and given them all individual constraints. Now, imagine there is a design change and you have to rip out a couple of labels and replace them with text fields. There goes all of your hard work because now you have to rip it all apart and put it all together again. Wouldn't it be cool if there was a way to be able to aggregate and remove objects and they all just automatically adjust? Well, you guessed it, UIStackView is to the rescue.

Creating a New Project and set up User Interface

To begin, open Xcode if you haven't already and click `Create a new Xcode project`. Double-click `Single View Application`, give it a name and save it anywhere.

On the left column select `Assets.xcassets` and drag all of your images under the `AppIcon` section.

Next, open up `Main.storyboard` and click on the `UIViewController` in Interface Builder.

To start building our UI, click the (+) button above the `Utilities` column to get to the "Object Library". Search for "UIView" and drag the "View" to the top of the `UIViewController`.

Pull on the white boxes to have it span the width of the `UIViewController` and shrink it to a height of 60. (You'll see a grey dimension box above the "View" you're dragging indicating the width (W) and height (H).

From the `Utilities` column on the right (with the Attributes Inspector icon selected at the top), find the "Background" dropdown and select "System Red Color" from the list to give our UIView a red background.

Now we need to pin this simulated navbar the to View Controller. Select the "Add New Constraints" icon ⊢□⊣ at the bottom right-hand side of the Interface Builder.

Let's pin it 0 from the left, 0 from the top and 0 from the right.

Then give a fixed height of 60 and click "Add 4 Constraints". (Figure 14.0)

Figure 14.0

Next, open up the "Object Library" again by clicking the (+) button above the `Utilities` column. Type `UIImageView` into the search and drag the `Image View` onto the View Controller.

Adjust the size to have a height of 130 and width of 130 by dragging the white squares but **do not** give the `Image  View` any constraints yet.

NOTE - You can also set the size by selecting the "Size Inspector" (Ruler icon) from the Inspector bar above the `Utilities` column. Enter the dimensions mentioned above into the 'Width' and 'Height'. (Figure 14.1)

Figure 14.1

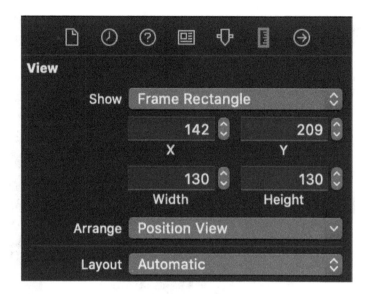

Place the image in the center of the View Controller and below the navbar with some space between the two.

Make sure the `Attribute Inspector` (downward triangle) is selected and choose the image from the drop-down menu next to the *Image* property. In this case the image's name is `Profile-Pic`.

Then change the change the `Content Mode` from `Scale to Fit` to `Aspect Fit`. (do **not** add any constraints yet)

Let's drag another `Image View` on to the View Controller right below our `Profile-Pic` and give it a width of 160, and a height of 50. In the Attributes Inspector, change the Image to `Add-User-Button`, and make sure the `Content Mode` is `Aspect Fit` as well. (Do **not** add any constraints yet).

Now, lets drag *another* `Image View` under our "Add User" button. Since this will merely be a subtle line to separate the screen, let's make the width 300, and the height 1. In the Attributes Inspector add a background color of "System Indigo Color". (Do **not** add any constraints yet).

Great! Now we're going to place 5 `Image Views` beneath our line. These should all be 50 by 50 respectively. You can either drag each one onto the View Controller individually, or configure 1, and then copy paste them next to each other 4 times. (Figure 14.2)

Figure 14.2

Now go ahead and place the remaining images into each `Image View` from the Attributes Inspector. Be sure to have their `Content Mode` set to `Aspect Fit`.

Lastly, add a text Label (search "label") from the `Object Library` with the text "View Bio." Just to make our UI look great, be sure to have the text color the same as your Navigation Bar & line.

Implementing Stack Views

If you'll notice we haven't added any constraints just yet. Running this project as is would probably result in these assets being offset and not entirely where we want them. Have no fear! That's about to change.

First, let's go ahead and select our `Profile-Pic` and look for the "Embed in" icon ⬇ on the bottom right of the Interface Builder and select the "Stack View" option.

Once you click it, you might notice the image may have slightly gotten bigger, or shifted. Don't worry! You just put the `Profile-Pic` into it's own stack view. Now go to the Attributes Inspector, and change the `Axis` to `Horizontal`.

It may not seem like much because we only have 1 element in our Stack View. Let's continue to do that for the `Add User Button` and the `line separator.` Remember to select them individually and change the `Axis` to `Horizontal`.

Now you're going to select all 5 of the circular icons. You can do this by click/dragging a box around them or clicking each of them while holding down `shift`. Once they're all selected, go ahead and click the "Embed in" button and select "Stack View". Set the `Axis` to `Horizontal`. (Figure 14.3)

Figure 14.3

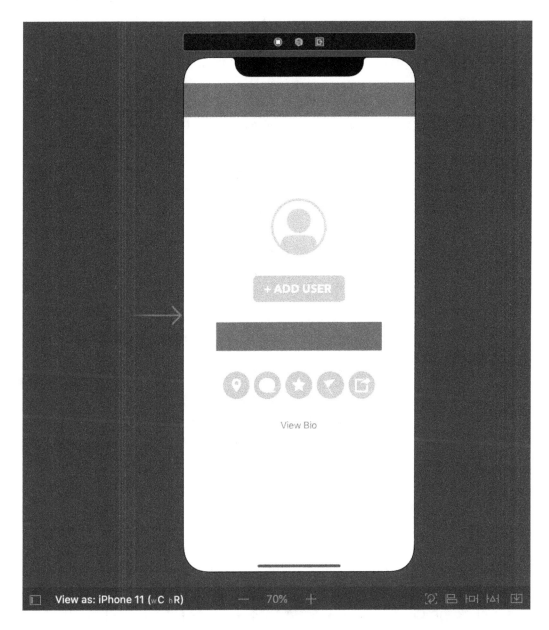

Lastly, go ahead and put the `View Bio` label in its own Stack View and set the `Axis` to `Horizontal`.

Now take all of your horizontal stack views you've just created (Profile-Pic, Add User Button, Line separator, Icons, and the View Bio label), and select them all in the left pane. With all of them selected, create another stack view but this time keep the`Axis Vertical`.

Whoa! What just happened? Let's break down exactly what we have done so far:

- We put all 5 elements into a Horizontal Stack View (Think 5 bars going across).
- We then put all those bars into a Vertical Stack View

Now all we need to do is configure them to iron out the UI!

With parent vertical stack view selected, in the Attributes Inspector, change the `Distribution` to `Equal Spacing`, and the `Alignment` to `Center`. This evenly spaces our elements with our parent stack view.

Now go ahead and click the `Align` ⊟ icon at the bottom of the Interface Builder and check "Horizontally in Container" and "Vertically in Container" and click "Add Constraints". Instead of pinning the edges of our stack view, this centers it Vertically and Horizontally in the container. This means no matter what we do, the stack view remains in the center of the view.

If you've ran the project at all during these steps you'll notice things are still a little whack. Have no fear! A few more tweaks and a touch of radness, the UI will look great!

So what's even cooler about stack views, is that we can adjust the spacing of our elements within it on the fly. With the parent stack view selected, find `Spacing` in the Attributes Inspector. From here we can increase or decrease the spacing in between elements. Let's take the `Spacing` to 35.

Now that we know we can equally space elements, lets do the same for our circle icons! Select the stack view with the circle icons, and make sure the `Distribution` is `Fill Equally`. Then increase the `Spacing` until they are a desired width apart. I'm going to set mine at **6**.

Lastly, we're going to want to fix this enormous line separator that was once our thin line separator. Select the `UIView` within the stack view, click the `Constraints` ⊡ icon, and give it a fixed height of 1 - then click "Add Constraints".

As you can see, since our line separators height becomes smaller, all the other elements within the stack view automatically adjust. If we were to delete any element within our parent stack view, all the elements would automatically fill the space equally, without us having to reset individual constraints! You're final UI should look like this (Figure 14.4). Go ahead an run the project now!

Figure 14.4

Wrapping Up

Stack views are incredibly powerful for building flexible UI. Of course, not every interface calls for the implementation of a stack view, but when it does, it will make your life a whole lot easier!

Exercise

Find some new icons and elements off of the internet, and re-create a profile screen similar to this using stack views.s

Chapter 15: Tipsy Tip Calculator App

Have you ever been at a restaurant with a group of people, received your check and felt embarrassed because you didn't know how much 15% of your bill was? You are about to save yourself a lot of heart ache while you watch all your friends experience anxiety. You are about to build the best looking tip calculator you have ever seen (in our humble opinion of course).

What you will learn

- In this chapter you will build an app that will give you your first real taste of MVC in a project. Take your time and have fun!

Key Terms

- MVC
- Model
- View
- Controller
- Data Encapsulation

Resources

Download here: https://github.com/devslopes/iOS13-book-assets/wiki/iOS13-Book

Model - View - Controller

When you, as an app user, open an application you are drawn to several buttons, a menu bar, some images and much more. You are looking at the User Interface or UI for short. When you see information on your phone's screen, you may have stopped to wonder where the data on your screen comes from and how it gets there. That data, as we call it, is all handled behind the scenes so the user doesn't have to worry about it. Where that data is stored is called the `Model` layer of the app. Data can't just appear out of thin air - it must be stored somewhere. The UI has to know where to find it and the `Model` has to know where to send it.

This communication between the `Model` and the View(UI) is handled in the `View Controller`. All three of these make up one of the most, if not most, used practices in iOS. It is called, Model - View - Controller or as you will hear all throughout the industry `MVC`.

Project creation and building the UI (User Interface)

Let's begin by creating a new project `Single View Application`, set the User Interface to `Storyboard` and call it whatever you would like. In this case we are calling it `TipsyTipCalculator`.

Once you have created the new project select `Main.storyboard` found in the project folder on the left hand side of Xcode.

Next, open up the "Object Library" by clicking the (+) button above the `Utilities` column. Type `UIView` into the search and drag the `Image View` onto the View Controller. From the Attributes Inspector click on the `Background` dropdown and select a whatever color you want. In this case we will be using #00CA79

Hint - You can set custom colors to elements! When you select the "Background" dropdown, click on "Custom" at the bottom of the list. A "color" window will appear and from there you can add/select any color.

If it is the first time you are opening the color selector you will most likely see a round color graph.

At the top of window you will see five different selections. You can choose from the circle graph the color you desire or click on the "Color Slider" icon and you will be able to enter the Hex Value provided above.

Ensure `RGB Sliders` is selected from the dropdown menu located above the sliders.

Now that you have chosen a color, drag the View to span the width of the View Controller. Now lets add some constraints. Select the "Add New Constraints" icon ⊦□⊣ at the bottom right-hand side of the Interface Builder. `Pin` it

```
0 from the left
0 from the top
0 from the right
```

Height of 60

Click `Add 4 Constraints`.

Now that we have the the top menu bar lets add a `UILabel` . Open up the "Object Library" by clicking the (+) button above the `Utilities` column. Type `UILabel` into the search and drag the `Label` onto the "navigation bar" we just created. Use the handy snap guides to position it horizontally and vertically centered.

To change the text in the label, click on it, and in the Attributes Inspector change where it says "Label" to say `Tipsy`. Press Enter so save that text.

To set a custom font and avoid using the yucky system font, from the Attributes Inspector, click the 'T' box on the right side of the `Font` property. Then click the `System  -  System` dropdown and change it to `Custom`.

At this point, you can choose whatever font you'd like and set the style and size. For this project, I'm using 'Avenir Next', 'Demi-Bold', size 30. After doing that, change the font color to white and change `Alignment` from "Left" to "Center".

If your label text has disappeared you need to increase the size of the "Label" field. To do so, click on the "Label" and drag the white boxes to enlarge the field until the text shows again.

Now we need to add some constraints to keep this label in the center of our navigation bar. When you add those constraints, they will be bound within the navigation bar.

Select the "Add New Constraints" icon at the bottom right-hand side of the Interface Builder. Check the `Width` and `Height` boxes to give the label a fixed width and height. Then click `Add  2  Constraints`.

Since we know we want this label to stay in the center of the view we are going to give it two more constraints.

Click the `Align` icon at the bottom of the Interface Builder and check "Horizontally in Container" and "Vertically in Container" and click "Add Constraints".

Now we need to start adding on the rest of our UI elements. We will make good use of `UIStackView` to make this process as simple as possible. No need to over-complicate things!

To begin, search for `UIStackView` in the Object Library and drag a `Vertical Stack View` on to the ViewController. Position it to take up the entire space below the navigation bar . Select the "Add New Constraints" icon ⊦□⊦ and pin it: (Figure 2.3.1).

0 from the top
0 from the left
0 from the right
0 from the bottom

Before you add the Constraints, be sure to check "`Constrain to margins`"

Figure 15.0

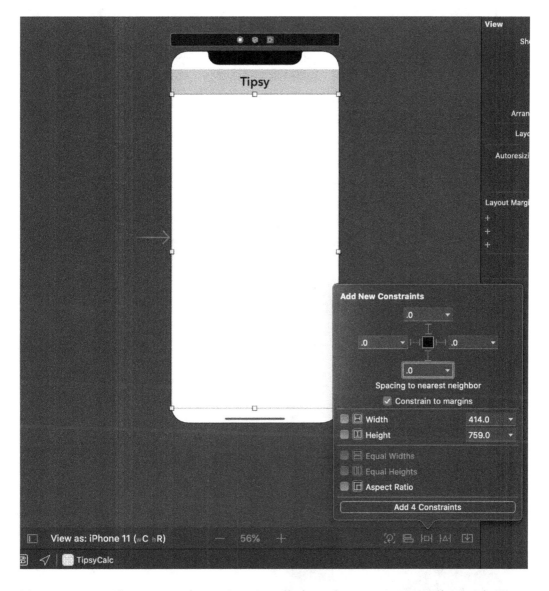

Now we need to start dropping in all the elements we will need. First, lets add a `UITextField` where the user will enter their bill amount. Search in the "Object Library" and drag on a `UITextField`. Drop it *into* the Vertical Stack View.

You probably notice that the TextField is massive and taking up the entire `UIStackView`. That will be fixed as we add more elements. Working with Stack Views can be tricky and takes persistent tweaking and modification but we'll get it to look great!

131

Click "Stack View" from the Document Outline to the left of Interface Builder. Then click on the Attributes Inspector if it isn't already.

Now we should add a slider for the user to modify with a label beside it to display the tip percentage. To do this we're actually going to drop a Stack View inside of our Stack View. Search for `Horizontal Stack View` in the "Object Library" and drag it into our original Stack View, but at the bottom so that it is beneath the `UITextField` (Figure 15.1)

Figure 15.1

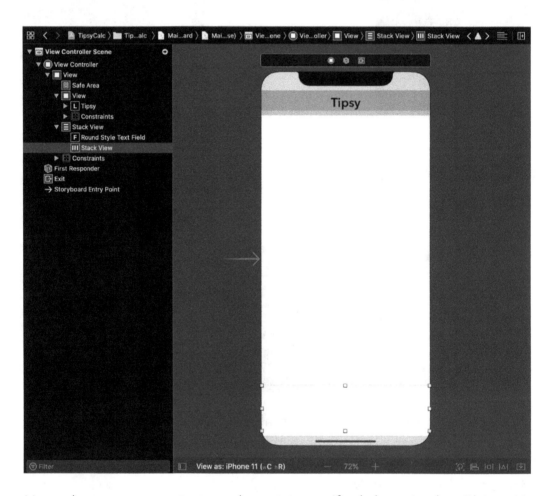

Now, drag on a `UILabel` and `UISlider` (find them in the Object Library) and drop them into the `Horizontal Stack View` you just created so that the label is on the left and the slider is on the right.(Figure 15.2)

Figure 15.2

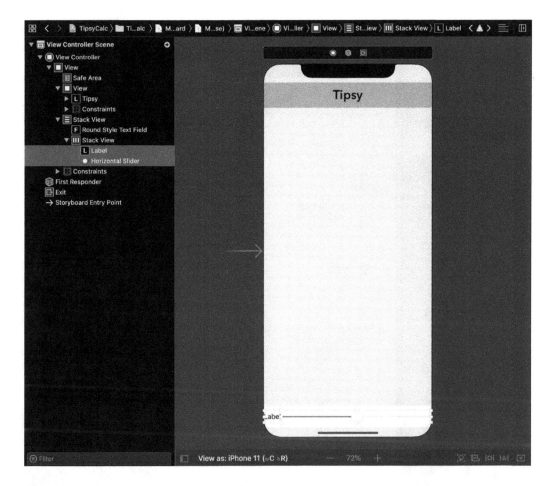

Now, let's keep on adding UI elements.

Next, beneath the slider we need to display the tip amount in dollars. To do this, we will add a nice little money icon, a label which simply says "Tip:", and another label which will update a dollar amount dynamically when the drag the slider. Just like before, we're going to use UIStackView!

Drag on another `Horizontal Stack View` beneath the previous Stack View (containing the label and tip slider), and place a `UIImageView` inside it. To the left of that `drag two UILabels side by side`. Your results may vary, but my labels were hidden by the UIImage-View. (Figure 15.3)

Figure 15.3

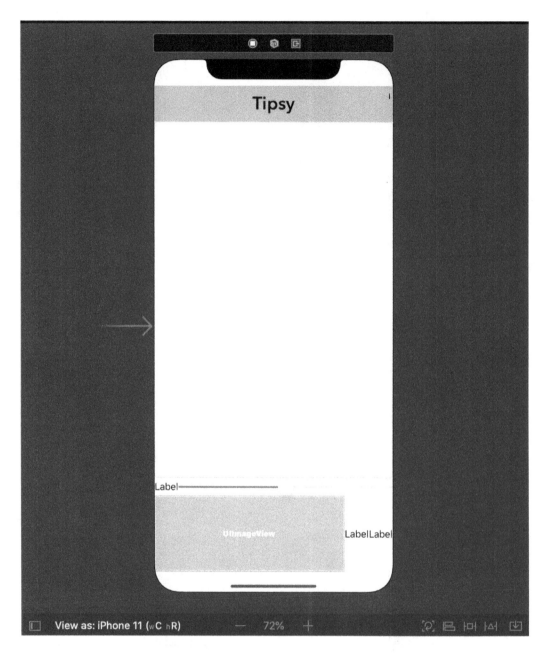

We want to make everything look nice and make sure that everything is visible so to do that, click the `UIImageView`, click the "Add New Constraints" icon ⊟, and give it a Width constraint of 60.

Do the same for the first label. While you're at it, click on the label, and in the Attributes Inspector change the text to `Tip:`.

We can leave the last label alone as it's width is fluid since we haven't changed anything about it. It is dependent on the other two elements which have their width locked thanks to constraints.

Beneath the lowest `Stack View`, we need another `Stack View` with duplicate contents so click on the `Stack View` in the Document Outline on the left, press ⌘ + C then ⌘ + V and you should see a duplicate `Stack View` appear below (Figure 15.4):

Figure 15.4

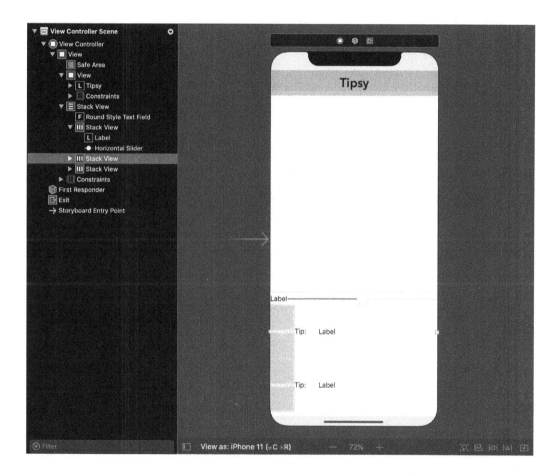

Alright, so now we have all the important UI elements we need for our app, but let's make them look better.

First of all, our main parent `Stack View` that is holding the `UITextField` and the other Stack Views is pinned to the outer edges of our screen and I think it would look better if we pulled it in a little from each side.

To do this, click the top-level parent Stack View in the Document Outline, click the "Size Inspector" 📏 icon above the `Utilities` column. In the "Constraints" section you can see the 4 constraints we created earlier.

Click the `Edit` button on the "Align Trailing to:" and set the Constant value to 30. Press Enter to lock it in place. Repeat this process for all three of the remaining constraints.

"Align Trailing to:" 30

"Align Leading to:" 30

"Align Top to:" 30

"Align bottom to:" 30

Now let's add some spacing between each vertical element of the main parent Stack View. Select it using the Document Outline and in the Attributes Inspector, change the `Spacing` property from 0 to 20.

Alright, now let's set up the `UITextField` so it isn't so massively tall.

Click on it and click the "Constraint" icon ⊢◻⊣ to add a `Height` constraint of 70, the click "Add Constraints".

Now, in the Attributes Inspector set the `Alignment` to `Center` and set the font to `Custom` and use any font you'd like.

In the `Placeholder` field, type "enter bill amount" and press enter. A little further down, change the `Keyboard Type` from `Default` to `Decimal Pad`.

At the moment, we are pinning our main outer Stack View to the bottom which is why it's pulling down the other two Stack Views inside. To fix that, we simply need to experiment with changing the `Constant` of the bottom constraint until the spacing looks right. So to do this, click on the parent 📏 Stack View from the Document Outline and click the Size Inspector 📏.

Click `Edit` to change the constant value for the `Bottom Space` constraint. Instead of 30 change it to something between 300-350. Whatever looks best to you.

Stack Views can be inconsistent in how it displays in Interface Builder, so let's make sure it will evenly space our two identical Stack Views (including the image view and two labels) by giving the three Stack Views nested inside the parent Stack View all a height constraint of 30. (Click the "Constraints" icon [icon] to add the height constraint). Your ViewController should look like Figure 15.5

Figure 15.5

Now let's change the color and text of the label to the *left* of our **slider**. Click on it and in the Attributes Inspector change the color to the same blue color as the UIView above (#88B5FF). Change the label text to say **Tip:**. Press Enter to save it. Then add a width "Constraint" [icon] of 60.

Change the color of the other two labels that say **Tip:** to match (#88B5FF).

It also looks as though we should change the Width constraint of the **Tip:** label (in the Stack View) to narrow spacing between it and the other label to the right of it. Click on the label, open the Size Inspector [icon], click **Edit**, and change the Constant value to 40 instead of 60.

Now we need to add some spacing to our two identical embedded Stack Views. In the Document Outline, select one of the Stack Views (containing the Image View and two labels) and in the Attributes Inspector change the **Spacing** property from 0 to 10. Then select the other Stack View and repeat this process.

Change the label in the bottom-most Stack View to say **Total:** instead of **Tip:**.

Now select every label we've made (except the "Tipsy" label at the top. You can do this from the Document Outline) and in the Attributes

Inspector change the font from the `System font` to whatever custom font you're using.

Finally, the very last thing we need to do is set our `UIImageViews` to the images we downloaded from the resources above. In Xcode, select `Assets.xcassets` and then open the *Tipsy Assets* folder from the downloaded resources. Drag in the image files from that folder.

Now, return to `Main.storyboard` and click on the top-most `UIImageView` next to the `Tip:` label. In the Attributes Inspector, in the `Image` text field, type `tipIcon` and press Enter to lock it in place.

Next, click `Content Mode` and change it to `Aspect Fit`.

Do the same process for the `UIImageView` beneath this one, but set the image to `totalIcon`. At the very end, your completed UI should look like (Figure 15.6)

Figure 15.6

Throw your hands in the air and yell something cool because the user interface is now done! Let's move into the fun stuff now - writing code!

Creating A Data Model

We're going to dive into the code by creating our data model. Remember, the model layer is all about data. It will be the "brains" of our calculator as it will help with storing and calculating the bill amount, tip percentage, tip amount, and total amount (after tip).

To get started, right-click on the yellow Model folder in the Project Navigator (far left column) and click `New File...`

On the pop-up that follows, click `iOS` in the top left, then double-click on `Swift File`. Name it "TipModel" and click **Create**.

You now should be looking at a blank `TipModel.swift` file in the Xcode code editor.

Let's begin by declaring the class. Beneath import Foundation type:

```
import Foundation


class TipModel {


}
```

This is the body of our model class. Next, we need to add some properties for data that needs to be stored and managed by our app. We will need to consider the bill amount, tip percentage, tip amount, and the total amount.

Add the following properties like so:

```
import Foundation


class TipModel {

    private var _billAmount: Double = 0

    private var _tipPercent: Double = 0

    private var _tipAmount: Double = 0

    private var _totalAmount: Double = 0

}
```

The reason why you've used the keyword private, is to render the variables above as, well, private... This means that they are not accessible from outside this class. We call this `Data Encapsulation` and it means that the way we're using this code is kept hidden from the user and the user can only do a limited number of things to this code by calling functions unique to this class. If you're wondering why we used underscores before the names of our variable, I will explain it in a moment.

In order to access the variables above we need to use *accessors* which are affectionally called *getters* and *setters*. Essentially, we will create four new variables which will have the same name as the private variables from above, just without the underscore. These variables will allow for you to read (get) the value of a variable and write (set) a new value to that variable. They also will be available to us outside of this class. They are sort of like an intermediary between us and the private variables.

To do that, add the following code beneath where you created the private variables:

```
class TipModel {

    private var _billAmount: Double = 0

    private var _tipPercent: Double = 0

    private var _tipAmount: Double = 0

    private var _totalAmount: Double = 0


    var billAmount: Double {

        get {

            return _billAmount

        } set {

            _billAmount = newValue

        }

    }


    var tipPercent: Double {

        get {

            return _tipPercent

        } set {

            _tipPercent = newValue
```

```
        }

    }


    var tipAmount: Double {

        return _tipAmount

    }


    var totalAmount: Double {

        return _totalAmount

    }

}
```

Whew, that was a lot of code! Let's unpack it now.

What we've done is create four new variables with the same names as the private variables above just without the underscore.

For the first two, `billAmount` and `tipPercent`, we used the `get` to return the value of `billAmount`. We used `set` to change the value of `billAmount` and used `newValue`.

`newValue` is built into Xcode and basically, when using a `setter` it sets the value of the private variable to whatever value a particular variable is changed to. However it's modified, the `newValue` will be equal to that value.

Since we don't need to write a value for the `tipAmount` and `totalAmount` variables, we didn't explicitly use *get* or *set*. In returning values we are essentially "reading" the values of those variables like when we use *get*.

"Now, when we use this data model later on, we will need to pass in values for billAmount and tipPercent. In order to make sure this happens, let's write an initializer function.

Writing A Custom Initializer

At the bottom of `TipModel`, beneath the variables we created, including getters and setters, write the following function:

```
init(billAmount: Double, tipPercent: Double) {

    self._billAmount = billAmount

    self._tipPercent = tipPercent

}
```

When we create an instance of `TipModel` in our `ViewController` later on (don't freak out, I will go over this in detail), we will use the `init(billAmount:tipPercent:)` function to give the instance some initial values to work with.

What we need to do to wrap up our data model is write a function to calculate the tip we need to pay. We can use the values passed in when `TipModel` is instantiated. Let's write that function now.

Writing A Function To Calculate the Tip Amount

So let's think about how we should calculate the tip amount. If we know the bill amount (i.e. $36.50) and the tip percentage (i.e. 15%), we can multiply the bill amount by the percentage to get the tip amount (i.e. $5.47).

So, using our variable names the formula would look like this:

```
tipAmount = billAmount * tipPercent
```

Beneath the *initializer* function, write the skeleton of the following function and the formula needed to calculate the tip amount:

```
func calculateTip() {

    _tipAmount = billAmount * tipPercent

}
```

Great! So now our formula can calculate the tip amount. But that isn't completely helpful in and of itself. We want to know the total amount for the meal and the tip included. To calculate that, we should add the following line of code to add the bill amount to the tip amount:"

```
func calculateTip() {

    _tipAmount = billAmount * tipPercent
```

```
    _totalAmount = billAmount + tipAmount
}
```

Now both values `tipAmount` and `totalAmount` will be set, thanks to their setters!

BOOM! Our model is done! Now we're going to set up the `View-Controller` (i.e. the Controller layer) to handle passing data to the View layer making our app interactive and fun!

Setting Up the ViewController

At the moment, we don't have a "Controller folder" to drag `ViewController.swift` into - you know, for organization's sake and all. Let's create one and do that. Right-click on the yellow `Model` folder in the Project Navigator (far left column) and click `New Group` and name the folder `Controller`.

Once you've done that, click on `ViewController.swift` and drag it into the folder. Click on the file again to assure it's selected and delete the commented-out line from within `viewDidLoad()`, but leave the function in place like so:

```
import UIKit


class ViewController: UIViewController {

    override func viewDidLoad() {

        super.viewDidLoad()


    }
}
```

At the top, `import UIKit` tells Xcode to include the `UIKit` framework which contains everything you will need for interacting and manipulating UI elements and much more.

The function `viewDidLoad()` is called after the controller is loaded into memory. To put it simply, the code in viewDidLoad() basically run as the app loads past the launch screen.

As you will see in later chapters, there are ways to call code before and after the view loads/appears. Now, we need to create some `@IBOutlets` so we can communicate with our UI elements like the slider, labels, and text field.

Creating @IBOutlets

Click on `Main.story``rd` and once it's opened, click on the "Adjust Editor Options" icon and select `Assistant` from the list. You will now have a split screen with the storyboard on the left and a code editor containing `UIViewController` on the right.

You might be feeling a little claustrophobic with all those views open in Xcode . Lets make some room by closing the two columns on the left and right side of Xcode. Click the right and left show/hide Navigator icons at the top right of the Interface Builder.

The `ViewController.swift` file should automatically load beside Interface Builder but in case it doesn't, save the project, close Xcode, and reopen the project. Sometimes Xcode gets lost day dreaming and forgets work correctly...

Now let's actually create some `@IBOutlets`. We'll start with the text field.

Right-click and hold on the `UITextField` and drag until the cursor is above `viewDidLoad()` but beneath the class declaration of `View-Controller` (Figure 15.7):

Figure 15.7

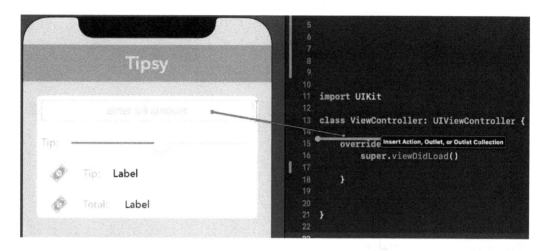

When you release the mouse, you will be presented with a pop-up just like in and an empty Name text field. Type "textField", make sure the `Connection` dropdown above says `Outlet` and press `Connect`. Now we've properly connected our text field so that we can read values from it.

Following the same steps, you will need to create `@IBOutlets`s for the following elements:

- `UISlider` - "tipPercentageSlider"
- `Tip` label to the *left* of the slider - "tipPercentageLabel"
- `Label` to the *right* of the `Tip:` - "tipLabel"
- `Label` to the *right* of the `Total:` - "totalLabel"

In all you should have the following `@IBOutlets` in your ViewController class:

```
import UIKit


class ViewController: UIViewController {


    @IBOutlet weak var textField: UITextField!

    @IBOutlet weak var tipPercentageSlider: UISlider!
```

```
@IBOutlet weak var tipPercentageLabel: UILabel!

@IBOutlet weak var tipLabel: UILabel!

@IBOutlet weak var totalLabel: UILabel!


override func viewDidLoad() {

    super.viewDidLoad()



    }

}
```

Setting Up UISlider

UISlider can be set up with a value, minimum, and maximum property.

The value property is what UISlider is first loaded with. It will display at this value. The *minimum* and *maximum* values are essentially the range that the UISlider can handle.

To modify these values, click on the UISlider and ensure that the Attributes Inspector is open (open the right column if needed from the show/hide Navigation icon). Set the Value property to 0.15 for a default tip amount of 15% (standard in the U.S.), the Minimum property to 0.1 and the Maximum property to 0.25.

Creating an Instance of our Data Model

Now, we're going to create an instance of our data model so that we can pass in values and calculate the tip as we'd like. To do this, add the following variable beneath the @IBOutlets:

```
var tip = TipModel(billAmount: 0.0, tipPercent: 0.0)
```

We've created an instance of the class TipModel. Since classes are reference types, we have created a reference to the original class (sort of like a link on a website).

We passed in a static amount of $0.00 and a tip percentage of 0% but we will change that later on. So the variables `billAmount` and `tipPercent` are now set and are ready for use by the rest of the class.

If you glance back in this chapter to when we created the `TipModel`, we wrote a function called `calculateTip()` which calculates our tip amount (believe it or not!) by multiplying the bill amount by the tip percentage which we now have.

We'll use this function momentarily, but first, we should set up some `@IBAction`s to control the changing of the bill amount text field and tip percentage slider value.

Setting up @IBActions

To create an `@IBAction`, we'll do the same thing we did when we created the IBOutlets. Simply right-click and drag from the element you want and drop it at the bottom of your class in the `UIViewController`. Do this for the `UITextField`.

When you get the pop-up, click on the `Connection` dropdown menu and change it from `Outlet` to `Action`. Give it a descriptive name like `billAmountWasChanged`. Since we're dealing with a `UITextField`, change the dropdown below from `Value Changed` to `Editing Changed`. We're doing this so that when we enter a value into the text field, it can update as we type. After that's done, click `Connect`.

> *Helpful Hint:*
>   *It is not mandatory to put @IBActions at the bottom of your code files, but it is fairly common to separate @IBOutlets and @IBActions like this.*

Now, we have an `@IBAction` for our `UITextField` and you probably noticed that it looks a lot like a function. That's because it is! Whenever the value is changed in the text field, we can call code to run! Let's just print a value for now. Inside of `billAmountWasChanged(_sender:)`, add the following line of code:

```
@IBAction func billAmountWasChanged(_ sender: Any) {

        print("My value changed!")
```

```
        }
```

Now when we run our app and enter a value and/or change it, the code inside the `@IBAction` will be called. Let's give it a shot!

Click the triangular "Play" button at the top-left side of Xcode to build & run the project. So far so good! As you enter and remove values, the console prints that the "value was changed".

"Now let's set up the UISlider's @IBAction and test it also. Switch back over to Xcode from the Simulator and in `Main.storyboard`. Right-click and drag from the `UISlider` to beneath the `@IBAction` `billAmountDidChange`.

Set the `Connection` to `@IBAction`, the Name to `tipPercentageDidChange` and the event to `Value Changed`. Click `Connect` and inside the brackets of `tipPercentageDidChange` add the following line to test if it's working:

```
@IBAction func tipPercentageDidChange(_ sender: Any) {

        print(tipPercentageSlider.value)

    }
```

Click the Build & Run button again to check if our slider is working properly. Once it builds and opens in Simulator slide the slider around a bit and check out what happens. You should see a list of values printing out to the console!

```
0.15622744

0.15731047

0.158574

0.16019855

0.1616426

    .

    .
```

As you can see, the value prints out whenever we move the slider at all which is exactly what we're looking for.

Updating the Labels in the View Layer

Now that we know our @IBActions are working, we will write a few functions to set the tip calculation values as well as update the user interface.

Above the `@IBActions` but beneath `viewDidLoad()`, add the following functions:

```
func setTipCalculationValues() {

    tip.tipPercent = Double(tipPercentageSlider.value)

    tip.billAmount = ((textField.text)! as
NSString).doubleValue

    tip.calculateTip()

}


func updateUI() {

    tipLabel.text = String(format: "$%0.2f",
tip.tipAmount)

    totalLabel.text = String(format: "$%0.2f",
tip.totalAmount)   tipPercentageLabel.text = "Tip: \
(Int(tipPercentageSlider.value * 100))%"

}
```

Let me explain the first function, `setTipCalculationValues()`. First, we call `tip` which is the instance of our data model. Then, we set it's `tipPercent` property to be the same as whatever the value of the `tipPercentageSlider` is.

We placed `tipPercentageSlider.value` inside of parentheses and wrote `Double` in front of it so that we are setting it as a double value instead of Float as provided by UISlider. Then, we set `tip.billAmount` to whatever value the `UITextField` has been set with.

The interesting thing is that a `UITextField` deals with values of type String, so we wrap `textField.text` in parentheses and use a ! to tell Xcode that we definitely have a value. We force it to be "downcast" as type `NSString`, which has a property `.doubleValue`. Essentially, we are converting a String (guaranteed to be a number) as a Double. At the end, we call `tip.calculateTip()` which sets the properties `tipAmount` and `totalAmount` in our data model. We use those values to modify the `UILabels` in our ViewController to show the tip and total values.

Next we call the function `updateUI()` which sets the text property of `tipLabel`, `totalLabel`, and `tipPercentageLabel`. We set the type of `tipLabel` and`totalLabel` to String but we use parentheses to include a custom feature which is displaying as U.S. currency ($).

For the `format` property, we wrote `"$%0.2f"` which is a way of telling Xcode that any number value we pass in will be converted to look like a U.S. currency value (i.e. 5 becomes $5.00). For the `tipPercentageLabel` we set it to say "Tip: " and then we use String Interpolation to pass in the value of the `tipPercentageSlider` and multiply it to get the percentage as a whole number (i.e. 0.1 * 100 = 10%).

Calling the Functions from @IBActions

As you know, functions don't do anything unless they are called from somewhere else, so let's do that. Our @IBActions are a perfect place to call them from.

When we enter in a value for the `billAmount`, we should call `setTipCalculationValues()` and `updateUI()` so that we can display a tip calculation every time we add or remove a value. We should call the same code when we change the value of the slider. Call both functions from each @IBActions like this:

```
@IBAction func billAmountWasChanged(_ sender: Any) {

        setTipCalculationValues()

        updateUI()

    }



@IBAction func tipPercentageDidChange(_ sender: Any) {

    setTipCalculationValues()

    updateUI()

}
```

There is one last place we need to call the `updateUI()` and `setTip-CalculationValues()` function - in `viewDidLoad()`! This is so that when our view loads the labels display $0.00 which is the amount we've entered when the app loads - nothing!

```
override func viewDidLoad() {

        super.viewDidLoad()

        setTipCalculationValues()

        updateUI()


    }
```

Testing

Click the triangular Build & Run button and let the app build and run in Simulator. Try it out! You should be able to add a value to the `UIText-Field` and the *tip* and *total* should display at the bottom. The *tip amount* to the left of the slider should also be displaying. If any element sizes seem off, go ahead and adjust them using the Size Inspector (■).

Making UISlider Snappier

When sliding the UISlider from 12% to 13%, for example, you probably notice that the tip and total amounts keep changing. Our UISlider is fluidly sliding from 12%-12.1%-12.2% and so on. We want to set it to snap at whole number values. We can do this with a bit of math.

Add the following code to the `tipPercentageDidChange` @IBAction:

```
@IBAction func tipPercentageDidChange(_ sender:
UISlider) {

        let steps: Float = 100

        let roundedValue = round(sender.value * steps) /
steps

        sender.value = roundedValue
```

151

```
setTipCalculationValues()

updateUI()

}
```

Don't worry if you don't fully understand this bit of code, but essentially we are creating a Float type variable set to a value of 100, representing 100 "steps" a UISlider can take (percentages).

Then, we round the value using a built-in Swift `round()` function. We take whatever value is being passed in and multiply it by steps (100). It is then rounded to the nearest whole number.

Next, we divide it by 100 to get it back down to a number `UISlider` can understand.

Here's an example: We set UISlider to 0.12223182 which is a bit over 12%. We can use this value in the @IBAction by calling `sender.value` (assuming that the sender is of type `UISlider`). You can change it to be in the @IBAction if yours is set to *Any*.

Then, we create the constant `roundedValue` by passing in `sender.value` (0.12223182) multiplied by 100 (steps) which equals 12.223182. Since this is inside the `round()` function, it is rounded down to the whole number 12. We then divide it by 100 (steps) and it equals 0.12 again. Next, we set `sender.value` to be equal to `roundedValue`, forcing it to snap into place at exactly 12%!

Take a look at the app you've just made! I know it was difficult to understand and work through this chapter, but you did it! A major milestone on your path to becoming a developer!

Figure 15.8

Wrapping up

You now have created an amazing app which can calculate the tip amount and total amount you need to know when paying your bill. This chapter taught the basics of `Model-View-Controller` and while we didn't dive in too deeply to the View layer, you will learn to rely on that much more heavily in the chapters to come. You will create custom view layers which can set a custom appearance for any of the UI elements.

For the scope of this chapter, you learned what the View layer is and will soon put that practice into practice.

We created a data model that stored and performed calculations on several important variables. We used our ViewController to work with the View layer to display and show values from the data model.

Exercise

Are you ready for a challenge? Of course you are! Using what you've learned in this chapter, add functionality to split bills using a UISlider and dividing totalAmount to split the bill between a group of people.

Chapter 16: UIScrollView & Paging

Many apps feature content that must be scrolled through or paged through, but not many coding teachers will teach you how to use `UIScrollView` to do this. In this book, you will learn how so you're prepared.

What you will learn

- Creating a `UIScrollView`
- Allowing `UIScrollView` paging
- Adding UIImageView as a Subview
- Setting `UIScrollView`'s `contentSize` property

Key Terms

- `UIScrollView`

Resources

Download here: https://github.com/devslopes/iOS13-book-assets/wiki/iOS13-Book

Apps like Devslopes original app use `UIScrollView` to allow a user to page between relevant content. In the case of the Devslopes app, you can scroll between pages including the different "Slopes" (Figure 16.0)

Figure 16.0

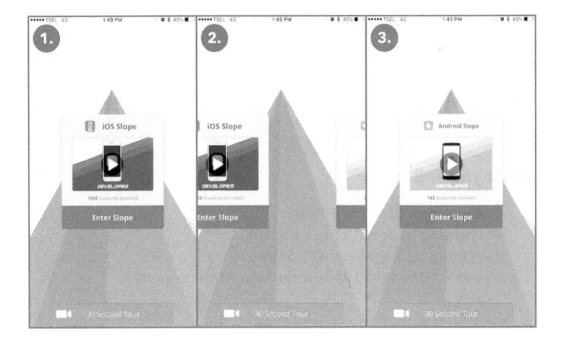

Setting up

Creating a new Xcode project

Let's begin by creating a new project, `Single View Application`, set the User Interface to `Storyboard` and call it whatever you would like. In this case we are calling it `PageTheScroll` .

Building the User Interface

Click on `Main.storyboard` to open up Interface Builder. Next, download the assets for this project from the link above. Then, click on `Assets.xcassets` and drag all downloaded assets inside like we've done before.

Adding a UIImageView

Now we need to give our app a background image. Next, open up the "Object Library" by clicking the (+) button above the `Utilities` column. Search for `UIImageView` and drag one onto our ViewController. Drag the elements edges so it spans the full size of the ViewController.

With the UIImageView selected, click the "Constraints" icon ⊢□⊣ at the bottom right-hand side of the Interface Builder. Add constraints pinning it a distance of 0 from all sides of the view. Make sure to check "Constrain to margins".

Next, click on the UIImageView and select the Attributes Inspector if it isn't selected already. Set the `Image` property to be "Sky" image and the `Content Mode` to be `Apsect Fill`. This is so that our image maintains it's aspect ratio, while filling to the edges of the UIImageView like a picture in a frame. It will look best on all screen sizes this way.

Next, drag on another UIImageView and position it in the top right corner. In the Attributes Inspector for this UIImageView, set the `Image` property to "Sun" and the `Content Mode` to be `Aspect Fit`.

Click the "Constraints" icon ⊢□⊣ at the bottom and pin it 0to the right and 20 to the top. Make sure you tick "Constrain to margins" and the `Height` and `Width` boxes to give it a fixed width and height so that it remains the size we want.

Drag on one last UIImageView and position it at the bottom like so (Figure 16.1):

Click the "Constraints" icon ⊢□⊢ at the bottom right-hand side of the Interface Builder. Pin it 0 to the bottom, left, and right sides. Also, tick the `Height` box to give it a fixed height.

In the Attributes Inspector ⬇, set the `Image` property to "Mountains" and the `Content Mode` to `Aspect Fill`.

Alright, so now we have a nice background for our app. We didn't have to spend time making this, but it's important to always make things look good in addition to running well.

Adding `UIScrollView`

Next, we are going to add in a `UIScrollView` which will perform all of the scrolling and paging we want for this app. Open the "Object Library" (+) and search for a "`UIScrollView`", and **drag one into the Document Outline on the left-hand side** of the Interface Builder, just beneath the "Mountains".

The reason we didn't drop the `UIScrollView` on top of the View-Controller is because *sometimes* there are issues with `UIScrollView` in Interface Builder, so adding it to the Document Outline ensures that we position it in the right place - as the top-most item in front of everything else.

Next, drag and position the `UIScrollView` so that it takes up the entire frame of the ViewController - just like we did for the UIImageView with the background image.

The `UIScrollView` is created transparent, but you should see the text "`UIScrollView`" in the center of element.

Next, with the `UIScrollView` selected, in the Attributes Inspector, **untick** the boxes for: `Shows Horizontal Indicator`, `Shows Vertical Indicator` and **tick** the box `Paging Enabled` (Figure 16.2).

Figure 16.2

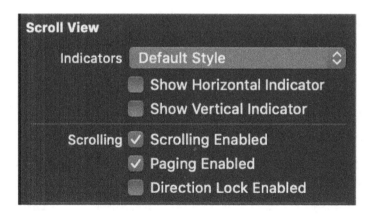

Adding content to `UIScrollView`

Great, now that we've added on a `UIScrollView` we need to give it some content so that it's useful! Click on `ViewController.swift` in the Navigator on the left-hand side of the Xcode window.

Next up, let's create an empty array of UIImageViews to contain all of our course icons from the **Assets.xcassets** folder. We'll also create a for loop to create images to store inside each UIImageView. Add the image array above `viewDidLoad()`, and the **for-in** loop within the **super.viewdidLoad()**:

```
import UIKit


class ViewController: UIViewController {


    var images = [UIImageView]()


    override func viewDidLoad() {
        super.viewDidLoad()


        for x in 0...2 {
            let image = UIImage(named: "icon\(x).png")
            let imageView = UIImageView(image: image)
            images.append(imageView)
        }

    }

}
```

So you just wrote the code to create an array of UIImageView. Then you wrote a **for-in** loop which cycles from 0 up until 2. After, you created a constant called **image** which creates a UIImage and passes in the value for **x** into the filename for the picture (icon0.png, icon1.png, icon2.png). Then we create a constant of type UIImageView and pass in the UIImage. At the end of the loop, we append a UIImageView (containing a UIImage) to our array called **images**.

So after the loop runs, we have the following inside the **images** Array:

- UIImageView -> UIImage -> icon0.png
- UIImageView -> UIImage -> icon1.png
- UIImageView -> UIImage -> icon2.png

If you build and run your app at this point, you will definitely see our nice mountain background image, but the icons are nowhere to be found. That's because we haven't placed them anywhere yet, we only created them.

Now let's get our images actually showing up in the `UIScroll-View`.

Before we move forward though, I want you to think of `UIScroll-View` like it's a magical window looking out into the world. When you drag your finger across the window, the world outside moves with your finger, instead of you needing to move your head to see what's outside.

`UIScrollView` has a property called `contentSize` which allows you to define how much content can be inside of a `UIScrollView`. As per the example above, the content size allows you to choose how big the world is through the window. We'll set the `contentSize` momentarily.

Connecting `UIScrollView` to our **ViewController.swift** file

Let's create an @IBOutlet so that we can interact with our `UIScroll-View` and add in those images.

Click on `Main.storyboard` and once it's opened, click on the "Adjust Editor Options" icon ▤ and select `Assistant` from the list. You will now have a split screen with the storyboard on the left and a code editor containing `ViewController.swift` on the right.

Right-click and hold on "Scroll View" from the Document Outline and drag the cursor over to `ViewController.swift`. Release the cursor above `viewDidLoad()`.

When you release the cursor give the @IBOutlet a name of `scrollView` and leave all other properties as is. Now we can interact with the `UIScrollView` and make it do cool things!

Positioning UIImageView on `UIScrollView`

Now we need to set up some code which will be responsible for helping us to scroll our content and contain pages of content, too.

Inside the `for-in` loop lets add the following lines of code:

```
for x in 0...2 {

    let image = UIImage(named: "icon\(x).png")

    let imageView = UIImageView(image: image)

    images.append(imageView)


    var newX: CGFloat = 0.0


    newX = view.frame.midX + view.frame.size.width *
CGFloat(x)

}
```

What we have done is create a variable of type CGFloat called `newX`. We then set it's value, but it may be confusing to a new programmer to understand these values with no explanation. Let me explain.

1.) `view.frame.midX` is a value that takes the current view (in this case, our screen) and looks for the size of it's `frame` (in this case, the same size as our screen). Then it calculates the midpoint on the X axis.

So, if your screen was 320 pixels wide, the `midX` point would be 160. Figure 16.3 shows how the grid actually works in iOS:

Figure 16.3

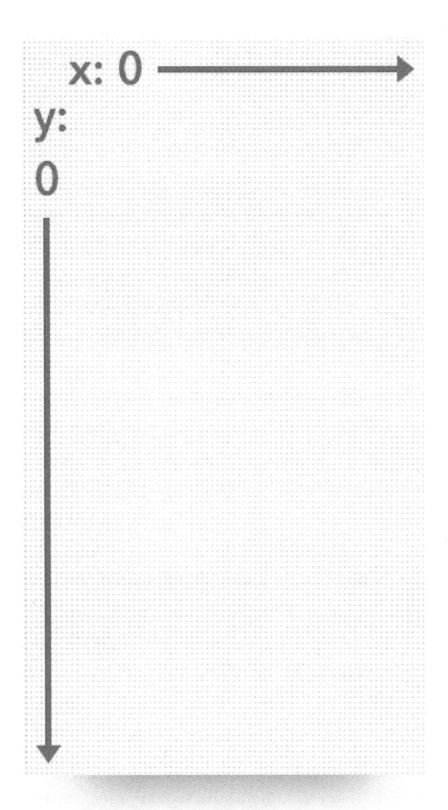

x: 0

y: 0

As you can see, the top left corner is `x: 0, y: 0` and as you move to the right or down towards the bottom the values increase.

2.) `view.frame.size.width` is a value that captures the width of our screen in this example. It looks inside of the view, then the frame, then captures it's size and stores the value for the width.

Since our imaginary screen is 320 pixels wide, it would return a value of 320.

3.) At the end we multiply `view.frame.midX + view.frame.size.width` by `CGFloat(x)`. Remember that we are in a `for-in` loop passing in values of 0, 1, and 2.

When the loop runs for the first time, we pass in the value 0 for `x`. Continuing with our example of a screen width of 320 pixels, `newX` calculation would go like this:

view.frame.midX = 160
    view.frame.size.width = 320
    CGFloat(0) = 0.0

So, for the first time through our loop we are calculating `160 + 320 * 0` which gives us a grand total of 160 if we follow the order of operations.

The loop runs again and our calculation changes. It now looks like this:

view.frame.midX = 160
    view.frame.size.width = 320
    CGFloat(1) = 1.0

We've just performed `160 + 320 * 1` which results in 480.

The loop runs one last time before stopping.

view.frame.midX = 160
    view.frame.size.width = 320
    CGFloat(2) = 2.0

We performed `160 + 320 * 2` resulting in 800. So by the end we have changed `newX` to first be equal to 160, then 480, then 800.

Remember when we discussed `contentSize` earlier? We need to offset each icon to have an entire screen width of space so that we can page between them properly. These `newX` values are what we will use to accomplish this.

We want our icons to show up in the middle of our screen which is why we are using `midX` as a property.

Adding each UIImageView as a Subview

Now that our loop creates a UIImageView and fills it with one of our icon images, we need to add it as a subview of `UIScrollView`. Think of this similarly to how you would add a page in a Microsoft Word or Pages document. At the bottom of the `for-in` loop, add the following:

```
for x in 0...2 {

    let image = UIImage(named: "icon\(x).png")

    let imageView = UIImageView(image: image)

    images.append(imageView)


    var newX: CGFloat = 0.0


    newX = view.frame.midX + view.frame.size.width *
CGFloat(x)


    scrollView.addSubview(imageView)

}
```

We also need to give our images a frame size so that they are bound to a certain size. Set up the `frame` property of UIImageView like so:

```
for x in 0...2 {

    let image = UIImage(named: "icon\(x).png")

    let imageView = UIImageView(image: image)

    images.append(imageView)
```

```
var newX: CGFloat = 0.0


    newX = view.frame.midX + view.frame.size.width *
CGFloat(x)


    scrollView.addSubview(imageView)


    imageView.frame = CGRect(x: 0, y:
view.frame.size.height / 2, width: 150, height: 150)

}
```

Now every UIImageView we make in our loop will be bound to a frame size of 150 x 150.

We've positioned it at 0 on the x-axis and the middle of the screen (view.frame.size.height / 2) on the y-axis. We want it to be in the middle of the x and y-axis but as of now it's only centered on the y-axis. We will modify the x-axis value using **newX** shortly.

Let's build and run our app at this moment to check and see how we did. You should now see our image showing up, but it's a little too low. That's because we set it's y-axis value to be `view.frame.-size.height / 2` meaning that the top of our UIImageView is positioned in the middle of our screen on the y-axis. We want it to be centered, so let's do that now by subtracting half of the height of our Angular image.

We know the height of our UIImageView is 150 because we set it to be so. We just need to subtract half of our UIImageView's height to bring it up to the center. Do that by surrounding `view.frame.-size.height / 2` with parentheses and subtracting 75 like so:

```
imageView.frame = CGRect(x: 0, y:
(view.frame.size.height / 2) - 75, width: 150, height:
150)
```

Build and run the app again and check to see how the positioning has changed. Awesome, centered now! Now let's make the image centered on the x-axis.

We already have the value in place to move our image to the center of the x-axis so change the **x** value in `imageView.frame` from 0 to use **newX** from earlier.

```
imageView.frame = CGRect(x: newX, y:
(view.frame.size.height /2) - 75, width: 150, height:
150)
```

Changing the x-axis value here works identically to how we changed the y-axis above - meaning that the left side of the image (0 on the x-axis) will be positioned in the center. To make the image appear centered on our screen, we need to subtract 75 just like before.

```
imageView.frame = CGRect(x: newX - 75, y:
(view.frame.size.height / 2) - 75, width: 150, height:
150)
```

Build and run to see if it worked. You should see the iOS course image in the middle of the screen. Woohoo! It's lookin' so good, but we still can't scroll. With everything centered and looking great, we only have a few more steps to go. Let's make that `UIScrollView` scroll and page, too!

Making `UIScrollView` **play nicely**

Like I said before, `UIScrollView` has a property called `contentSize` which operates sort of like a magic window that allows us to move the world behind it as we move our finger across the glass. If we have content that is three times the width of our screen, we can set our `UIScrollView` to understand that.

Let's create a property to store the width of our content and change it's value based on the loop we created so it expands as each UIImage-View is created.

Add the following to `ViewController.swift`:

```
import UIKit


class ViewController: UIViewController {
```

```swift
    var images = [UIImageView]()

    var contentWidth: CGFloat = 0.0


    @IBOutlet weak var scrollView: **UIScrollView**!


    override func viewDidLoad() {
        super.viewDidLoad()


        for x in 0...2 {
            let image = UIImage(named: "icon\(x).png")
            let imageView = UIImageView(image: image)
            images.append(imageView)


            var newX: CGFloat = 0.0


            newX = view.frame.midX +
view.frame.size.width * CGFloat(x)


            contentWidth += newX


            scrollView.addSubview(imageView)


            imageView.frame = CGRect(x: newX - 75, y:
(view.frame.size.height / 2) - 75, width: 150, height:
150)
        }
    }
```

```
}
```

As you can see, we added a variable of type `CGFloat` called `content-Width` and set it equal `0.0`. Then, inside of the `for-in` loop we incremented it's value by `newX` each time the loop runs. This creates enough space for a page for each image.

All we need to do now is to set the `contentSize` on our `UIScrollView` by adding a line of code beneath the `for-in` loop like so:

```
override func viewDidLoad() {

    super.viewDidLoad()


    for x in 0...2 {

        let image = UIImage(named: "icon\(x).png")

        let imageView = UIImageView(image: image)

        images.append(imageView)


        var newX: CGFloat = 0.0


        newX = view.frame.midX + view.frame.size.width *
CGFloat(x)


        contentWidth += newX


        scrollView.addSubview(imageView)


        imageView.frame = CGRect(x: newX - 75, y:
(view.frame.size.height / 2) - 75, width: 150, height:
150)

    }
```

```
    scrollView.contentSize = CGSize(width: contentWidth,
height: view.frame.size.height
```

```
}
```

Build and run the app to see how if our `UIScrollView` is now scrollable. You should now be able to scroll from page to page seeing all three of our images snap nicely into place.

Wrapping up

At this point, you've learned all that you need to know about `UIScrollView` and I hope you can see how useful it can be to make accessing your content dynamic and fun in iOS apps.

Exercise

Currently, our app scrolls when we scroll on the UIScrollView. Extend this app by figuring out a way to make the entire screen page left and right instead of just being able to scroll on the UIImageView. *Hint*: Check out the Chapter in Section 3 about "Gestures" and how to use `UIGestureRecognizer` in iOS.

Chapter 17: MyHood App

A fun app to record images and details to be displayed in a table view. We will focus on saving and retrieving data using UserDefaults.

What you will learn

- Use Table Views
- Store data and images with UserDefaults
- Style images
- Encode and decode data

Key Terms

- UserDefaults
- TableView
- Table View Cell
- Protocol and Method
- Singleton
- Encode and Decode

Resources

Download here: https://github.com/devslopes/iOS13-book-assets/wiki/iOS13-Book

In this chapter, we are going to build an app called `MyHood`.

This is a fun little app that you can use to document your neighborhood (or with different branding, anything really!) by taking pictures and adding descriptions. The images and descriptions will be saved to your apps ****UserDefaults****, which is a way to permanently save data to your device, for as long as the app is installed. So lets get started!

Sneak peak (Figure 17.0 A & B)

Creating an Xcode project

Let's begin by creating a new project `Single View Application`, set the User Interface to `Storyboard` and call it whatever you'd like. In this case we're calling it `MyHood`.

Getting started with the Data Model

We are going to start building our app now. And you can start with the data model or the user interface. Sometimes it makes more sense to do it one way or the other, but often its best to start with the data model. So that is what we are going to do here!

Now if you go back and reference the final product in Figure 2.5.0 (A & B), you see that we have a number of posts in a `TableView`, and each post has a Title, Description, and an Image.

Now, you would not normally save a bunch of images to your app using `UserDefaults`. `UserDefaults` is best used for a small amount of data, like setting your username and password. But because the purpose of this app is to learn about `UserDefaults`, we will be using it extensively to teach the principles involved with this class.

Also keep in mind, that what we are saving to `UserDefaults` for the image, is actually the `path` to the saved image on disc. So do keep in mind, that in the future when working with images and large amounts of data, you would want to use something like an online database or CoreData.

So, lets start on the data model. Right-click on your project (Yellow folder in the far left column) and select 'New Group' and name that new group "Model".

Then right-click on the `Model` folder and select `New File` This will open a new window. Make sure `iOS` is selected at the top, and we want a `Swift File`. Select `Next`, then name the file `Post` and click `Create`.

We just created the file that will become the custom class that will hold all the information displayed in each post in the table view.

Inside the `Post.swift` file, it should be empty save a lonely `import Foundation` line, so let's give it some company. Remember, a custom class is like a blue print. So what do we want each post to be able to have? An image path, a description, and a title.

We'll add those as private variables then create an initializer as follows.

We want every post to be required to have a title, description and an image, so we'll include all three in the initializer.

Note that you should not use the reserved keyword `description` when naming properties, that is why we went with *postDesc*.

```
class Post {


    fileprivate var imagePath: String

    fileprivate var title: String

    fileprivate var postDesc: String


    init(imagePath: String, title: String, description: String) {
        self.imagePath = imagePath

        self.title = title
```

```
        self.postDesc = description

    }

}
```

Now when a new Post is initialized, the properties will be assigned the values that are passed into the initializer. Now we can start on the UI, so hop on over to your `Main.storyboard` file.

User Interface

Referring back to Figure 2.5.0 A, we can see we'll need a `TableView` to display the posts, and a View to contain the banner and navigation controls.

So go ahead and search for `uiview` in the `Object Library` and drag one to the top of your ViewController. Drag it so it spans the width of the device.

In the `Attributes Inspector`, change the background color to any color you choose, but I will be using #2E87C3.

Then in the `Size Inspector` 📏, change the height to 65.

Now let's add some constraints. With the `UIView` selected, click on the "Constraints" icon ⊬⊐⊬ at the bottom right of the Storyboard.

Make sure `Constrain to margins` is *not* checked and set the left, top, and right constraints to 0.

Then set the height constraint to 65 by checking the Height box. Click `Add Constraints`.

Now is as good a time to add our assets. Download them from the resource link at the beginning of this chapter and drag them into the `Assets.xcassets` folder.

Now head back to the `Main.storyboard` file, and add an `Image View` from the "Objects Library" to the blue View we added previously.

In the Attributes Inspector in the Utilities pan on the right, set the Image to `bannerlogo` and set the Content Mode to `Aspect Fit`.

Resize it to your liking so it fits in the blue banner. Then we'll add our constraints.

Select the "Constraints" icon ⊬⊐⊬, and set the Width and Height constraints. Click `Add Constraints`.

Then select the `Align` tool , and check `Horizontally in container` and `Vertically in container`. This will align the banner image smack dab in the center of the View it is contained within.

Next lets add the camera button. In the "Object Library" (+), search for *button*. Then select and drag a button to the top right of our banner. In the Attributes Inspector remove the default *Button* text, and change the Image to *camera*.

You will need to resize the button. I found 30 tall and 40 wide looks good. You can change these dimensions in the "Size Inspector" . Lastly lets add some Constraints . Pin it 8 from the right and bottom, then tick the width and height to set it.

Next we need to add the `TableView`. In the "Object Library" search for `TableView`, and drag it into your View Controller below the banner bar (which is what I will refer to the top blue view from now on).

Be sure not to grab a Table View Controller.

Add constraints and (with "Constrain to margins" checked) pin it 0 from the left and right, and 20 from the top and bottom. Then press `Add 4 Constraints`. You'll notice it resized it for us.

If, after you have added constraints, the element has orange dotted lines as seen below, this means that the constraints you added are different from what were previously displayed in the Storyboard.

So you need to update frames. This can be done by clicking the `Resolve Auto Layout Issues` button, and selecting `update frames`, or the keyboard shortcut `command + alt (option) + =`.

Now, we need to add a `Table View Cell`. In the "Object Library", search for a `Table View Cell` and drag it into the Table View. It will snap to the top of the `TableView` with the words "Prototype Cells" above it.

Select the Content View under `TableView` cell in the Document Outline and in the Attributes Inspector change the `Background` to blue (#2E87C3).

This is just so we can see the contents of the cell we are working with more easily, once we have all the elements inside it, we will change it back. At this point it should look like the contents of Figure 17.1.

Figure 17.1

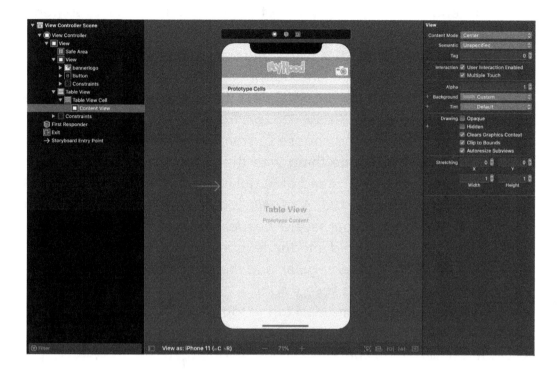

We need the cell to be a little bigger. Select the `Table View Cell` from the Document Outline and in the Size Inspector ▥, uncheck "Automatic" and set the `Row Height` property to 100.

Now we can start adding our necessary elements. In each post, there is an image to the left and two labels to the right. So go ahead and add an Image View and two Labels from the "Object Library" as shown in Figure 17.2

Figure 17.2

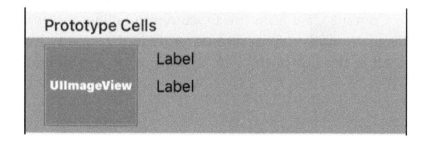

Select the Image View, and from the Attributes Inspector change the Image to 'barrel-water-bridge' from the assets we added earlier. This is just a placeholder image for now. Set the `Content Mode` to `Aspect Fill` and check the box `Clip To Bounds` if it isn't already.

Then add constraints ▣ with `Constrain to margins` checked, and pin it 0 from the top, left, and bottom and set the width to 83.

Now lets work with the labels. Select the top label and change the `Color` property to `Dark Gray Color` from the list. Then click the 'T' from the `Font` property and choose *Custom* and the Family of *Helvetica Neue* is good. Do the same thing with the second label, except make the "Style" property Light instead of Regular.

Design tip: Black text color is usually too black. It is better to go with a dark gray. And, when you have a header and text below it, you may think, "make the header bold and the text below regular". But it is actually better to make the header regular, and the text below light. That is why we made the second labels style = light.

Now lets add constraints ▣ to the top Label.

Pin it 8 from the left, 0 from the top, and 0 from the right, with `Constrain to margins` checked and set height to 20.

For the bottom Label set the constraints ▣ with `Constrain to margins` checked. Pin it 8 from the left, 8 from the top, 0 from the right, and 0 from the bottom.

With the bottom label still selected, select the Attributes Inspector ▽ and set the number of `Lines` property to 3, and below that the `Autoshrink` property to *Minimum Font Size* and in the input below it set the value to 9.

This makes it so that if there is a long description, it wont truncate at first. It will shrink the font trying to fit the whole text until it gets down to font size 9, at which point it will finally truncate it.

Finally, it's time to change our blue Content View back to Default. Select the Content View from the Document Outline and from the Attributes Inspector ▽ change the `Background` property back to Default (located at the top of the list). By now, your app should look like Figure 17.3

Figure 17.3

Working in the View Controller

Now what we need to do, is head into our `ViewController.swift` and start adding `IBOutlets` and `Delegates` so that we can work with the elements we just added to our Storyboard. For this part, I'm going to show you a different method for creating and connecting @IBOutlets - for the sake of learning new things!

First lets add the `IBOutlet` for the `TableView` by adding to the View Controller the following code above `viewDidLoad()`:

```
@IBOutlet weak var tableView: UITableView!
```

Then in your `Main.storyboard`, hook up the `TableView` to the `IBOutlet` by right-clicking `View Controller` cell from the Document Outline and dragging from the `tableView` outlet to the `Table View` in the Storyboard. as shown in Figure 17.4

Figure 17.4

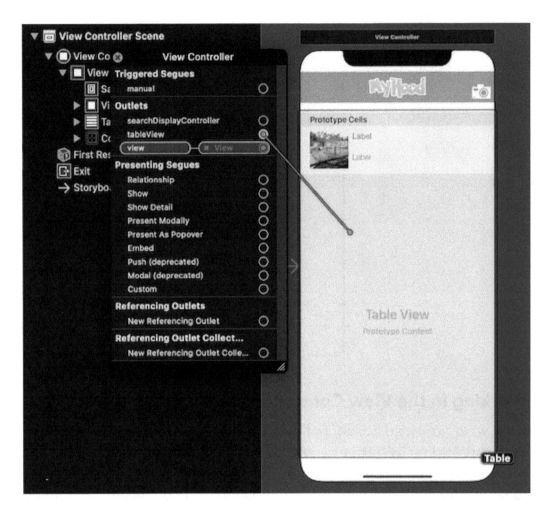

Now to work with the Table View in the View Controller, we need to add some **Protocols** and **Methods**.

A **Protocol** is used to declare a set of methods that a class adopts. It is a way of saying, "here is a set of behavior that is expected of an object in a given situation."

The **Methods** we implement then carries out the expected behavior.

Select the **ViewController.swift** file. So for a Table View we need to add two **Protocols** to the class of View Controller like this:

```
class ViewController: UIViewController,
UITableViewDelegate, UITableViewDataSource {
```

Once you have added those, you will have an error that says, "Type
ViewController does not conform to protocol UITableViewData-
Source".

So, we need to add some methods and other information to fix this.
Go ahead and add the following code to your viewDidLoad():

```
override func viewDidLoad() {

        super.viewDidLoad()

        tableView.delegate = self

        tableView.dataSource = self

}
```

Then we need to add the methods. Depending on the protocol, there
are required and optional methods. For Table Views we are required
to provide information on how many rows there will be and a function
to create the cells.

These methods below your viewDidLoad():

```
func tableView(_ tableView: UITableView, cellForRowAt
indexPath: IndexPath) -> UITableViewCell {


        return UITableViewCell()

}


    func tableView(_ tableView: UITableView,
numberOfRowsInSection section: Int) -> Int {


        return 10

}
```

So lets digest these two functions real quick. The first one you can get to
autocomplete by typing "cellForRowAt" and the rest will pop up.

The second function you can get to autocomplete by typing "numberOfRowsInSection".

Now there are a number of optional `methods` that you can use besides these ones which implement further functionality.

For example - what happens when a cell is clicked on, or how many sections you want, or define cell size dynamically? These two will be sufficient for us.

The first function is where we'll initialize and display our custom Posts. For now I have a simple `return UITableViewCell()` to complete the function.

Later on we'll return a custom cell that is initialized based on posts that are created and saved by the user.

The second function manages how many rows there will be in the Table View. I currently have it hard-coded at 10.

But what we *really need* is an array of type Post, and return the size of that array. So lets do that.

Below the `tableView IBOutlet`, declare a variable `posts` as follows:

```
var posts = [Post]()
```

and change the `numberOfRowsInSection` method to:

```
func tableView(_ tableView: UITableView,
numberOfRowsInSection section: Int) -> Int {

      return posts.count

   }
```

Now that you have the required `Methods` for the implemented `Protocols`, you will see that any errors have gone away.

Custom Cell

What we need to do now is create a custom class for the cell. If you look at the Storyboard, and the cell that we have our images and labels in, we need a way to communicate with those elements and have them update based on the data saved to our posts variable.

So to do that, right-click your project folder (yellow folder) in the far left column, and create a "New Group" called *View*. (just like we did with our Posts Model). Then right-click the *View* directory and create a "New File".

Now this time, select `Cocoa Touch Class` and press `Next`. Make sure the `Subclass` is `UITableViewCell` (from the dropdown) and name it *PostCell*. Then press `Create`.

The PostCell file should open and look like this:

```
import UIKit


class PostCell: UITableViewCell {


    override func awakeFromNib() {

        super.awakeFromNib()

        // Initialization code

    }

    override func setSelected(_ selected: Bool,
animated: Bool) {

        super.setSelected(selected, animated: animated)


        // Configure the view for the selected state

    }

}
```

You can go ahead and delete the `setSelected` function. Now, this custom class is meant to communicate with the cell in Storyboard, so we need to add some `IBOutlets` as follows. Go ahead and copy/paste these into your code and we'll connect them later.

```
class PostCell: UITableViewCell {
```

```swift
@IBOutlet weak var postImg: UIImageView!

@IBOutlet weak var titleLbl: UILabel!

@IBOutlet weak var descLbl: UILabel!


override func awakeFromNib() {

    super.awakeFromNib()

    // Initialization code

}

}
```

As you can see we have an outlet for the image, title, and description found in the Storyboard cell. Now lets go into `Main.storyboard` and hook those up the same way we did for the button.

But first we have to do something very important. And that is to change the Class of the `Table View Cell` to our newly created *PostCell* class.

Do that by selecting the `Table View Cell` in the Document Outline, then click the Identity Inspector ▣ (next to the Attributes Inspector). At the top of the column, find the `Class` property and from the dropdown change it to our custom *PostCell* class.

Now over in the Attributes Inspector ⬇ you'll see an `Identifier` property, type in *PostCell* to give it the same name as our custom class.

This identifier will be used later to identify which cell to use when creating and displaying cells in the `Table View`.

Now let's hook up the @IBOutlets we created earlier for the Table View Cell. Right-click on `PostCell` from the Document Outline and drag the outlet to its corresponding UI element as shown in Figure 17.5. Do this for each outlet we created in `PostCell`.

Figure 17.5

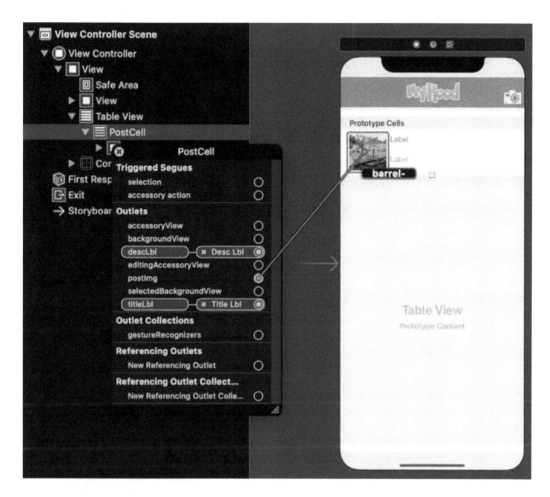

Image = postImg
   Top Label = titleLbl
   Bottom Label = descLbl

While we are in the Storyboard, lets go ahead and remove the `TableView` separators. Select the large `TableView`, go to the Attributes Inspector ⬇, find the `Separator` property and select None from the dropdown.

Now, we want to be able to configure a cell in the *PostCell* file.

To do that, we first need to modify the Post file. So head over to the Model directory, click the `Post` file and make the following changes:

```
fileprivate var _imagePath: String!
```

```swift
fileprivate var _title: String!

fileprivate var _postDesc: String!


var imagePath: String {

    return _imagePath

}


var title: String {

    return _title

}


var postDesc: String {

    return _postDesc

}


init(imagePath: String, title: String, description:
String) {

    self._imagePath = imagePath

    self._title = title

    self._postDesc = description

}
```

Lets talk about these changes real quick. When we first made this class, we made the properties private. Which is good practice because you don't want other files to be able to change these without special permissions.

However, we need to be able to have some way of accessing these properties, so we needed to create *getters*. So we modified the declaration of the private variable by adding a _ to the start of the variable name, then created *getters* for each. This practice is called "data encapsulation".

Now that we have our *getters*, or sometimes called *accessors*, we're able to go onto the next step. Open your PostCell file, and add the following function beneath the `awakeFromNib()` function:

```
func configureCell(_ post: Post) {

        titleLbl.text = post.title

        descLbl.text = post.postDesc

    }
```

This function takes in a *post* as a parameter. Then sets the title and description labels that we set in the Storyboard to the values of that specific post we pass in.

We aren't going to worry about the image for a while, it will just display our placeholder image we put in the Storyboard.

So where do we use this function? Lets go back to the `ViewController` file and update the `cellForRowAt` function to the following:

```
func tableView(_ tableView: UITableView, cellForRowAt
indexPath: IndexPath) -> UITableViewCell {


        let post = posts[indexPath.row]

        if let cell =
tableView.dequeueReusableCell(withIdentifier:
"PostCell") as? PostCell {

            cell.configureCell(post)

            return cell

        }

        return PostCell()

    }
```

Now lets run through this.

First we declare a constant post that is created from the posts array.

Next we grabbed the specific post that corresponds to the row that we are looking at in the `TableView`. (That's what `IndexPath.row` refers too).

For example, if there are 10 entries in our posts array, there will be 10 rows in our table view, and each row corresponds exactly with its `IndexPath.row` property.

Then we are creating an *implicitly* unwrapped variable called `cell`, and setting it equal to `tableView.dequeueReusableCell(withIdentifier: "PostCell") as? PostCell`.

What is happening here, is with `TableViews`, they don't load all the data into cells. If you had thousands of posts in your posts array, that would crash the app. So what it does is only load into memory as many as needed to be shown on the screen at a time.

Then it will *dequeue* the cells as they go off the screen and push the new data into new cells as they come onto the screen.

We are also telling the `Table View` which cell to use with the 'identifier' of `PostCell` that we added in Storyboard. And finally we cast it as a PostCell class.

We take that newly created cell, and we call the function we created in the PostCell `configureCell()` and pass in the post from the posts array that corresponds to that row. This will update the title, description, and eventually the image information that we created in the Storyboard.

Then we `return` the `cell`. Lastly, in the unlikely event that there is no *dequeued* cell available, we `return` an empty `PostCell()`.

Whew! I know that is a lot to take in and there are a lot of moving pieces here, so take some time and follow the bread crumbs to understand everything.

Now, we got everything set up, and we can run it, but we don't even have any data in our posts array, so lets add some test data.

In our ViewController file, in the `viewDidLoad()`, add the following:

```
let post = Post(imagePath: "", title: "Post 1",
description: "Post 1 Description")

    let post2 = Post(imagePath: "", title: "Post 2",
description: "I am the second post. Yipeee!")

    let post3 = Post(imagePath: "", title: "Post 3",
description: "I am the most important post.")
```

```
posts.append(post)

posts.append(post2)

posts.append(post3)

tableView.reloadData()
```

All we are doing here is creating three test entries of type Post, adding them to the posts array, and then reloading the Table View data.

You want to use `reloadData()` any time you make a change to your data, this notifies your table view that changes have been made so it will call your `cellForRow` and `numberOfRows` and any other **methods** related to table view and reload the Table View.

Run the project and make sure it's working. You should see the following:

Figure 17.6

Second View Controller

So we can see that it is working! Congratulations! You have done a lot so far, but now we need a way to add posts. Lets create a second View Controller for that.

Create a `New Group` in your project called *Controller*, by right clicking on the *MyHood* directory in the left pane. Then right click on the new group *Controller* folder and select `New File`, select `Cocoa Touch Class` and click `Next`. Set the subclass to `UIViewController` and name it *AddPostVC*.

Delete the comments and the `didReceiveMemoryWarning` function.

Before we begin building our second VC (View Controller) in Storyboard, lets revisit our finished product and remember what the "Create New Post" screen looks like (Figure 17.0 B). We have our banner at the top, an image, two text fields, and a button.

Go to `Main.storyboard` and add a new View Controller by searching for `view controller` in the object library.

Drag it into the Storyboard next to our existing View Controller.

Then set the `Class` property to `AddPostVC` in the Identity Inspector. You can type "AddPostVC" into the class field to find it faster.

We can also add our *Segue* from the first screen to the second screen by control dragging from our Camera button to the new View Controller we added. A `segue` defines a transition between two view controllers in your app's storyboard file. Select `Show` from the popup.

Then select the segue (as it appears as an arrow connecting the two View Controllers), Click the Attributes Inspector and in the `Identifier` property name the segue *AddPostVC*.

Now lets go ahead and add our banner bar to the *AddPostVC*.

This can be done by selecting the banner bar in the original VC, copying it with `cmd + c` , then selecting the new VC and pasting it with `cmd + v`.

Then drag it to the top, add some "Constraints" and pin it 0 to the left, top, and right. Check `Constrain to margins` and add the constraints.

You can delete the Camera button and the banner image. Add a Label from the "Object Library" to the banner bar. From the Attributes Inspector set the text to "Make New Post". Change the color to white, and change the font to *Helvetica Neue*.

Next, add some "Constraints" and pin it 8 from the bottom, set the width and height. Click "Align" and center it `Horizontally in Container`.

Next we need a button to cancel and go back to the original screen if we decide to. Drag a button from the "Object Library" to the left of the banner, and change the text to "Cancel", the color to white, and the font to *Helvetica Neue*. Add constraints ⌯ and pin it 8 from the left, 8 from the bottom, and set width and height.

Next we need to add an image to the `AddPostVC`. Drag an Image View from the "Object Library" onto the screen. From the Size Inspector ▤ change the size to 240 x 240. Give it constraints ⌯ and pin it 35 from the top, then set width and height. Click "Align" ▤ and center it `Horizontally in Container`.

Go ahead and select the image, and from the Attributes Inspector ⬇ set the image to our test image, "barrel-water-bridge".

Set the `Content Mode` property to `Aspect Fill`, and make sure the `Clip To Bounds` is checked in the Attributes Inspector. This image is what we'll click to add the images to be displayed in the Table View, so we need a way to click on it.

We can accomplish this by simply adding a Button over the top of the image and making it the same size as the image.

Drag a new button from the "Object Library" onto the `AddPostVC` and make it the same size as the image, 240 x 240. Change the font to white, make the text say "+ Add Pic".

Next, select both the image and the button from the Document Outline and in the "Constraints" ⌯, select `Equal Widths` and `Equal Heights`.

Then in the Align tool ▤ select `Horizontal Center` and `Vertical Centers`. NOTE - Not to be confused with *Horizontally in Container* & *Vertically in Container*!

Now we need to add a couple text fields below the image so we can enter the Title and Description of our Post. Add two text fields from the Objects Library below the image and span their width to be a littler wider than the image as seen in the following Figure 17.7.

Change the color to *Dark Gray Color* and change the font to *Helvetica Neue*. Add a Placeholder text "Enter Title" for the top text field and "Enter Description" for the bottom text field.

Figure 17.7

For the top text field, add constraints, pinning it 0 from the left and right, and 20 from the top. Then set height. Make sure `Constrain to margins` is checked and add the constraints.

For the Description text field, add constraints, pinning it 0 from the left and right, and 8 from the top. Then Set height. Make sure `Constrain to margins` is checked and add the constraints.

Now we need a button that will make the post once the information is added. So drag in a new button from the Objects Library below the text fields. Change the button text to "Make Post", change the Text Color to White. Set the background to Blue. Add constraints 8 from the top, set height to 30 and width to 170. Click Align and `Center Horizontally in Container`.

Now we are ready to get into some code and hook up these elements. Open the AddPostVC file and above the `viewDidLoad()` function add the following outlets:

```
@IBOutlet weak var titleField: UITextField!
```

```
@IBOutlet weak var postImg: UIImageView!
```

```
@IBOutlet weak var descField: UITextField!
```

Then below the `viewDidLoad()` add the IBAction for the Make Post, AddPic, and Cancel buttons:

```
@IBAction func addPicBtnPressed(_ sender: UIButton) {


    }
```

```
@IBAction func makePostBtnPressed(_ sender: UIButton) {


    }
```

```
@IBAction func cancelBtnPressed(_ sender: UIButton) {


    }
```

Now switch back to the `Main.storyboard`, right-click on the Add-PostVC and drag from the Outlets to the corresponding UI elements as seen in Figure 17.8.

Figure 17.8

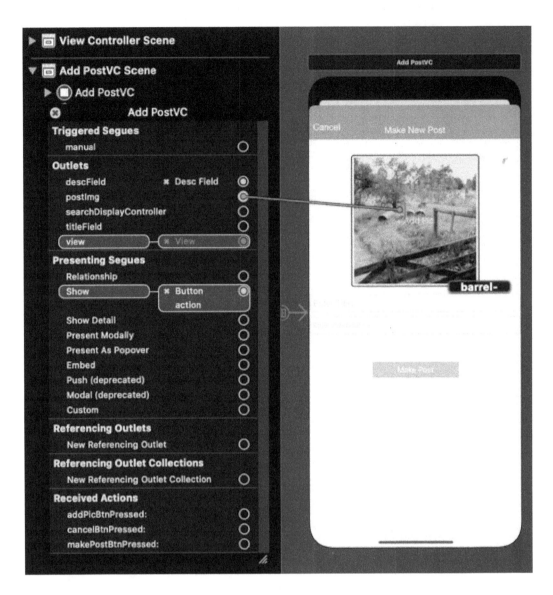

postImg -> Image
    titleField -> top text field
    descField -> bottom text field
    When we hook up the IBActions for the Cancel, Make Post, and AddPic buttons, we also need to select the type of action, which is 'Touch Up Inside'.

Figure 17.9

addPicBtnPressed -> *button/image*
  makePostBtnPressed -> *bottom button*
  cancelBtnPressed -> *cancel button*

So at this point, you should have hooked up the Outlets for the post-
Img, titleField, and descField, and hooked up the IBActions for the add-
Pic, Cancel, and Make Post buttons.

Now, real quick lets make it so that when we tap the + Add Pic button, it looks like the button goes away. We'll do this by just removing the button text. So in back in the `AddPostVC.swift` file, in the `addPicBtnPressed` function modify it to the following:

```
@IBAction func addPicBtnPressed(_ sender: UIButton) {

        sender.setTitle("", for: .normal)

    }
```

Next lets make the cancel button takes us back to the initial screen when pressed. This is easy enough to do, simply modify that IBAction to the following:

```
@IBAction func cancelBtnPressed(_ sender: UIButton) {

        dismiss(animated: true, completion: nil)

    }
```

At this point, lets run it and make sure that we are able to click on the camera button in the first screen and segue to the second screen. Make sure when we click on the + Add Pic button in the second screen the button title disappears, and last, make sure clicking on the Cancel button takes you back to the initial screen.

All right, hopefully that's working out just awesome for you!

Lets add a little styling to the main image on the second screen, and make it a circle. So in `viewDidLoad()` add the following:

```
postImg.layer.cornerRadius = 120
```

All we're doing here is setting the `cornerRadius` of the image to 120 which is one half the width of the image, effectively turning it into a circle.

At this point we can remove the test image from the `Post Img` Image View. Select it from the Document Outline, select the `Image` property in the Attributes Inspector and delete the text inside the field. Then set the `Background` property to `Light Gray Color`. Feel free to bump up the font size of "+ Add Pic" if you want.

Now lets add a little styling to the images in the table View. In the `PostCell.swift` file, in the `awakFromNib()` function add the following code:

```
override func awakeFromNib() {

    super.awakeFromNib()

    postImg.layer.cornerRadius = 15

}
```

This gives the image in each post a subtle rounded edge which looks nice.

Adding UIImagePicker

Now we're going to write the code that will allow us to click on the Add-Pic button and select an image from our camera roll. This is done by means of a `UIImagePickerController`, so under your IBOutlets in the `AddPostVC.swift` file, declare the following variable

```
var imagePicker: UIImagePickerController!
```

Then in `viewDidLoad()` initialize it below everything else in that function:

```
imagePicker = UIImagePickerController()
```

We also need to add a couple protocols that are required to work with the imagePicker, so modify your class as follows:

```
class AddPostVC: UIViewController,
UIImagePickerControllerDelegate,
UINavigationControllerDelegate {
```

and just like we did with the Table View earlier, we need to add the delegate for the `imagePicker` in `viewDidLoad()` which should look like this:

```
override func viewDidLoad() {
```

```
super.viewDidLoad()


postImg.layer.cornerRadius = 120

imagePicker = UIImagePickerController()

imagePicker.delegate = self


    }
```

Now we need to add a method as follows. You can add this to the bottom of the AddPostVC below the IBActions:

```
func imagePickerController(_ picker:
UIImagePickerController, didFinishPickingMediaWithInfo
info: [UIImagePickerController.InfoKey : Any]) {

  let selectedImage = info[.originalImage] as? UIImage

  imagePicker.dismiss(animated: true, completion: nil)

  postImg.image = selectedImage

}
```

What this function is doing is listening for when the **imagePicker** is presented, then when the user selects a picture, it takes that picture and assigns it to the constant **selectedImage** and casts it as a **UIImage**, then assigns that to the **postImg.image** so that it can be displayed and used later. Then it dismisses itself.

   Now we need to present the imagePicker View Controller when the **addPicButton** is pressed:

```
@IBAction func addPicBtnPressed(_ sender: UIButton) {

    sender.setTitle("", for: .normal)

    present(imagePicker, animated: true, completion:
nil)

    }
```

And lastly, before we can test this, we need to add a permissions to the `info.plist` file.

Open the `info.plist` from the left hand pane. The file is near the bottom of the list. In the last entry, when you hover over the cell you'll see a + sign appear.

Click on it and type `Privacy`, and you should get some auto completed entries, we're looking for `Privacy - Photo Library Usage Description` then on the right, in the "Value" column, there is an input available to enter a message to the user why you would like to access their photos. Say something like "MyHood needs to access your photos."

Figure 17.10

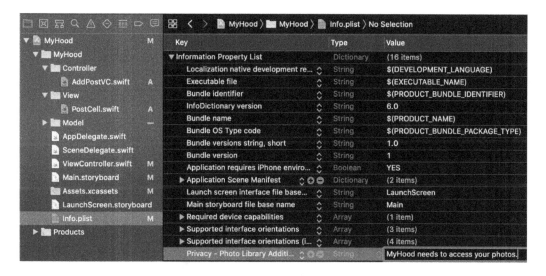

Go ahead and run it, and verify that when you click the Add Pic button, you are asked to allow access to photos, then when you click a photo, it returns to the AddPostVC and the image you selected is now displayed.

DataService

In our original View Controller file, we have our variable of `posts` array. But that is not globally accessible. So what we want to do is introduce a new data model called a `Singleton`, which is a single instance of data that is globally accessible.

So create a new group in your file tree like we did with Model, View, and Controller, and name it "Services". Inside the new folder, create a new **file** > select **Swift File** > and name it **DataService**.

Once the file is opened modify it as follows:

```
import Foundation

import UIKit


class DataService {

    static let instance = DataService()


    private var _loadedPosts = [Post]()


    var loadedPosts: [Post] {
        return _loadedPosts
    }


    func savePosts() {
        //TO DO
    }


    func loadPosts() {
        //TO DO
    }


    func saveImageAndCreatePath(image: UIImage) {
        //TO DO
```

```
    }

    func imageForPath(path: String) {
        //TO DO
    }


    func addPost(post: Post) {
        //TO DO
    }
}
```

Let's talk about what we have here. We've laid the groundwork for the functions we'll need to make this all work together. We've created and instantiated an instance of the **DataService**.

We have created a private array of posts, and created the getter for that array. Then we have created empty functions for saving and loading posts, as well as saving images and creating the path for the image, a function to fetch that image given a path, and finally a function to add posts that are created.

As we move forward, each of these functions will get fleshed out. In fact we can start with the last **addPost** function.

Since we know that once we add a post, we'll be adding it to the _loadedPosts array, then saving the posts, then reloading them, we can modify that function to be:

```
func addPost(post: Post) {

    _loadedPosts.append(post)

    savePosts()

    loadPosts()

}
```

These functions we added aren't doing anything yet, but again we're laying the foundation.

Lets work on the `savePosts()` function. We're going to be using the `UserDefaults` class to save and load data, in conjunction with the `NSKeyedArchiver`. So modify the `savePosts()` function as follows:

```
func savePosts() {

    let postsData = try?
NSKeyedArchiver.archivedData(withRootObject:
_loadedPosts, requiringSecureCoding: true)

    UserDefaults.standard.set(postsData, forKey:
"posts")

}
```

What we're doing here is taking the `_loaded` posts array and using the `NSKeyedArchiver` class to transform that array into data.

Then we are using `UserDefaults` to save that data to a key we are calling "posts". And finally, using `UserDefault` method to save the data to disc.

Next we can work on the `loadPosts()` function, so modify it as follows:

```
func loadPosts() {

    if let postsData =
UserDefaults.standard.object(forKey: "posts") as? Data {


        if let postsArray = try?
NSKeyedUnarchiver.unarchivedObject(ofClasses:
[Post.self], from: postsData) as? [Post] {

            _loadedPosts = postsArray

        }

    }
```

```
    NotificationCenter.default.post(Notification(name:
Notification.Name(rawValue: "postsLoaded"), object:
nil))

}
```

Here we are essentially reversing the process we took to save the posts.

First we are using `UserDefaults` to load the archived and saved data in the `savePosts()` function, then un-archiving it and casting it to an array of type `Post`, then setting `_loadedPosts` equal to that newly restored `postsArray`.

Now, we have a challenge to overcome. We can add a post, which will then save, and in turn load the posts. However, there is currently no way of letting the Table View know that there has been any change. So lets fix that.

First lets go into the `AddPostVC.swift` file and make it so we can actually make posts. Modify the `makePostBtnPressed` action as follows:

```
@IBAction func makePostBtnPressed(_ sender: UIButton) {

        if let title = titleField.text, let desc =
descField.text, let _ = postImg.image {

              let post = Post(imagePath: "", title:
title, description: desc)

              DataService.instance.addPost(post: post)

        dismiss(animated: true, completion: nil)

    }

}
```

Lets break this down. First we have a string of `if   let` to check that there's in fact something inside each of the text fields and Image View.

Since we are requiring there to be an entry for each, the action will not continue if there's not.

Then we create a post based on the input of the text fields (we're still not ready to test images, so it is an empty string).

Then we call the `DataService.instance.addPost` function and pass into it the newly created post. And remember that when the add-

`Post` function is called, that post is then added to the `loadedPosts` array, and so are the **savePosts** and `loadPosts` functions. Last, we dismiss the view and return to the initial screen to see the `TableView`.

So now lets continue solving the problem of the Table View not knowing when a new post has been added. We're going to solve this by using notifications.

Back in the `DataService.swift` file modify the `loadPosts()` function by adding:

```
func loadPosts() {

        if let postsData =
UserDefaults.standard.object(forKey: "posts") as? Data {


        if let postsArray = try?
NSKeyedUnarchiver.unarchivedObject(ofClasses:
[Post.self], from: postsData) as? [Post] {

            _loadedPosts = postsArray

        }


NotificationCenter.default.post(Notification(name:
Notification.Name(rawValue: "postsLoaded"), object:
nil))

        }



NotificationCenter.default.post(Notification(name:
Notification.Name(rawValue: "postsLoaded"), object:
nil))

    }
```

What we're doing here is using `Notification`   `Center` to signal whenever this function is called. So it sends a signal out that posts have been loaded, and now we need to implement the listener in the `ViewController.swift` file that contains the Table View.

We can remove all the test data we used before as well as deleting `var posts = [Post]()` since we'll be using the data from the singleton now. Modify the `viewDidLoad()` function as follows:

```
override func viewDidLoad() {

        super.viewDidLoad()

        tableView.delegate = self

        tableView.dataSource = self


        NotificationCenter.default.addObserver(self,
selector: #selector(ViewController.onPostsLoaded(_:)),
name: NSNotification.Name(rawValue: "postsLoaded"),
object: nil)

}
```

We have deleted the test data, and added the `Notification` Observer.

This function is listening for the signal sent by the function we created just prior in the `loadPosts()` function. When it receives the signal, it will then call the function **onPostsLoaded** which we will create now. Below your other functions add:

```
@objc func onPostsLoaded(_ notif: AnyObject) {

        tableView.reloadData()

  }
```

This one is simple enough. Once the observer receives word that new posts have been loaded, it will call this function which will then reload the data.

We deleted the test data and the posts array we were using, so we need to change a couple functions as follows, swapping out **posts** for `DataService.instance.loadedPosts`:

```
func tableView(_ tableView: UITableView, cellForRowAt
indexPath: IndexPath) -> UITableViewCell {
```

```
        let post =
DataService.instance.loadedPosts[indexPath.row]

        if let cell =
tableView.dequeueReusableCell(withIdentifier:
"PostCell") as? PostCell {

            cell.configureCell(post)

            return cell

    }

    return PostCell()

}


func tableView(_ tableView: UITableView,
numberOfRowsInSection section: Int) -> Int {

        return DataService.instance.loadedPosts.count

}
```

The last thing we can do, before we test that our posts are being saved is prepare the **Post** class to be encoded and decoded by the Archiver and Un-archiver. Now, when using UserDefaults, you can save and re-trieve simple objects very very easily. For example the following works right out of the box:

```
UserDefaults.standard.set("Mark W", forKey:
"userNameKey")


  if let name = defaults.string(forKey: "userNameKey") {

            print(name)

    }
```

No need to add any encoding or decoding. This works for Strings, inte-gers, booleans, Double, Floats, and URLs.

```swift
let defaults = UserDefaults.standard

        defaults.set("JRadness", forKey: "userNameKey")

        defaults.set(32, forKey: "age")

        defaults.set(true, forKey: "isRad")

        defaults.set("This is a string", forKey:
"string")


        if let name = defaults.string(forKey:
"userNameKey") {

            print(name)

        }
```

But when you want to save more complex data such as custom classes you have to be very explicit and tell `UserDefaults` how to encode and decode each property of the class. Let's go to the **Post.swift** file and do that.

First off we have to modify the class to inherit from **NSObject** and **NScoding** as follows:

```swift
class Post: NSObject, NSCoding {
```

Then after the initializer add the following:

```swift
override init() {


}
```

```swift
    func encode(with aCoder: NSCoder) {

        aCoder.encode(self._imagePath, forKey:
"imagePath")

        aCoder.encode(self._postDesc, forKey:
"description")

        aCoder.encode(self._title, forKey: "title")
```

```
    }


    required convenience init?(coder aDecoder: NSCoder)
{

        self.init()

        self._imagePath = aDecoder.decodeObject(forKey:
"imagePath") as? String

        self._title = aDecoder.decodeObject(forKey:
"title") as? String

        self._postDesc = aDecoder.decodeObject(forKey:
"description") as? String

    }
```

We are required to add that `override init()`.

Then what we are doing is simply providing keys for each property to be encoded, then upon decoding explicitly stating what type of object they should be `decoded` to. It looks a little scary, but if you look at just one line at a time, its not too bad.

Now we're ready to test it out! Run it and make sure that you are able to add a picture, set title and description, then press `Make Post` and it should return to `TableView` and display the post you just made!

The image in the Table View isn't updated yet because we have not yet implemented that code, but we are getting there. And just to recap what is going on behind the scenes here, when we press `Make Post`, it is taking the information you input into the image, title, and description fields, creates a new post with that information, then calls the `DataService` function, `addPost()` which takes the new post, and adds it to the `loadedPosts` array in the `DataService`.

It then saves the entire `postsArray` which encodes the posts into data and saves it to a `UserDefault` key.

Then `loadPosts()` is called which retrieves the data that was just saved, un-archives it and turns it back into an array of usable posts, at which point we send a notification to the initial View Controller that the `loadedPosts` have been updated. So it should reload the `Table View` data.

Then we see the newly added posts! Whew!

The last thing we have to do is get those images working!

Saving and retrieving images

I said earlier, that when I say we're saving an image to `UserDefaults`, what we're actually saving is a reference to the location of that image.

So we need a way to get the path to that image we saved. In the `DataService.swift` file, at the very bottom add this function:

```
func documentsPathForFileName(_ name: String) -> String
{
        let paths =
NSSearchPathForDirectoriesInDomains(.documentDirectory,
.userDomainMask, true)

        let fullPath = paths[0] as NSString

        return fullPath.appendingPathComponent(name)

}
```

Basically happening here is we're passing in a file name and saying go into my file directory and return to me the path of that file.

Then we're appending that path string to the file name we passed in. So for example say I passed in `image001.png` into this function.

It goes and finds the path, then appends that path to my file name and returns `user/jradness/images/image001.png` (or whatever the path would look like).

Next we need to update the `saveImageAndCreatePath` function as follows:

```
func saveImageAndCreatePath(_ image: UIImage) -> String
{
        let imgData = image.pngData()

        let imgPath = "image\
(Date.timeIntervalSinceReferenceDate).png"

        let fullPath = documentsPathForFileName(imgPath)

        try? imgData?.write(to: URL(fileURLWithPath:
fullPath), options: [.atomic])
```

```
        return imgPath

}
```

Let's break it down. We pass into this function an actual image of type **UIImage**. We the turn that image into data. We create an image path and use the **Date.timeInterval** function to ensure that each time we save an image it will have a unique path name.

Then we pass that path into the **documentsPathForFileName** function we just created and use that path that's returned to write to disc the image data! Then we return the **imgPath**.

Now lets get ready to retrieve an image from storage by updating the **imageForPath** function as follows:

```
func imageForPath(_ path: String) -> UIImage? {

    let fullPath = documentsPathForFileName(path)

    let image = UIImage(named: fullPath)

    return image

}
```

In this function we're passing in a path and returning an actual **UIImage**.

We get the **fullPath** by way of our **documentsPathForFileName** function and then create an image from the path, then return the image. Not too bad!

Now we're ready to modify our **makePostBtnPressed** action to work with images, so head on over to the **AddPostVC.swift** file and modify it as follows:

```
@IBAction func makePostBtnPressed(_ sender: UIButton) {


    if let title = titleField.text, let desc =
descField.text, let img = postImg.image {

        let imgPath =
DataService.instance.saveImageAndCreatePath(img)
```

```
        let post = Post(imagePath: imgPath, title:
title, description: desc)

        DataService.instance.addPost(post: post)

        dismiss(animated: true, completion: nil)

    }

}
```

What we did here was create the variable `imgPath` and use the **save-ImageAndCreatePath** function in **DataService** which takes an image, turns that image into data, returns a String that contains the path to that file.

Then we use that `imgPath` string in the initializer of our post to save the path.

Next we need to update the `configureCell()` function in the **PostCell** file so that when we reload the data, the image in the cells load the saved image corresponding with each cell. Modify the **configureCell** function as follows:

```
func configureCell(_ post: Post) {

        titleLbl.text = post.title

        descLbl.text = post.postDesc

        postImg.image =
DataService.instance.imageForPath(post.imagePath)

}
```

Here we are using the **imageForPath** function we created to take the **imagePath** we just saved, and retrieving the data and turning it into a UIImage that will be displayed in the Table View cell.

Finally, add one last thing to add to the **viewDidLoad()** function in **ViewController.swift** file. This is so that when we load the Table-View we are loading the posts. Add this right above the **NotificationCenter Observer**:

```
DataService.instance.loadPosts()
```

Wrapping up

And that's it! I know this was a bit of a journey, but look how much you've learned! You know how to use `TableViews`, how to `encode` and `decode` data using `UserDefaults`, how to use `Notifications`, and much more.

If things are still hazy, I encourage you to read through this chapter again to help solidify this knowledge. Way to go, give yourself a pat on the back and keep on learning.

Exercise

Now that you have learned about Table Views and Segues, your exercise for this section is when you click on one of the Table View entries, it takes you to a new View Controller detail screen about that entry. Display the information and the picture in a larger format. Happy coding!

Chapter 18: AutoLayout Size Classes

AutoLayout is already an incredibly helpful tool in developing iOS apps, but the ability to use Size Classes will make it even more helpful for you as a developer.

What you will learn

- How to use AutoLayout size Classes
- Implementing device-specific features

Key Terms

- `Size Classes`: a way of configuring a user interface with device-specific features.

Resources

Download here: https://github.com/devslopes/iOS13-book-assets/wiki/iOS13-Book

AutoLayout in Xcode is an amazing tool in regards to building apps that look beautiful on all screen sizes, but we can customize AutoLayout using `size classes` to make specific changes or UI decisions based on the screen size. Some things that look great on iPhone don't always look as great on an iPad (seriously, check out the Twitter app for iPad), but `size classes` allow us to fix this.

Creating a new Xcode project

Let's begin by creating a new project `Single View Application`, set the User Interface to `Storyboard` and call it whatever you'd like. In this case we're calling it `AutoLayoutSizeClasses` .

Next, open up `Main.storyboard` and click on `View as: iPhone xx (wC hR)` (Figure 19.0) at the bottom of the window. `wC` means "Width: Compact" and `hR` means "Height: Regular".

213

Figure 18.0

Note that the initial device loaded in Xcode is an iPhone in Portrait mode which has a width skinner than it's height – therefore it's width is compact. It's height is considered "regular" because it is in Portrait orientation. If we rotated the device, it's height would then be compact.

Now click on the square box next to "View as: iPhone" and what you'll see is a row of different screen sizes an iOS device can have.

We'll talk about these in a moment, but for now let's place some things on our ViewController so we can later modify them for different screen sizes.

Adding items & constraints to ViewController

Review of AutoLayout

Drag a `UIView` onto your ViewController from the Objects Library and add any background color for it. Then add some constraints and pin it `0` from the top and left, set the width and height both to `128`, check `Constrain to margins`, and add the constraints.

Now, if you click on one of the device options at the bottom, you can see what it looks like on different screen sizes. Click through the different screen sizes and see that our view maintains the same size and position.

Using AutoLayout is nothing new at this point in the book, but we needed to set up an example for using `size  classes`. Let's do that now.

Using Size Classes in Interface Builder

In the same list of devices you see at the bottom, select the `iPhone  8` for this example. Click the landscape orientation button at the far right to rotate our device in Interface Builder.

If you look closely, you will see that now our iPhone 8 has a compact width and compact height. "View as: iPhone 8 (wC hR)"

We will use `size classes` to change our UIView based on the width of the device. Click the `Vary for Traits` button from the bottom row of devices and tick the `Width` box.

Now anything that we change will affect the devices and orientations shown in blue. Click on the landscape-oriented iPhone and select the UIView in the ViewController. Make sure that the Size Inspector is selected and double-click on the `Width Equals:` constraint to edit it.

You should now see a list of properties all relating to our width constraint (Figure 19.1):

Figure 18.1

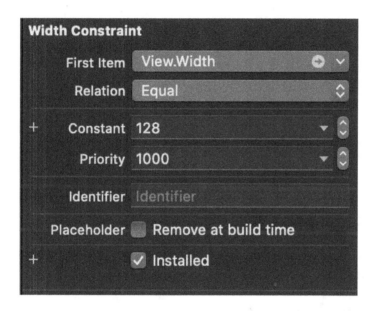

There's a little plus sign (+) next to the 'Constant' property. We want to change this value so that our UIView will be wider when the screen is wider. Click the plus sign and set both the width and height dropdowns to be 'Compact'. Leave 'Gamut' alone as we don't need to change that. Click `Add Variation`.

Now we have two 'Constant' properties that we can modify. One is named 'wC hC' and affects our UIView `only` when it's width and height are both compact. The other is named 'Constant' and affects it in every other circumstance. Change the value of 'wC hC' from 128 to 300 and notice how it changes in Interface Builder.

Here is where the magic happens... Click on the Portrait-oriented iPhone at the bottom of the window. Notice that the UIView is back in it's original form of being a square. Why the change?

Well, the iPhone now has a compact width and regular height. We have it set to stretch to a width of 300 only when `both` the width and height are compact! So cool!

To finish up this example, click 'Done Varying' on the blue Size Class menu at the bottom of the window:

A note about iPad and iPhone Plus Models

If you were to switch devices to an iPad, you probably noticed that the height and width are both regular. The iPhone X/Plus models are different in landscape mode than any other iPhone because it has a bigger screen size.

Here is a helpful table to help you remember it all:

Vertical Size Class	Horizontal Size Class
`iPad Portrait`	Regular	Regular
`iPad Landscape`	Regular	Regular
`iPhone Portrait`	Regular	Compact
`iPhone Landscape`	Compact	Compact
`iPhone X/Plus Landscape`	Compact	Regular

These devices can sometimes cause headaches when trying to get your UI to look nice on both iPad and iPhone. Knowing what size classes to use is definitely a step in the right direction!

A more useful example

Now that we've used `size classes` to make changes depending on the screen width, let's make something a little more useful.

Setting up the UI

Select and delete the UIView that we've been modifying so that we have a blank ViewController again. Drag on a UITableView from the Object Library and position it so that it fits in the ViewController like so (Figure 18.2):

Figure 18.2

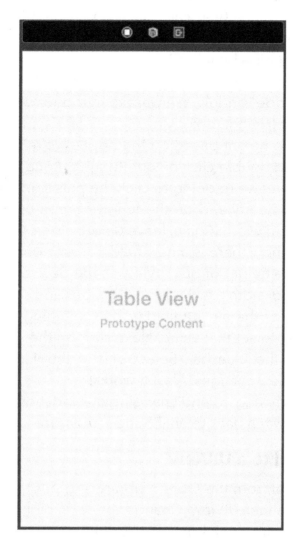

Let's add some constraints to our UITableView and pin it 55 from the top and 0 from the left, right and bottom. Make sure `Constrain to margins` is *unchecked* and then add the constraints.

Drag on a UIView from the Object Library and size it to take up that white space above our UITableView. This will be our banner bar.

Give it a background color of your choice. Then give it some constraints by pinning it 0 from the top, left and right. Then set the height and add the constraints.

Now, drag on a UITableViewCell so that we aren't just looking at a grey box that says 'Table View'.

Modifying the UI for iPad

Our banner's height is great for an iPhone-sized device, but on an iPad it looks a bit too skinny (you can check if you want by clicking on the iPad at the bottom of the screen). Let's make it so that when we're using an iPad, the banner is a bit taller.

Click on the UIView banner, then click `Vary for Traits` at the bottom of the Xcode window. We want to introduce variations based on height, so tick the 'Height' box.

To change the height based on the device we're using, click on the Size Inspector and double-click on our `Height Equals:` constraint.

Just like before, we're going to click the plus sign button (+) next to the `Constant` property and on the following pop-up, select `Regular` for both height and width. Again, leave `Gamut` alone. Click `Add Variation` and notice how there is a new field beneath `Constant` where we can customize the height of our UIView as the device we're using has a regular height and width (i.e. iPads of all shapes and sizes).

Set the value of the `wR hR` field to be something taller than 52, like 100. Press `Enter` to set that value. Next, click on the arrows to the right of the device in the blue bar. Select one of the iPads and see if the height of our UIView changes. Alas! It works!

Click 'Done Varying' to end changing our variation and then click on the iPhone 8 to switch back to an iPhone screen size.

Adding a label to a UIView

Drag on a UILabel from the Object Library and position it in the center of our colorful banner UIView. Change the text color to something that shows up nicely with the banner background color you've chosen and change the Label to say "True Blue".

Next, we need to add some constraints to keep the UILabel where we want it. Click on the `UILabel` and pin it 15 from the top. Next, we need to make sure that our label stays centered. To do this, click the `Align` button and tick the `Horizontally in Container` box. Click 'Add 1 Constraint'.

Now our label is staying put. But what if on iPad, we wanted the font size to display bigger? It looks pretty silly at the moment being so small.

Let's change the font so it's bigger on a larger devices. Click on the UILabel and ensure that the Attributes Inspector is selected.

To change the font size on iPad, we don't even need to click the 'Vary for Traits' button but instead we can click the plus sign (+) to the left of the Font property in Xcode.

On the pop-up, choose 'Regular' for both width and height. Leave 'Gamut' alone again. Click 'Add Variation' to add our font variation.

Now, we see a duplicate font selector beneath the standard one named wR hR meaning "Width: Regular" and "Height: Regular". If we change the font size on wR hR, it will only affect iPad. Try it out and bump the font size up to 30. Now the font size is much easier to read on an iPad screen.

Showing/Hiding elements on different devices

Another cool thing we can do is create a label for some subtitle text beneath our app name 'True Blue' and have it show up on iPad but leave it out of the iPhone interface.

To do this click on the iPad in the Device menu at the bottom of the window. Drag on a UILabel beneath the center of the other label already on the screen. Change the Label to say "The bluest of all apps".

Click on the label, and pin it 8 from the top. Then Click the Align icon check Horizontally in Container and add the constraint.

Now, this looks fine on an iPad, but what does it look like on an iPhone? Click on an iPhone model in the Device menu to check.

Yikes! That's not what we're looking for. We need to set our label to show on iPad only, so click on an iPad in the device menu again. Then click on the subtitle label if it isn't selected anymore.

In the Attributes Inspector, scroll down to the very bottom. You should see a tick-box named 'Installed'. Click the plus sign (+) to add a variation for regular height and regular width just like before.

You should now see two tick-boxes - both labeled 'Installed' but one with an extra label saying wR hR. Leave that box ticked, but untick the default box. This is basically saying that we want this label to only show on iPads, but everywhere else it shouldn't even be loaded.

Let's go check to see if the subtitle label has been removed from our iPhone. Click on any iPhone from the Device menu at the bottom of the window. If you don't see the Label on iPhone, it worked!

Wrapping up

This chapter contained a few basic examples of how `size classes` work together with AutoLayout to make building user interfaces for multiple devices and screen sizes even easier. We learned how to make changes to our UI determined by screen height or width. We showed a subtitle label on iPads but not on iPhone screens. We made our banner taller on iPad screens as well.

Being able to make our UI this flexible is a very powerful advantage Apple has over other platforms of development. I'm sure you can see how useful this could be when designing full-fledged apps.

The best apps are made by developers who are attentive to detail and care about how the app is experienced on iPhone and iPad. If you're able to make an app that tailors to both devices, your app will be way ahead of many other apps out there now.

Exercise

Extend this app by adding a + button to the upper right-hand corner of our app as if we were to add a post or image to our imaginary app. Give it some constraints to keep it in place. Switch to an iPad in Interface Builder and add in some more buttons to the left of the + button. Set them so that they are only installed on an iPad device with a regular height and regular width.

Chapter 19: Working with Maps - Park.ly App

Apps using the iPhone's GPS capabilities help us get from place to place, give us to-the-minute traffic updates, and much more. In this chapter, we will build a useful tool which saves our parking spot on a map and gives us walking directions back to it.

What you will learn

- Using MKMapView
- Implementing MKMapViewDelegate Methods
- Creating the ParkingSpot Model Class
- Conforming to MKMapViewDelegate/CLLocationManager-Delegate with Extensions
- Using and adding MKAnnotation/MKAnnotationView/MKPin-AnnotationView
- Creating a LocationService Singleton

Key Terms

- MKMapViewDelegate
- CLLocationManagerDelegate
- Table View Cell
- Singleton

Resources

Download here: https://github.com/devslopes/iOS13-book-assets/wiki/iOS13-Book

If you're anything like me, the following scenario will sound familiar: You drive to the store, mall, or some other place. You go in and do whatever it is that you went there to do. When walking out to go home, you look around helplessly as you have forgotten where you parked. This can be a very frustrating event and I happen to forget where I've parked all the time.

We're going to build a nice little app in this chapter called Park.ly which will allow you to drop a pin on your location and tap on the pin to pull up GPS walking directions back to your car. The features of MapKit and MKMapView are many, and this chapter will cover the basics of using maps and location services in iOS. Here's a screenshot showing you what this app will look like when we're done building it:

Figure 19.0

Creating an Xcode project

Let's begin by creating a new project `Single View Application`, set the User Interface to `Storyboard` and call it whatever you'd like. In this case we're calling it `Park.ly`.

Building the User Interface

Click on Main.storyboard to open up Interface Builder. Next, download the assets for this project from the link above. Then, click on `Assets.x-cassets` and drag all downloaded assets inside.

Modifying Info.plist

What you are about to do doesn't have to be done first by any means, but it's a very small step that can easily be overlooked and will hinder your ability to use Maps in iOS, so I like to do this step from the beginning so that I don't forget down the road.

In the Project Navigator, you should see a list of your files. Click on `Info.plist` file near the bottom and open it. You should see a screen with 3 columns and a bunch of rows/cells. In the empty area below the cells, `right-click` and select "Add Row" from the list of options.

As soon as you've click `Add Row`, an editable field will appear as a new row in the column of other properties. We need to give permission for `When In Use` Maps usage. This means that our app will only be able to track our location when we're actively using the app. To do this, type "Privacy - Location When In Use Usage Description" and press `Enter`. What you will see is a new String property with no value.

Helpful Hint:

MapKit, which we will be using in our app, has two usage capabilities: When In Use and Always. Think of an app like Google Maps as one that would use your location all the time since it monitors your location when you're using the app and when you request GPS directions. Even when you're phone is locked and you're not directly using Google Maps, it's still tracking your location to give you turn-by-turn directions.

Apple requires developers to give a reason for why they are requesting certain services such as access to the Photos library, Contacts, Touch ID, etc. We will type our reason as the value for the `When In Use` property we just added - "We need your location to save parking pins, thanks!"

Press `Enter` to save that value. Now we've successfully added the required properties to `Info.plist` that our app needs to successfully use the MapKit framework. Let's move on to building our UI.

Building the Park.ly User Interface

Open up `Main.storyboard` from the Project Navigator and you'll see a blank ViewController. Search for a UIButton from the Objects Library (+). Drag the UIButton onto the ViewController and place it in the center near the bottom. Drag the sizing boxes to make it approximately 75 x 75. Now let's add some constraints and pin it 30 from the bottom and set the width and height to 75.

Next, with the UIButton still selected click the Align button, select `Horizontally in Container`, and click `Add 1 Constraint`.

Open up the Attributes Inspector and click on the UIButton. We need to change our button to look like the design. First, delete the `Button` text, then set the button `Image` property to "parkCar" and press `Enter`. Now, scroll down to the bottom of the Attributes Inspector panel and click `Background` property under the *View* section and choose White Color. The background color is up to you, but white is what I thought looked best for contrasting the Map View.

Next up, we need to add a UIImageView to show the Park.ly logo. In the Object Library, search for UIImageView and drag it onto the Storyboard.

Position it so that it looks the same as Figure 19.1. Use the handy snap guides in Interface Builder to position it equally from the left, right, and top.

Figure 19.1

Next, click on the UIImageView and ensure that the Attributes Inspector is opened. In the `Image` property box, type "park.ly-logo" and press `Enter`. For the `Content  Mode` property, change the mode to `Aspect Fit`.

Let's give the UIImageView some constraints and pin it 0 from the top, and 10 from the right and 10 from the left. Be sure to check `Constrain to margins` then add the constraints.

We're now at the last step of creating our UI - adding the `Map View`! In the Object Library, search for "Map Kit View" and drag it into the center of the Storyboard. If you try to drag and resize it to the four corners of the ViewController, you'll notice the Map View covers up the logo and the button. We need to change that.

It's a simple fix - In the Document Outline, drag the `Map View` to be above the Button and Park.ly Logo cells.

Now add some constraints to the Map View and pin it 0 from all sides, double check `Constrain to margins` is _unchecked_ and add the constraints.

Finally, before we dive into the code we need to allow our Map View to show the User Location. Click the Map View and in the Attributes Inspector, tick the box labeled `User Location`. Excellent! Now we have a nice, simple User Interface for our app. (Figure 19.2)

Figure 19.2

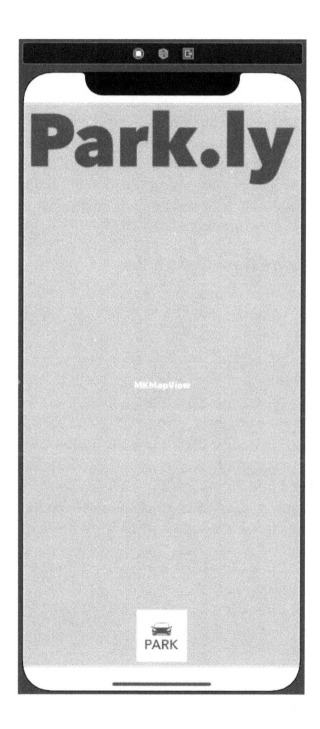

Custom UIButton/UIImageView Classes

Setting Up MVC Folders

In the completed app screenshot above, the Park Car button is circular and has a nice drop shadow. The Park.ly logo also has a drop shadow. We're going to make two quick, little subclasses to make that happen.

First, we should set up our project with some folders. We'll use the standard Model-View-Controller setup by creating `New   Groups` in Xcode for each of the three components. Go to the Project Navigator on the left and then right-clicking on the yellow park.ly folder -> select `New   Group` -> name it "Controller", and do the same process for the other two folders -> naming them "View" and "Model".

Creating Custom View Class Files

Right click on the `View` folder and click `New   File....`, double-click `Cocoa   Touch   Class`. Give it a Subclass of: UIButton and name it "RoundButton". Ensure that Swift is selected for the language and click Next. The following pop-up window asks you where to save the file. Save it in the default location by clicking Create but make sure that the Park.ly box is ticked under Targets.

Open `RoundButton.swift` from within the View folder and delete the commented out code so that the RoundButton class is empty. To set up our custom round button, we only need to override one function and add a few lines of code.

Add the following code to override `awakeFromNib()`. Don't forget that you can use Xcode's speedy autocomplete feature to make this faster and easier.

```
override func awakeFromNib() {

        //TO DO

}
```

You may be wondering why we're overriding the default implementation of `awakeFromNib()`. According to Xcode's Quick Help: *"Typically, you implement awakeFromNib for objects that require additional set up that cannot be done at design time. For example, you might use this method to customize the default configuration of any controls to match user preferences or the values in other controls. You might also use it to restore individual controls to some previous state of your application."*

Customizing the default controls is exactly what we want to do! So let's do it. Inside the `awakeFromNib()` function, we need to change a property called cornerRadius. We can use this to make rounded corners, but in our case we want a completely round button.

What we can do is we can set the corner radius to be half of the height of the button. That means that the corners will be rounded perfectly to the middle. If our button was 50 pixels tall and we rounded each corner 25 pixels (half it's height), they would each meet in the middle making the button appear to be perfectly circular.

To set the cornerRadius property, add the following code to `awakeFromNib()`:

```
override func awakeFromNib() {

    self.layer.cornerRadius = self.frame.height / 2

}
```

In that one line, we are setting the property `cornerRadius` to be the height of the button divided by 2. No matter what height we make our button in the future, it will always perfectly circular!

In order for our UIButton to use this code, we need to set its subclass `RoundButton`. To do this, click `Main.storyboard` and click on the UIButton at the bottom of the ViewController. Click on the Identity Inspector ▣ and in the `Class` property in the _Custom Class _section, type "RoundButton" and press `Enter`.

Testing and Fixing ViewController.swift

We should build and run the app to check if we were successful. Before we do that though, there's a tiny thing we need to do to keep our app from crashing. Since we're using a Map View from MapKit, we need to actually tell the ViewController how to handle that. So before we can run this app at all, we need to import MapKit in our ViewController.

Click `ViewController.swift` file and import the MapKit:

```
import UIKit
```

```
import MapKit


class RoundButton: UIButton {

    override func awakeFromNib() {

        self.layer.cornerRadius = self.frame.height / 2

    }

}
```

And that's all we need at the moment to get our app running...for now. Go ahead and Build and Run the project (or press ⌘ + R) and wait for the app to open in Simulator.

Great! So our UIButton is now rounded. Let's give it a nice pillowy drop shadow. In `RoundButton.swift` file add the following code to `awakeFromNib()`:

```
override func awakeFromNib() {

    self.layer.cornerRadius = self.frame.height / 2

    self.layer.shadowRadius = 20

    self.layer.shadowOpacity = 0.5

    self.layer.shadowColor = UIColor.black.cgColor

}
```

After adding that code, Build & Run once more to check to see our beautiful view code in action. Well......? It's looking great so far?! Believe it or not, the UI part of our app is complete.

For an extra challenge: See if you can make a custom view class for UIImageView just like we did for UIButton and set the same code (be sure to delete the line of code changing the cornerRadius) inside of `awakeFromNib()`. Then go to `Main.storyboard` and set the custom class in the Identity Inspector.

Setting Up A Data Model

For our app, we will be saving a location to a map, so we need to create a data model class which we will instantiate later on to create and save a location on our Map View. Let's dive in!

First, right-click the `Model` folder in the Project Outline. Click `New File...` -> double click `Cocoa Touch Class` -> set it to subclass `NSObject` and name it "ParkingSpot". Click Finish then Create to save it to your project. It will open automatically as you probably know by now.

We haven't subclassed NSObject before and the reason we're doing that is because of MKAnnotation.

According to `Xcode's Quick Help`, *"The MKAnnotation protocol is used to provide annotation-related information to a map view."*

We we'll be using MKPinAnnotation later on to display the pin information on our map and the MKAnnotation to capture the location to help the pin know where it should drop and display itself on the map.

So, as you may have guessed, we need to inherit from MKAnnotation to use ParkingSpot on our Map View. We also need to import MapKit. Change the declaration of the ParkingSpot class to look like this:

```
import UIKit

import MapKit


class ParkingSpot: NSObject, MKAnnotation {

    //TO DO

}
```

After doing this, you'll immediately be shown an error. Xcode is warning you that you aren't conforming to the protocol MKAnnotation - and you're not yet. All we need to do is create three properties for the title, location name, and coordinate of the Map View annotation. Then initialize them.

Add the following code to the ParkingSpot class:

```
class ParkingSpot: NSObject, MKAnnotation {

    let title: String?
```

```
    let locationName: String?

    let coordinate: CLLocationCoordinate2D


    init(title: String, locationName: String,
coordinate: CLLocationCoordinate2D) {

        self.title = title

        self.locationName = locationName

        self.coordinate = coordinate

    }

}
```

As you can see in the code sample above, we create three constants. Two of these constants are optional and one is required. If you look deeper into MKAnnotation, you will see that it requires a coordinate value but it's title and subtitle are optional.

Then, we create an initializer function to initialize the values for title, locationName, and coordinate when an instance of ParkingSpot is created.

I just told you that MKAnnotation has an optional subtitle property, but how should we handle it? It's simple! We'll just use a variable called subtitle and brackets to return locationName as it's value. This way we're actually setting the subtitle property of MKAnnotation and not creating a separate variable of the same name. Do this like so:

```
class ParkingSpot: NSObject, MKAnnotation {

    let title: String?

    let locationName: String?

    let coordinate: CLLocationCoordinate2D


    init(title: String, locationName: String,
coordinate: CLLocationCoordinate2D) {

        self.title = title
```

```
        self.locationName = locationName

        self.coordinate = coordinate

    }


    var subtitle: String? {

        return locationName

    }

}
```

The last thing we need to do before our data model is done is add a function that will pass in a coordinate (CLLocationCoordinate2D) and return an MKMapItem which encapsulates information about a specific point on a map.

The function will set up that specific point for our function.

Write `import Contacts` beneath `import MapKit` at the top of `ParkingSpot.swift` file and add the following code at the bottom, then I'll break down what we wrote:

```
func mapItem(location: CLLocationCoordinate2D) ->
MKMapItem {

        let addressDictionary =
[String(CNPostalAddressStreetKey): subtitle]

        let placemark = MKPlacemark(coordinate:
location, addressDictionary: addressDictionary as
[String : Any])

        let mapItem = MKMapItem(placemark: placemark)

        mapItem.name = title


        return mapItem

}
```

In this function, we pass in `location` as a CLLocationCoordinate2D. This is simply a GPS coordinate with a latitude and longitude property. Next, inside the function we declare a constant called `addressDic-`

tionary which, as you probably guessed is a dictionary that holds addresses.

Then we create **placemark** of type MKPlacemark. This takes in a coordinate (which we have) and an addressDictionary (which we also have) and creates specific point and connects it to a specific address. In our case, we won't be using an address but will be using a message describing the location name.

Finally, we create **mapItem** which is of type MKMapItem and we pass in the **placemark** we created earlier. We set the **name** property of **mapItem** with the value of ParkingSpot's **title** property. Then, we return **mapItem**.

Now when we instantiate ParkingSpot, we can call **mapItem(location:)** to create an MKMapItem for our Map View to understand. We'll use it later so you can see how it's really used in context. We needed to import the Contacts framework so that we could access CNPostalAddressStreetKey which gives us a String value containing the street name.

And just like that, our data model is complete! We're now set to start programming our ViewController! Pat yourself on the back and yell something cool *REALLY* loud…

Setting Up The ViewController

In the Project Navigator, click on **ViewController.swift** to open it in the code editor. We've already imported the MapKit framework, but there's one other key framework we need - CoreLocation. Update **ViewController.swift** to include CoreLocation:

```
import UIKit

import MapKit

import CoreLocation


class ViewController: UIViewController {

    override func viewDidLoad() {

        super.viewDidLoad()

    }
```

```
}
```

Alright, so we can't interact with our ViewController without the proper @IBOutlets and @IBActions so let's switch over to `Main.storyboard` and set them up. Once you've selected `Main.storyboard`, click on the "Adjust Editor Options" icon and select `Assistant` from the list. You'll now have a split screen with the storyboard on the left and a code editor containing `UIViewController` on the right.

Lets make some room by closing the two columns on the left and right side of Xcode. Click the right and left show/hide Navigator icons at the top right of the Interface Builder.

Creating @IBOutlets/@IBActions

In order to interface with the elements in our UI, we need to create two @IBOutlets – one for UIButton and one for Map View.

You already know how to do this. Either right-click and drag from the UIButton to the code file or manually type the @IBOutlet code and then drag from the little circle to the UIButton on the Storyboard. I'm going to drag from the UI element on the Storyboard to the code file just above the `viewDidLoad()` function to create the @IBOutlets.

Now create an @IBOutlet for the MKMapView by doing the same thing you did for the UIButton. You can name the @IBOutlets:

UIButton -> parkBtn

MapView -> mapView

Let's set up an @IBAction now for our UIButton so that we can drop pins on our map when we tap on it.

Right-click and drag from the UIButton to beneath `viewDidLoad()` and let go. Be sure to change @IBOutlet into @IBAction by clicking on the drop-down menu and changing the connection type. Name it something like "parkBtnWasPressed". It's important to name your @IBActions descriptively relating to what's being done to trigger the action. We won't put any code inside of it yet, but soon enough we will. Your code should look like this:

```swift
import UIKit

import MapKit

import CoreLocation


class ViewController: UIViewController {

    @IBOutlet weak var parkBtn: RoundButton!

    @IBOutlet weak var mapView: MKMapView!


    override func viewDidLoad() {

        super.viewDidLoad()

    }


    @IBAction func parkBtnWasPressed(_ sender: Any) {

        //TO DO

    }

}
```

Creating The LocationService Singleton

A singleton is one of my favorite things in programming. A singleton is actually a software design pattern that only allows a class to be instantiated with one object. This means that we can create one instance of a class and save information to it and use it throughout our class without needing to instantiate it.

We will use a singleton as a LocationService which will:

1.) Set up and configure a CLLocationManager to our liking.

2.) Manage our location and persistently update the coordinate property so our app can use our current GPS coordinate however and whenever we like.

We won't dive deep into detail about how singletons work or anything too complex, but you can certainly see how singletons work and imagine how useful they could be in your apps.

Let's begin by creating a new group and file in Xcode. Right-click on the yellow park.ly folder and click `New Group`. Name it Services. Then, right-click the Services folder and click `New File....`. Double-click on Swift File and name it "LocationService". Click `Create` to save it.

Importing CoreLocation

Open `LocationService.swift` and directly beneath `import Foundation` add the line `import CoreLocation`. Now we can access all the fun location-related stuff we need!

"Creating A Singleton Class"

We'll create the most simple of `singletons` first, then expand on it.

First, add the following class declaration to your Swift file:

```
class LocationService {

    static let instance = LocationService()

}
```

By declaring `instance` as `static` we are giving it the ability to "live" across the entire run of our app. Which is perfect if we want to be able to use the values in this class wherever and whenever we want. At the moment our singleton doesn't do anything, so let's give it some properties and methods.

First off, we need to have it inherit from NSObject and `CLLocationManagerDelegate`. Those are both needed when wanting to get a user's location because `CLLocationManagerDelegate` relies upon NSObject to work properly. Add the following code:

```
class LocationService: NSObject,
CLLocationManagerDelegate {

    static let instance = LocationService()

}
```

Next, we're going to add some variables - one which will manage our location and then other which we will save our current location to.

Add the following lines of code:

```
class LocationService: NSObject,
CLLocationManagerDelegate {

    static let instance = LocationService()

    var locationManager = CLLocationManager()

    var currentLocation: CLLocationCoordinate2D?

}
```

The `locationManager` variable is instantiated and going to help us in managing our location. If you press press ⌘ and click on **CLLocation-Manager**, you can see all the fun location managing functions we can use! Our currentLocation variable is not yet instantiated, but it will be in a moment.

Overriding The Initializer

When we use this `singleton`, we want it to have certain properties saved like how our locationManager should work and set specific settings so that we don't have to write extra code in our ViewController. We can do this by overriding the initializer for the `singleton` class. We're going to set values for some properties of `locationManager` in addition to declaring the singleton as it's delegate. Add this code to override the initializer:

```
class LocationService: NSObject,
CLLocationManagerDelegate {

    static let instance = LocationService()

    var locationManager = CLLocationManager()

    var currentLocation: CLLocationCoordinate2D?


    override init () {

        super.init()

        self.locationManager.delegate = self

        self.locationManager.desiredAccuracy =
kCLLocationAccuracyBest
```

```
        self.locationManager.distanceFilter = 50

        self.locationManager.startUpdatingLocation()

    }

}
```

So what did we just do? We told LocationService that when it is instantiated by `static let instance = LocationService()` to set the `locationManagers` delegate to be LocationService. Then we tell it what level of accuracy we'd like with `kCLLocationAccuracyBest`. We set a distance filter to tell CLLocationManager when it should update our location. We'll talk more about that one in a couple paragraphs. Finally, we tell our locationManager to start updating our location.

Now to finish this up, there is one delegate method we need to use to to update our location in our app and it is called locationManager(manager:didUpdateLocations locations:).

Add it to the bottom of the `singleton` class we just made:

```
class LocationService: NSObject,
CLLocationManagerDelegate {

    static let instance = LocationService()

    var locationManager = CLLocationManager()

    var currentLocation: CLLocationCoordinate2D?


    override init () {

        super.init()

        self.locationManager.delegate = self

        self.locationManager.desiredAccuracy =
kCLLocationAccuracyBest

        self.locationManager.distanceFilter = 50

        self.locationManager.startUpdatingLocation()

    }
```

```
    func locationManager(manager: CLLocationManager!,
didUpdateLocations locations: [AnyObject]!) {

        //TO DO

    }

}
```

Awesome, now let's discuss what we will do with this. Earlier we set a property called `distanceFilter` to a value of 50. That means that every 50 meters CoreLocation will trigger a location update. We can use the delegate method we just added to run code every time our location is updated. Pretty cool!

All we need to do is save our current coordinates to our `current-Location` variable and we're good to go.

To do that add in the following code:

```
func locationManager(manager: CLLocationManager!,
didUpdateLocations locations: [AnyObject]!) {

        self.currentLocation =
locationManager.location?.coordinate

}
```

Awesome. So now, whenever our location is updated and CLLocation-Manager notices, this function is called saving our GPS coordinates to our very own `currentLocation` variable. Once we've granted location services to our app (more on that later), we'll be able to pull our GPS coordinates and use them whenever we want!

Let's move on to doing that. Click on ViewController.swift to open it up in the code editor.

Let's go ahead and do that. Click on `ViewController.swift` to open it up in the code editor.

Creating Our ParkingSpot

We'll need to create a variable of type `ParkingSpot` so that whenever we tap the "Park" button, a pin annotation is made with our current location and dropped on the map appropriately. To do this write a single variable above `viewDidLoad()` like so:

```
var parkedCarAnnotation: ParkingSpot?
```

We'll instantiate and it and set the **coordinate** property when the users location is updated, but that will be later on in this chapter."

Checking And Requesting Location Services

In order for us to actually get a user's location data to show up on the Map View, we need to request permission first. At the beginning of this chapter, we added a property to **Info.plist** with the message we will show when requesting location permissions, but now let's actually write the code to request it.

I wrote a function called **checkLocationAuthorizationStatus()** to put everything in my **viewDidLoad()** function look a little neater. Plus, I could reuse this elsewhere in this ViewController if I needed to. Add the following function beneath the @IBAction called **parkBtnWasPressed**:

```
func checkLocationAuthorizationStatus() {

        if CLLocationManager.authorizationStatus()
== .authorizedWhenInUse {

            mapView.showsUserLocation = true


LocationService.instance.locationManager.delegate = self


LocationService.instance.locationManager.desiredAccuracy
= kCLLocationAccuracyBest


LocationService.instance.locationManager.startUpdatingLo
cation()

        } else {


LocationService.instance.locationManager.requestWhenInUs
eAuthorization()

        }

    }
```

This function will check to see if we are authorized for location services. If we are not, it will request "When In Use" authorization. If we are already authorized, it will show the users location on the Map View and tell our LocationService to start updating our location. In order for our app to work properly, we need to call this function from `viewDid-Load()` as well as set the delegate of our Map View.

In `viewDidLoad()` call the function you just wrote and set the delegate of `mapView` like so:

```
override func viewDidLoad() {

        super.viewDidLoad()

        mapView.delegate = self

        checkLocationAuthorizationStatus()

    }
```

The delegate is `self` (referring to our ViewController) because, "a map view sends messages to its delegate regarding the loading of map data and changes in the portion of the map being displayed" according to Xcode's Quick Help. It makes sense that the delegate is set to be our ViewController because that is the thing that cares what is being displayed and how and when.

Creating A Function To Center MKMapView

When I was building this app for the first time, I thought it would be the best user experience if the users location was centered on the screen and it would be great on the code side to be able to center the map on the user's location at will.

To achieve this, you will write a little function which takes in a location property of type CLLocation (basically just a coordinate including longitude and latitude properties). Then you will create a coordinate region which tells the map what size it should zoom to. Then we set the region and it will animate automatically. MapKit gives us that for free.

First, we need to create a variable called `regionRadius`. This property will tell our function the length in meters (500) it should zoom in to on our map. You will see how it's used in a moment.

Add the following property beneath the @IBOutlets:

```
let regionRadius: CLLocationDistance = 500
```

Then, add the following function to the bottom of the ViewController class:

```
func centerMapOnLocation(location: CLLocation) {

        let coordinateRegion =
MKCoordinateRegion.init(center: location.coordinate,
latitudinalMeters: regionRadius * 2, longitudinalMeters:
regionRadius * 2)

        mapView.setRegion(coordinateRegion,
animated: true)

}
```

As you can see the **coordinateRegion** property is created using the coordinates from the location we pass in (as a center coordinate), and two other values for longitudinal meters and latitudinal meters which are set using the **regionRadius** we created earlier with a value of 500 meters. Feel free to mess around with this value and tweak it to your liking.

Adding MKMapViewDelegate and CLLocationManager-Delegate Extensions to ViewController

MKMapViewDelegate Extension

To get the functionality we want, we need to conform to CLLocation-ManagerDelegate and MKMapViewDelegate. We could add these to the end of our class declaration or for the purpose of writing clean code, we can create extensions of **ViewController** at the bottom of our code file which conform to the protocols we need.

Go to the bottom of **ViewController.swift** and beneath the closing brackets of the ViewController class add an extension of ViewController which conforms to MKMapViewDelegate like so:

```
extension ViewController: MKMapViewDelegate {

    //TO DO

}
```

Now we can call some methods from `MKMapViewDelegate` that we need. First call **`mapView(mapView:viewFor annotation:)`** inside our extension like so:

```
extension ViewController: MKMapViewDelegate {

    func mapView(_ mapView: MKMapView, viewFor
annotation: MKAnnotation) -> MKAnnotationView? {

        if let annotation = annotation as? ParkingSpot {

            let identifier = "pin"

            var view: MKPinAnnotationView

            view = MKPinAnnotationView(annotation:
annotation, reuseIdentifier: identifier)

            view.canShowCallout = true

            view.animatesDrop = true

            view.pinTintColor = UIColor.orange

            view.calloutOffset = CGPoint(x: -8, y: -3)

            view.rightCalloutAccessoryView =
UIButton.init(type: .detailDisclosure) as UIView

            return view

        } else {

            return nil

        }

    }

}
```

We're doing a lot in the code above. First, we use an `if let` to create an annotation but only if it is of type `ParkingSpot`. We then set up an identifier ("pin"), create a view variable of type `MKPinAnnotation-View`, and then proceed to set various settings and customizations.

When we set `view.rightCalloutAccessoryView` we're telling our app that when we tap the pin, on the white pop-up that follows we want there to be a Detail Disclosure button on the right-hand side. You can see that in Figure 18.3 below. At the very end, we return `view` which is of type MKAnnotationView.

This function creates an MKAnnotationView which is the fancy code-name for the view which holds the pin and the callout pop-up in the Apple Maps app. In the screenshot of our completed app above, this is what an MKAnnotationView looks like including the "callout" - the white view that pops up when tapping the pin.

Figure 19.3

Next, we need to handle what happens when we tap on the pin then tap on the Detail Disclosure button. We want it to copy the current location and send it to the Apple Maps app (bonus points if you can figure out how to send this to Google Maps instead).

To do this, we will add another delegate method of `MKMapView-Delegate` *underneath* the other `mapView` function we just wrote, but still inside of the extension:

```
func mapView(_ mapView: MKMapView, annotationView view:
MKAnnotationView, calloutAccessoryControlTapped control:
UIControl) {

        let location = view.annotation as! ParkingSpot

        let launchOptions =
[MKLaunchOptionsDirectionsModeKey:
MKLaunchOptionsDirectionsModeWalking]

        location.mapItem(location:
(parkedCarAnnotation?.coordinate)!).openInMaps(launchOpt
ions: launchOptions)

}
```

This function handles what happens when we tap on the Detail Disclosure button on the white pop-up view after tapping on the pin we drop."

We create a constant called `location` which we set with `view.annotation` and we downcast it with the type `ParkingSpot`. Then we created another constant called `launchOptions` which is a dictionary that MapKit uses to tell the Apple Maps app what type of directions we want to use.

You can choose default, driving, walking, or transit. I used walking directions because most people will be walking to find their car. Finally, using the `mapItem()` function of `ParkingSpot`, we pass in our `location` from `parkedCarAnnotation` we created earlier and set it to open in Maps by calling the function `openInMaps(launchOptions:)` and passing in our dictionary of launch options. All this to send our location to the Maps app.

CLLocationManagerDelegate Extension

Now we will create an extension for `CLLocationManagerDelegate`. Beneath the closing brackets of the `MKMapViewDelegate` extension add the following extension:

```
extension ViewController: CLLocationManagerDelegate {

    //TO DO

}
```

Inside, we're going to call one delegate method that is called when the user's location is updated. It is a perfect time to save our location to our LocationService `singleton` and also a perfect time to instantiate our `parkedCarAnnotation` and pass in our location so that we have an accurate pin drop every time. Add the following code inside the `CLLocationManagerDelegate` extension:

```
func mapView(_ mapView: MKMapView, didUpdate
userLocation: MKUserLocation) {

        centerMapOnLocation(location:
CLLocation(latitude: userLocation.coordinate.latitude,
longitude: userLocation.coordinate.longitude))
```

```
        let locationServiceCoordinate =
LocationService.instance.locationManager.location!.coord
inate


        parkedCarAnnotation = ParkingSpot(title: "My
Parking Spot", locationName: "Tap the 'i' for GPS",
coordinate: CLLocationCoordinate2D(latitude:
locationServiceCoordinate.latitude , longitude:
locationServiceCoordinate.longitude))

}
```

In this function, we're first calling `centerMapOnLocation(loca-tion:)` and passing in the current user location (via `userLocation.-coordinate.latitude/longitude`) provided to us by `CLLoca-tionManagerDelegate`.

Every time our location updates, the map will now center on our location.

Next, we create a constant called `locationServiceLocation` and set it to our LocationService `singleton` which is persistently managing our location and updating the `currentLocation` value with our current GPS coordinates. We use a variable like this so that we don't have to type `LocationService.instance.locationManager.lo-cation!.coordinate` twice as it's really lengthy.

Afterward, we set the value of `parkedCarAnnotation` to be of type ParkingSpot and we instantiated it with all the values it requires like a title, locationName, and latitude and longitude values which we take from `locationServiceCoordinate`.

For the `locationName` property I wrote "Tap the 'i' for GPS" which is what the Detail Disclosure button looks like. If the user taps on that it loads up the Maps app with GPS directions. We're using `location-Name` as a subtitle for the MKAnnotation that shows up when tapping the pin.

Adding Code To Our @IBAction

Wait a minute! We haven't written any code to execute when our UIButton is pushed. Let's do that to ensure that our app actually does something.

Inside of the @IBAction named `parkBtnWasPressed`, add the following code to check and see if there's any annotations in our mapView. If there's not, we'll add an annotation to drop a pin on the map and change the UIButton's image to the red 'X' reading "FOUND CAR".

If there is, we'll remove it and set the UIButton's image back to the one with grey "PARK" text and the car icon. At the end, we'll center the map on the current user's location. Scroll to the top of our `ViewController.swift` and add this code to the @IBAction `parkBtnWasPressed`:

```
@IBAction func parkBtnWasPressed(_ sender: Any) {

    if mapView.annotations.count == 1 {

        mapView.addAnnotation(parkedCarAnnotation!)

        parkBtn.setImage(UIImage(named:
"foundCar.png"), for: .normal)

    } else {

mapView.removeAnnotations(mapView.annotations)

        parkBtn.setImage(UIImage(named:
"parkCar.png"), for: .normal)

    }

    centerMapOnLocation(location:
LocationService.instance.locationManager.location!)

}
```

If you're confused by why I checked to see if `mapView.annotations.count` was equal to 1, let me explain. When MKMapView is created, it stores a default annotation in an array of MKAnnotations. So when we start up the app, the array `mapView.annotations.count` is already equal to 1.

Since that's the case, we call `addAnnotation` and pass in `parked-CarAnnotation`. Then we set the button image and center the Map View. At this point, `mapView.annotations.count` is equal to 2.

When we press the button again to delete the pin, we check the count of the annotations array and since it is not equal to 1, we enter the `else` block, remove any annotations in our `mapView`, and set the button image back to the default grey "PARK" image.

Building, Running, & Wrapping Up

At this point, you should be ready to build and run your app! Press ⌘ + R to run it and see how we did.

The app should pop up, request location services, and then center in on your location. If you're not building to a physical device, ensure that you have a location set.

To do this go up to the macOS Menu Bar when in Simulator, click Debug and scroll down to Location. Set one of the predefined locations like Apple or paste in an address of your own. You can also drop a pin and then set "City Bicycle Ride" or one of the other options to simulate the user's location moving on the screen.

MapKit is extremely useful and versatile. It can be used in a number of ways and we've just barely scratched the surface of what can be done. You also learned about and used `singletons` which wasn't necessary, but it definitely showed how they can be used and how useful they are!

Nicely done! This app introduced some new ideas and features of iOS you haven't used before. If you've made it thus far you should celebrate all the amazing learning you're doing. Keep it up!

Exercise

To extend this app, do your homework to enable this app to:

- Provide an option to open your parking spot pin in Google Maps and Apple Maps.
- Utilize UserDefaults to save and retrieve the pin even if the app is quit or crashes.

Chapter 20: Working with Gestures - Tanstagram App

You will use UIGesture Recognizers to make images expand, shrink, rotate and move around the screen. You will also be able to tap an image to save a screenshot of the current view to your camera roll on your iPhone.

What you will learn

- How to add gesture recognizers to your `UIImageViews`.
- How to Rendering UIImageView to UIImage
- How to save an image to the camera roll.

Key Terms

- UIGestureRecognizer
- UIPinchGestureRecognizer
- UIPanGestureRecognizer
- UIRotateGestureRecognizer
- UITapGestureRecognizer

Resources

Download here: https://github.com/devslopes/iOS13-book-assets/wiki/iOS13-Book

Getting Started

Lets begin with starting a new `Single View Application` and name it whatever you would like. You should be very familiar with this process by now. For this project we are going to name it `Tanstagram`.

Next, download the assets for this project from the link above. Then, click on `Assets.xcassets` and drag all downloaded assets inside.

Now click on the `Main.storyboard`. Search for `UIImageView` from the Objects Library and drag the `Image View` onto the View Controller.

With the `UIImageView` selected, head on over to the Attributes Inspector. Since we'll be pinching, zooming, and rotating, we'll want to check off `User Interaction Enabled` and `Multiple Touch` under the `Interaction` section. Let's also change the `Content Mode` to **Aspect Fit**.

Now let's put an image in our UIImageView! Select a shape from the `Image` dropdown in the Attributes Inspector. Once the shape appears, you'll want to resize the UIImageView so it "hugs" the shape, leaving as little whitespace as you can.

We'll need to make 6 more `UIImageViews` for the other shapes, so go ahead and copy and paste 6 more and fill them with their respective shapes. Don't forget to double check that they are all **Aspect Fit**, and `User Interaction Enabled` and `Multiple Touch` is checked off! Once done, you should have 7 shapes total. (Figure 20.0)

Figure 20.0

Note: These shapes do not need to be any exact size, just as long as you resize the `UIImageView` to fit around the shape as best as possible.

Click on the "Adjust Editor Options" icon and select `Assistant` from the list. You will now have a split screen with the storyboard on the left and a code editor containing `ViewController.swift` on the right. Go ahead and close the right and left columns to make some more room.

Now we're going to do something a little different here. We're going create an `@IBOutlet Collection` for all the images.

Go ahead and click on a shape in your Storyboard. We'll want to control drag on to our `ViewController.swift` right above `viewDidLoad`. Set the `Connection` to "Outlet Collection" and name it images. You now have an array of `UIImageView`.

Once connected, you'll notice a small dot next to your `@IBOutlet`. Hovering over it will turn it into a small plus symbol, and highlight the recently connected shape in the Storyboard. All we need to do now is click the plus, and drag it onto the rest of the shapes to add it to the array of `@IBOutlet Collection`. Once you are done connecting all the shapes, hovering over the small plus symbol will show all the shapes highlighted in the Storyboard.

Now let's dive into some code! First, let's add the `UIGestureRecognizerDelegate` after `UIViewController`. This will allow us to access some of the built in functions for UIGestureRecognizer. These should be comma separated.

```
import UIKit


class ViewController: UIViewController,
UIGestureRecognizerDelegate {


    @IBOutlet var images: [UIImageView]!


    override func viewDidLoad() {
        super.viewDidLoad()


    }

}
```

Pinch Gesture

Create a function called `addPinchGesture` with a parameter called `imageView` of type `UIImageView`. Create the UIPinchGestureRecognizer and add it to the UIImageView we pass into the function like so:

```
func addPinchGesture(imageView: UIImageView) {

        let pinchGesture =
UIPinchGestureRecognizer(target: self, action:
#selector(ViewController.handlePinch))

        imageView.addGestureRecognizer(pinchGesture)

}
```

You might notice we're getting an error. Don't worry! Before we fix it, let's break down what the return function is actually doing:

`target`: We're basically telling the function that it needs to look at `self` for the UIPinchGestureRecognizer.

`action`: This is what actually happens when we execute when the gesture. `#selector`: the selector looks for the function that the action will execute. In this case, we are telling it to look for a function called `handlePinch`.

This is the reason we are getting an error. We haven't created the function `handlePinch` yet! Let's do that now. Go ahead and write out the function **handlePinch** that takes a parameter called **sender** of type **UIPinchGestureRecognizer**:

```
@objc func handlePinch(sender: UIPinchGestureRecognizer)
{

        sender.view?.transform =
(sender.view?.transform)!.scaledBy(x: sender.scale, y:
sender.scale)

        sender.scale = 1

}
```

Since we've created the parameter (sender) of **UIPinchGestureRecognizer**, we can access some of it's properties and functions using dot notation. In this function we're basically looking to the view of the sender and accessing **transform**. Then we're telling it to scale both the x and y axis, specifically by 1, so when you put two fingers on the screen and expand or contract, the shape will react proportionally on a 1 to 1 ratio.

Now let's apply the `pinchGesture` function to our shapes! Create a function called **createGestures**. Inside it, we'll create a `for   loop` and pass each **image** into our **addPinchGesture** function:

```
func createGestures() {

    for image in images {

        addPinchGesture(imageView: image)

    }

}
```

Now all we need to do is add `createGestures` to `viewDidLoad` so the function runs!

```
override func viewDidLoad() {

    super.viewDidLoad()

    createGestures()

}
```

Run your project and you'll see you can pinch your shapes! Great work!

If your wondering how the heck to test this since you can't actually pinch/zoom your computer screen - on your Storyboard, place one of the shape in the center of the UI.

Now when you run your project and the simulator pops up, hover the mouse over the center shape and hold `option` , then click and drag the mouse in any direction. #BOOM - the shape should resize!

Looking at our code, you might notice it's broken up into 3 main parts - setting up the gestures, handling the gestures, and then applying them. Before we add our other two gestures, let's organize our code a little bit.

Add the following comments above their respective functions so we know what each block is responsible for:

```
// Set Gestures

    func addPinchGesture(imageView: UIImageView) {
```

```
        let pinchGesture =
UIPinchGestureRecognizer(target: self, action:
#selector(ViewController.handlePinch))

        imageView.addGestureRecognizer(pinchGesture)

    }



    // Handle Gestures

    @objc func handlePinch(sender:
UIPinchGestureRecognizer) {

        sender.view?.transform =
(sender.view?.transform)!.scaledBy(x: sender.scale, y:
sender.scale)

        sender.scale = 1

    }



    // Create Gestures

    func createGestures() {

        for image in images {

            addPinchGesture(imageView: image)

        }

    }
```

Now all we need to do is add the rotation and pan gestures. These are in a very similar format as our pinch gestures. I encourage you to pause here and see if you can figure out how to add it on your own! Then you can cross reference your work with the code below:

Add these two functions beneath the first function under // Set Gestures:

```
func addPanGesture(imageView : UIImageView) {

        let panGesture = UIPanGestureRecognizer(target:
self, action: #selector(ViewController.handlePan))
```

```
        imageView.addGestureRecognizer(panGesture)

}



func addRotationGesture(imageView: UIImageView) {

    let rotateGesture =
UIRotationGestureRecognizer(target: self, action:
#selector(ViewController.handleRotation))

        imageView.addGestureRecognizer(rotateGesture)

}
```

Add these two functions beneath the first function under // Handle Gestures:

```
@objc func handlePan(sender: UIPanGestureRecognizer) {

        let translation = sender.translation(in:
self.view)

        if let view = sender.view {

            view.center = CGPoint(x: view.center.x +
translation.x, y: view.center.y + translation.y)

        }

        sender.setTranslation(CGPoint.zero, in:
self.view)

    }



@objc func handleRotation(sender:
UIRotationGestureRecognizer) {

    sender.view?.transform =
(sender.view?.transform)!.rotated(by:
sender.rotation)

        sender.rotation = 0

}
```

Add modify the `createGestures()` function beneath `// Create Gestures` like so:

```
func createGestures() {

    for image in images {

        addPinchGesture(imageView: image)

        addPanGesture(imageView: image)

        addRotationGesture(imageView: image)

    }

}
```

If you'll notice, the `addPanGesture` and `addRotationGesture` are essentially the same as our `addPinchGesture`, except we're calling different functions in action. We're still setting the target as `self` to look for the gestures.

Similarly to our `addPinchGesture`, we need to create the functions `handlePan` and `handleRotation`. The `handlePan` function basically moves the center point of the shape upon the UIPanGestureRecognizer, which is exactly what we want! The `handleRotation` function rotates our shape upon UIRotationGestureRecognizer.

Run your project and make sure you can pinch, rotate, and pan your shapes!

Rendering UIImageView to UIImage & Adding to Camera Roll

You should have an image in your `Assets.xcassets` folder called "savePhotosButton." Let's go into the `Main.storyboard` and drag a `UIImageView` from the Object Library.

Place it in the center at the bottom of the ViewController. Go to the Attributes Inspector and make the image the "savePhotosButton." Make sure the `Content Mode` is set to `Aspect Fit`, then resize your UIImageView on your Storyboard to eliminate the white space.

Now let's add some constraints. First, let's set it to a fixed width and height, and pin it 8 from the bottom. Next, let's make sure the button stays in the center for any device. Click Align and check `Horizontally in Container` then add the constraint.

Believe it or not, there's more than one way to add gestures! Instead of doing it programmatically, we're going to switch things up and add it from the Storyboard.

Search for the "Tap Gesture Recognizer" in the Object Library, and drag it directly on to your "Save To Photos" image.

You'll notice the Tap Gesture Recognizer is now added to the top of the View Controller with a small blue icon. (Figure 20.1)

Figure 20.1

Reopen the Assistant Editor if you closed it so you have the split screen with the Storyboard on the left and code editor containing the `View-Controller.swift` on the right.

Now let's control drag from the Tap Gesture Recognizer from the bar above the Storyboard to our `ViewController.swift`. Place it right below `viewDidLoad()`. Be sure to change the `Connection` to `Action`, and `Type` to `UITapGestureRecognizer`. Then name it "save-ToPhotosTapGesture".

Next, we need to enable `Interactions` in the Attributes Inspector. While the `SavePhotosButton` image is selected, check `User Interaction Enabled` and `Multiple Touch`.

Let's test our button to make sure things are working. Go ahead and write a print statement (i.e. `print("Hello Save Button!")`) in your `saveToPhotosTapGesture` and run your project! Tap the button and make sure your print statement is showing up.

Rendering The Image View

First, let's create a function called `renderContainer()` that holds two constants, `renderer` and `image`. You can add this just below our `saveToPhotosTapGesture` function:

```swift
func renderContainer() {

        let renderer = UIGraphicsImageRenderer(size:
view.bounds.size)

        let image = renderer.image { (context) in

                view.drawHierarchy(in: view.bounds,
afterScreenUpdates: true)

        }

        UIImageWriteToSavedPhotosAlbum(image, self,
#selector(ViewController.image(_image:didFinishSavingWit
hError:contextInfo:)), nil)

}
```

Our **renderer** constant is assigned to UIGraphicsImageRenderer, which will render at the specified size. In this case, we are specifying the size as the **view.bounds.size**.

Then we create our **image** constant, which will render the image in the correct **view.drawHierarchy**. Last, our function is going to save the image with UIImageWriteToSavedPhotosAlbum. Let's go ahead and create that function now. The purpose of this function is to let the user know that the image has either been saved successfully, or if an error has occurred. You can add this function below the **renderContainer()**.

```swift
@objc func image(_image: UIImage,
didFinishSavingWithError error: Error?, contextInfo:
UnsafeRawPointer) {

        if let error = error {

            // we got back an error!

            let alert = UIAlertController(title: "Save
error", message: error.localizedDescription,
preferredStyle: .alert)

            alert.addAction(UIAlertAction(title: "OK",
style: .default))

            present(alert, animated: true)

        } else {
```

```
        let alert = UIAlertController(title:
"Saved!", message: "Your image has been saved to your
photos.", preferredStyle: .alert)

        alert.addAction(UIAlertAction(title: "OK",
style: .default))

        present(alert, animated: true)

    }

}
```

Don't forget to replace our print statement with our `renderContainer()` function in the `saveToPhotosTapGesture`! Now let's run our project!

Uh Oh, if you clicked the "Save To Photos" button it crashed! Let's read the error message in our console.

```
Tanstagram[31901:3158634] [access] This app has crashed
because it attempted to access privacy-sensitive data
without a usage description.  The app's Info.plist must
contain an NSPhotoLibraryAddUsageDescription key with a
string value explaining to the user how the app uses
this data.
```

All we need to do is add NSPhotoLibraryAddUsageDescription in our `Info.plist`. We basically need to prompt permission for Tanstagram to access our users Photo Library.

In the Project Navigator, click on `Info.plist` file near the bottom and open it. Right-click the empty area below the column/rows and "Add Row".

Add NSPhotoLibraryAddUsageDescription as a key. You'll notice when you hit enter, Xcode will register the key as "Privacy - Photo Library Additions Usage Description".

Under the "Value" column, let's write "Saving image to your camera roll!"

This is just a description that will be in the Alert View when we prompt for permission.

Now run your project and click the Save To Photos button! Success!

Wrapping up

As you can see, there's so much we developers can do with gestures. We've learned how to pan, pinch, and rotate images, as well as rendering our images to be saved to our camera roll. With the endless possibilities with a touch screen, the concepts presented here can be applied in numerous creative ways. Code on!

Student Project - 2

Sweet! You made it through section 2 and now have a good understanding of the fundamentals of Swift! That wasn't so bad, right? Now let's put your skills to the test.

Requirements:

1. Create a new Xcode project.
2. In the initial ViewController made in Main.storyboard, create a login screen similar to this:

Hint: You will need to use `UIButton`, `UILabel`, `UIImageView`, and `UIStackView`.

3. Rename this initial ViewController to `LoginVC`.
4. In Interface Builder, drag on a UITabBarController which will act as our main app UI. Rename "Item 1" to say "Home" and "Item 2" to say "Settings".
5. Make the UITabBarController the "Initial ViewController" by dragging the arrow from LoginVC to be on top of the Tab Bar Controller until it turns blue like so:

6.) Create a new Cocoa Touch Class file by right-clicking on the project folder on the left-hand side of Xcode. It's class should be called "HomeVC" and it's subclass should be UIViewController. Be sure to delete the extra "ViewController" text it automatically adds in to the Class field. Click 'Next', click 'Create' and return to Main.storyboard. Click on the "Home" ViewController in the Tab Bar Controller and click the Identity Inspector. Set the identity of the "Class" to be "HomeVC" and press `Enter`.

7.) Drag a UITableView into HomeVC and drag a custom UITableViewCell inside. Create a custom cell like this Instagram-style post like so:

This app will need to contain several photo posts. Our app will not be able to make posts, but will need to read from static data (for the purposes of this challenge). So, you will need to create a data model to store several posts. Create a data model to store:

- A Dictionary containing usernames (key) and posts (value).
- An Array of Photos (obtain nice free photos from pexels.com
  - no attribution required.)
- Use UIImage here
- The UIButtons don't need to actually do anything.

Helpful Hint:

Be a good programmer. Do your research, read back through the chapters in this section. Struggling through this is the best way to learn and retain what you've learned. Good programmers are always seeking to learn and improve their practice.

Chapter 21: SimpleWeather

Learn all about communicating with APIs and using CoreLocation in this app that will provide current weather details in a beautiful UI.

What you will learn

- Communicate with an API
- Use URLSession to make web requests
- How to use closures
- How to work with JSON
- How to use LocationServices

Key Terms

- Closure
- API
- JSON
- URLSession

Resources

Download here: https://github.com/devslopes/iOS13-book-assets/wiki/iOS13-Book

In this chapter, we are going to build a simple weather app called SimpleWeather. It will display the weather at your current location with a beautiful UI that communicates with the open weather API system.

Here is a sneak peak at the finished product!

Figure 21.0

Creating an Xcode Project

Let's begin by creating a new project `Single View Application`, set the User Interface to `Storyboard` and call it whatever you'd like. In this case we're calling it `SimpleWeather` .

Setting up the Interface

With this app we are actually going to start out building the interface first since it is pretty simple. So go to your `Main.storyboard` file and first thing we are going to do is give the background a nice blue color. Select the ViewController in the interface builder, and change the background color to #51A4FF.

Next, referring back to (Figure 21.0) it looks like we have several labels and one image view. They are all lined up vertically, so I think this would be a good time to use our old friend Stack Views. So from the `Objects Library` lets add the three Labels, then an Image View, then one more Label. They don't have to be placed exactly or anything, since we'll be dropping them in a Stack View.

Next, we'll style the Labels a little. Select all 4 labels, go to the `Attributes inspector`, and change the color to white, the font to `Custom`, family to `Avenir Next`, and the Style to `Medium`.

Next add titles to the labels as follows in (Figure 21.1). You can also refer to (Figure 21.0) for a visual reference. This is just placeholder text to let us know how to space things out. Change the font size of the second from top Label to `64` and make the Style `bold`. Change the size of the Image View to 100 x 100 from the Size Inspector.

Figure 21.1

```
UILabel -> "Today's Date"

UILabel -> "77.0"

UILabel -> "City"

UIImageView

UILabel -> "Clear"
```

Next select all elements, and add them to a `Stack View` by clicking on the `Embed in` button and selecting `Stack View`.

With the stack view selected, make sure the Axis is `Vertical`, Distribution is `Fill`, Alignment is `Center`, and Spacing is `10`. Then give it alignment constraints of `Horizontally` and `Vertically in container` to center it.

And that's our whole UI!

Now lets jump over to `ViewController.swift` file and make some IBOutlets and hook up those elements to our code. Just above the `viewDidLoad` function add the following:

```
@IBOutlet weak var dateLabel: UILabel!

@IBOutlet weak var currentTempLabel: UILabel!

@IBOutlet weak var locationLabel: UILabel!

@IBOutlet weak var currentWeatherImage: UIImageView!

@IBOutlet weak var currentWeatherTypeLabel: UILabel!
```

Then as we have done so many times, go back into Storyboard, and right-click on the ViewController in the Project Navigator and drag from the IBOutlets to the corresponding UI elements.

Now all our labels and elements are hooked up and we are ready to start talking about `APIs`!

OpenWeather API

What is an `API`? `API` stands for "Application Programming Interface" and provides a way for programmers to communicate with a certain application.

There are many many useful `APIs` available. Some are from well known companies like Facebook, Google, Twitter and YouTube.

There are ones for getting information about StarWars, Pokemon, and the weather. What's important to know is that, whatever `API` you use, you have to follow their rules. An `API` is able to provide only the specific information that it was built to provide, and the programmer must communicate with the `API` in a very specific way to get the results they want.

In this app we are going to be working with an `API` that can be found at 'OpenWeatherMap.org'

Go ahead and check out the website, as we will be creating an account and using it extensively.

On the website homepage, click on the `API` tab and you will see the `Current weather data` service description which includes:

- Access current weather data for any location including over 200,000 cities

- Current weather is frequently updated based on global models and data from more than 40,000 weather stations

- Data is available in JSON, XML, or HTML format

- Available for Free and all other paid accounts

That is the one we want. But first we need to sign up, so click the sign up button and follow the instructions:

Figure 21.2

Fill in the **Create New Account** form and click **Create Account**. The next screen will ask you the purpose for using this API. Go ahead and select **Mobile app development** from the **Purpose** dropdown menu.

Figure 21.3

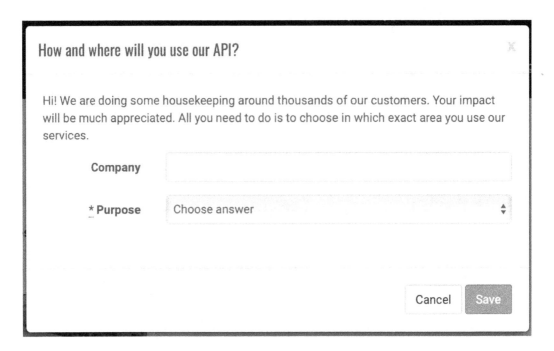

When you're finished you will land on a dashboard, then select the `API keys` menu option. Your `API` key is very important, without it, you would not be able to use the service. This is a common practice with `APIs` and is used to track usage for `APIs` that charge. Don't worry though, unless you switch to a paid plan you will not be charged for your account. Now copy your `API` key and navigate back to the `API` Page. Find the 'Current Weather data' section and click on the 'API doc' button.

Figure 21.4

Current weather data

API doc Subscribe

- Access current weather data for any location including over 200,000 cities
- Current weather is frequently updated based on global models and data from more than 40,000 weather stations
- Data is available in JSON, XML, or HTML format
- Available for Free and all other paid accounts

Then scroll down to the header 'By city name' and click on the first example link.

```
api.openweathermap.org/data/2.5/weather?q=London
```

Go ahead and click on the URL in your browser and at the end of the url you will see a long string of numbers. This is the special API key used to display samples only.

```
https://samples.openweathermap.org/data/2.5/weather?
q=London,uk&appid=b6907d289e10d714a6e88b30761fae22
```

Go ahead and replace that API key (everything after '&appid=') with your API key we copied earlier, and reload it. You should now see a bunch of information that may seem difficult to read. If you look in the

URL you will see 'london,uk'. If you want, you can change the city and get different results.

So what you are looking at here, is called JSON, which stands for JavaScript Object Notation. It is defined as a "lightweight data-interchange format. It is easy for humans to read and write. It is easy for machines to parse and generate."

Now it says it's easy for humans to read, but let's make it a little easier shall we. Copy the JSON and go to https://jsonformatter.curiousconcept.com

Paste the raw JSON data into the JSON Formatter window and press Process:

This will take you down to the formatted JSON view and look something like this:

```json
{
    "coord":{
        "lon":-0.13,
        "lat":51.51
    },
    "weather":[
        {
            "id":300,
            "main":"Clouds",
            "description":"light intensity drizzle",
            "icon":"09d"
        }
    ],
    "main":{
        "temp":283.157,
        "pressure":1012,
        "humidity":81,
```

```
"temp_min":279.15,

"temp_max":281.15

},
```

Now let's take a closer look here. JSON is arranged with keys and values. The keys are strings, and the values could be objects like strings, ints, or bools.

So taking a look at the above snippet you see that it is arranged in a kind of nested format. There is an opening parentheses that contains the entirety of the data. Then within that there are other groups of data. For instance, there is a key of "weather" that has a value of type array. That array has within it keys with values. Among which is the key "main" and the value of "clouds". A little further down is the key "main" with a dictionary of keys and values. One of which is "temp". BINGO! We have located our temperature within this jumble of JSON.

You can kind of think of JSON like a Russian nesting doll, only instead of one doll in each, there may be many. The outermost doll is the entire data set. Then you open it up and you might find the doll called "main" and you find a bunch of other dolls inside it, then you find the doll named "temp" open it and find the value of 283.157. And thats what you do for every value you are looking for.

Scroll through the formatted JSON and familiarize yourself with it. Most APIs these days will return JSON data. And the way to request that data is through a web request. Just like you entered the url with your key into the web browser to get this data, we are going to make a web request from your app to retrieve this JSON data, extract the necessary information, then display the data in our UI.

Remember in the URL you included the city information? You can imagine how you could have a variable for a city, then include that in the API request to retrieve the information for a specific city. We are going to actually use your current location to do that, but we'll get into that later.

So let's jump back into Xcode and get working on it! Create a new Swift file and name it CurrentWeather. This is going to be our custom class that contains all the class properties and API call. So what are we going to need? We will need private variables and getters for the city name, the date, the weather type, and the current temperature. Add this to the CurrentWeather file:

```
class CurrentWeather {
    fileprivate var _cityName: String!
    fileprivate var _date: String!
    fileprivate var _weatherType: String!
    fileprivate var _currentTemp: Double!


    var cityName: String {
        if _cityName == nil {

            _cityName = ""

        }
        return _cityName

    }


    var date: String {
        if _date == nil {

            _date = ""

        }


        let dateFormatter = DateFormatter()
        dateFormatter.dateStyle = .long
        dateFormatter.timeStyle = .none
        let currentDate = dateFormatter.string(from:
Date())
        self._date = "Today, \(currentDate)"
        return _date
```

```
    }


    var weatherType: String {

        if _weatherType == nil {

            _weatherType = ""

        }

        return _weatherType

    }


    var currentTemp: Double {

        if _currentTemp == nil {

            _currentTemp = 0.0

        }

        return _currentTemp

    }

}
```

The city name, weather type, and temperature are straight forward. We declare the properties, and then create the getters and do a check to see if the value is nil, and if so, we set it equal to an empty string so we don't get any crashes.

The date is a little more involved so lets break that down. First we create a `DateFormatter()`. This is a class that helps create string representations of NSDate objects. It has a number of functions as seen in the next two lines. First we set the `.dateStyle = .long` which specifies a long style, typically with full text, such as "January 1, 2020". Then since we are not really interested in the time we set `.timeStyle = .none`. Then we create the date by using `dateFormatter.string(from: Date())` where we take the current date as created by `Date()` and turn it into a string based on the `dateFormatter` parameters we set.

Setting up the API Call

Now that we have our current weather properties we need some way to get the data and assign it to our class properties.

But first we need to think about how this is going to work. We could put the API call directly in the ViewController file, assign the properties, then update the UI. But it is not considered best practice to have the controller also be retrieving and managing data. So we want the API call to be in the CurrentWeather custom class.

But that introduces a new challenge. Web requests are asynchronous. For example, suppose I have three lines of code A, B, and C. And B is a web request that retrieves information, and C is the function that takes that information and updates the UI. But because B is asynchronous, we don't know when that information will be available. It could be milliseconds, it could be minutes, depending on connection speed and the service or site being contacted. So then, B fires off the web request, and C immediately tries to use information that may or may not be there, potentially causing crashes.

So what we need is a way to know when a web request has completed, and we do that by way of closures. A closure is basically a block of code, that is self contained and can be passed around in your code, and that we can call at a pre-determined time. We are going to create a custom closure that we can use to determine when the download is complete.

So create a new Swift file, and call it Constants. And add the following:

```
typealias DownloadComplete = () -> ()
```

The syntax to create a closure is:

```
var closureName: (ParameterTypes) -> (ReturnType)
```

Our custom closure, does not have any parameter types, nor are we returning anything hence the empty parentheses. And typealias is just a way of renaming an existing type.

Now we are ready to create our function that we will eventually call in the ViewController file that will update the UI. So go back to CurrentWeather.swift and add the following below your getters:

```
func downloadWeatherDetails(completed: @escaping
DownloadComplete) {

    //TO DO

}
```

We name our function, then we name our closure `completed` and then we include our custom `closure` DownloadComplete. But first we have the `@escaping`. An escaping `closure` is often used in asynchronous operations like the web request we are going to be dealing with. So lets build that web request!

First we need to have a URL to point to. At this point we are just going to call it `CURRENT_WEATHER_URL`. This will go inside the `downloadWeatherDetails` function we just created. Later on we will add the URL to the Constants file when we are ready.

```
let url = URL(string: CURRENT_WEATHER_URL)!
```

Then add `let session = URLSession.shared`. The `URLSession` class is the Apple class that provides the `API` for downloading content. It provides all the necessary delegate methods we will need later on such as serializing `JSON` data and capturing the data and error responses.

Then we need to call a `dataTask` which retrieves the contents of our URL, and supplies the data, response, and error in a completion handler. When you auto complete `session.dataTask` there will be code completion prompts, press return, then rename the data, response, and error parameters. The `.resume()` is necessary to kick off the task of making the request.

So our `downloadWeatherDetails` function should now look like this:

```
func downloadWeatherDetails(completed: @escaping
DownloadComplete) {


    let session = URLSession.shared

    let url = URL(string: CURRENT_WEATHER_URL)!
```

```
session.dataTask(with: url) { (data, response,
error) in


    } .resume()

}
```

Next we need to take the response from the web request, and turn it into useable JSON data. So we are going to use the JSONSerialization.jsonObject method as follows.

```
session.dataTask(with: url) { (data, response, error) in

    if let responseData = data {

        do {

        let json = try
JSONSerialization.jsonObject(with: responseData,
options:
JSONSerialization.ReadingOptions.allowFragments)

        print(json)

    } catch {

        print("Could not serialize")

    }

    }

} .resume()
```

The JSONSerialization.jsonObject can fail, so it needs a **do-catch** block. If it fails, we simply print out that it could not serialize. Now we have an object JSON that contains all the information from the point of API call and can start drilling down into the JSON to acquire the information we need.

But first we need an actual url. If you recall CURRENT_WEATHER_URL was just a placeholder. So lets go back to our **API** website http://openweathermap.org/api and return to the 'Current weather data' API docs.

Then scroll down to the 'By geographic coordinates' section. If you recall, we want our app to give us the weather based on our current location. This section provides us with the information we need to make that type of call. It provides the base `API` call: `api.openweathermap.org/data/2.5/weather?lat={lat}&lon={lon}`

This route tells us what parameters we need, `lat` and `lon` (latitude and longitude). And gives an example of an `API` call: `api.openweathermap.org/data/2.5/weather?lat=35&lon=139`

Go ahead and plug that into your browser, and remember to replace the invalid `API` key at the end with your own.

This will provide the following `JSON` data:

```
{

    "coord": {

        "lon": 138.93,

        "lat": 34.97

    },

    "weather": [{

        "id": 803,

        "main": "Clouds",

        "description": "broken clouds",

        "icon": "04n"

    }],

    "base": "stations",

    "main": {

        "temp": 295.139,

        "pressure": 1021.33,

        "humidity": 100,

        "temp_min": 295.139,

        "temp_max": 295.139,
```

```
        "sea_level": 1030.63,

        "grnd_level": 1021.33

    },

    "wind": {

        "speed": 2.11,

        "deg": 68.0001

    },

    "clouds": {

        "all": 68

    },

    "dt": 1477077361,

    "sys": {

        "message": 0.1611,

        "country": "JP",

        "sunrise": 1476996953,

        "sunset": 1477036867

    },

    "id": 1851632,

    "name": "Shuzenji",

    "cod": 200

}
```

So let's copy the base API call and paste it into our Constants file as follows, including the required http:// portion of a URL.

```
let CURRENT_WEATHER_URL = "http://
api.openweathermap.org/data/2.5/weather?lat={lat}
&lon={lon}"
```

Then from playing with the URLs in the browser, we know we need to end with &appid= then your API key.

So now your URL should look something like:

```
let CURRENT_WEATHER_URL = "http://
api.openweathermap.org/data/2.5/weather?lat={lat}
&lon={lon}&appid=42a1771a0b787bf12e734ada0cfc80cb"
```

We're getting closer now. But you see that we now need to know the longitude and latitude parameters to pass into the URL. So lets work on that next.

Getting Current location

Our location anywhere on the planet can be determined by latitude and longitude. Your phone has GPS (global positioning system) and our app can take advantage of the phone GPS by using the Apple library Core-Location.

Let's create another custom class that will hold our current location. Create a new Swift file and name it `Location` and add the following:

```
import CoreLocation


class Location {

    static var sharedInstance = Location()

    private init() {}


    var latitude: Double!

    var longitude: Double!

}
```

First we import the CoreLocation library that is necessary to provide the required methods and delegates we will need.

Then we create a static `sharedInstance` of the `Location` class and set up an initializer. And the only two properties we need in this class are latitude and longitude. So we are good here!

Next we need to go to our `ViewController.swift` file and get ready to calculate our current location when the app opens. First up, import the CoreLocation library and add the 'CLLocationManagerDelegate'.

```
import CoreLocation
```

```
class WeatherVC: UIViewController,
CLLocationManagerDelegate {
```

Then we need to instantiate and declare a `locationManager` and a `currentLocation`. Add these right below the IBOutlets and above the `viewDidLoad` function.

```
let locationManager = CLLocationManager()
```

```
var currentLocation = CLLocation()
```

So, what is a locationManager? Apple defines it as "the central point for configuring the delivery of location- and heading-related events to your app. You use an instance of this class to establish the parameters that determine when location and heading events should be delivered and to start and stop the actual delivery of those events. You can also use a location manager object to retrieve the most recent location and heading data."

So basically it is in charge of all the location acquisition, parameters like accuracy, requesting permission to use GPS, and more.

`currentLocation` is a variable of class `CLLocation` which represents the location data generated by the `locationManager`

Next we need to add some settings for our `locationManager` so in `viewDidLoad` add the following:

```
locationManager.delegate = self
```

```
locationManager.desiredAccuracy =
kCLLocationAccuracyBest
```

```
locationManager.requestWhenInUseAuthorization()
```

```
locationManager.startMonitoringSignificantLocationChange
s()
```

First we are setting the delegate like we are used to doing, then we are choosing the desired accuracy which we are selecting the best available. The next line `locationManager.requestWhenInUseAuthorization()` generates the pop up that asks the user if they will allow our app to access their location. Then we have `locationManager.startMonitoringSignificantLocationChanges()` which monitors location changes and will update the locationManager delegates as needed.

Next we need to add two more functions. The first one is a method of `locationManager` and tells the delegate whether or not the app has permission to use the location services.

```
func locationManager(_ manager: CLLocationManager,
didChangeAuthorization status: CLAuthorizationStatus) {

    locationAuthStatus()

}
```

We also want to call this function whenever the view appears in **viewDidAppear(_ animated:)**, so that the temperature will be updated:

```
override func viewDidAppear(_ animated: Bool) {

    super.viewDidAppear(animated)

    locationAuthStatus()

}
```

`locationAuthStatus()` is a function we create that checks whether or not the app has permission to use location services. If it does, then we will set the current location, extract the latitude and longitude and set those equal to the custom class `Location` properties for latitude and longitude. If we do NOT have access, then we will request access.

```
func locationAuthStatus() {

    if CLLocationManager.authorizationStatus()
== .authorizedWhenInUse {

    currentLocation = locationManager.location
```

```
    Location.sharedInstance.latitude =
currentLocation.coordinate.latitude

    Location.sharedInstance.longitude =
currentLocation.coordinate.longitude

    } else {

    locationManager.requestWhenInUseAuthorization()

    }

}
```

We also need to add permissions to our `info.plist` so head over there, hover over the last entry until a '+' sign pops up. Click on it to create a new entry and start typing 'Privacy-Location' and select the one that says 'Privacy - Location When In Use Usage Description' and then to the right, under 'Value' add a message that will be displayed to the user when it opens, something like "We need your location to give you relevant, up-to-date weather information."

While we are in the `info.plist` we also need to add permissions for web requests to non-https websites, as OpenWeather is. So again, hover over the last entry in the plist, and press the '+' button. Select "App Transport Security Settings" then click the small arrow on the left that is pointing to the right, so that it points down, and click on the '+' button again, which will create a sub entry. Here select 'Allow Arbitrary Loads' and set the value to YES. Now our app is able to communicate with any website.

So, remember where we were when we started down this rabbit hole? Let's recap. We created a custom class for CurrentWeather, we started implementing the `API` call using `URLSession`, and we got to the point we are ready to make the call, so then we went to our `API` documentation and saw we need to know a longitude and latitude, so we created a Location custom class, then implemented the code to request access to location services, and if granted, set the current location latitude and longitude to our instance of custom class Location.

Whew! So now, we can circle back to our Constants file and insert the longitude and latitude parameters from our Location instance, and it should now look something like this:

```
let CURRENT_WEATHER_URL = "http://
api.openweathermap.org/data/2.5/weather?lat=\
(Location.sharedInstance.latitude!)&lon=\
(Location.sharedInstance.longitude!)&appid=42a1771a0b787
bf12e734ada0cfc80cb"
```

except with your API key at the end.

Lets head back to our CurrentWeather file. We have our URL and the next thing to do is extract the desired values from it. So lets take a look at the example result we had earlier, only I'm going to throw it into the JSON formatter we talked about earlier:

```
{
    "coord":{
        "lon":138.93,
        "lat":34.97
    },
    "weather":[
        {
            "id":803,
            "main":"Clouds",
            "description":"broken clouds",
            "icon":"04n"
        }
    ],
    "base":"stations",
    "main":{
        "temp":295.139,
        "pressure":1021.33,
        "humidity":100,
        "temp_min":295.139,
```

```
        "temp_max":295.139,

        "sea_level":1030.63,

        "grnd_level":1021.33

    },

    "wind":{

        "speed":2.11,

        "deg":68.0001

    },

    "clouds":{

        "all":68

    },

    "dt":1477077361,

    "sys":{

        "message":0.1611,

        "country":"JP",

        "sunrise":1476996953,

        "sunset":1477036867

    },

    "id":1851632,

    "name":"Shuzenji",

    "cod":200

}
```

We want the name of the city, the temperature, and the weather conditions. Remember our analogy of the Russian nesting dolls? We open the first doll and we see all this, inside it is a doll with the label "name" on it and inside it is the value of the city. In this case "Shuzenji". For the weather type we have to go down two levels, first to the key "weather" then to the key "main" which has the value of 'Clouds'.

So are you seeing how you drill down to the values you want?

Lastly we need the temperature which is in 'Main' then down one more level to 'Temp' with the value of 295.139.

So that is the path you take looking at it visually, but what does that look like in code. Inside our `downloadWeatherDetails` function we have created our session, data task, and serialized the response data into `JSON`.

So the next step is to turn that `JSON` into a dictionary, then use implicit unwrapping to unwrap and cast to dictionaries one layer at a time until we get the values we need. So modify your `downloadWeather-Details` as follows. These additions are inside the **do** block.

```
if let dict = json as? Dictionary<String, AnyObject> {


    if let name = dict["name"] as? String {

    self._cityName = name.capitalized

    }



    if let weather = dict["weather"] as?
[Dictionary<String, AnyObject>] {

        if let main = weather[0]["main"] as? String {

        self._weatherType = main.capitalized

    }

    }



    if let main = dict["main"] as? Dictionary<String,
AnyObject> {

    if let currentTemperature = main["temp"] as? Double
{

        let kelvinToFarenheitPreDivision =
(currentTemperature * (9/5) - 459.67)

        let kelvinToFarenheit = Double(round(10 *
kelvinToFarenheitPreDivision/10))
```

```
        self._currentTemp = kelvinToFarenheit

    }

    }

}
```

We start out by converting the JSON into a dictionary of type `<String, AnyObject>`. Then just like we discussed above, we drill down to each level, implicitly unwrapping as we go, until we reach the desired value, at which point we set it equal to the CurrentWeather property.

The temperature is a little more involved as it requires some math to convert Kelvin to Fahrenheit. Next we need to add one last thing related to the `closure`.

Remember how we named the `closure` `completed`? This is what determines when the asynchronous call is done. When we call this function from the ViewController it is going to look for when it reaches `completed()` then execute the next block of code. So we need to place it inside the request and after all the JSON has been assigned to the class properties. One level inside the `.resume()` should be good. So your final **downloadWeatherDetails** function should look like this:

```
func downloadWeatherDetails(completed: @escaping
DownloadComplete) {


    let session = URLSession.shared

    let url = URL(string: CURRENT_WEATHER_URL)!


    session.dataTask(with: url) { (data, response,
error) in

        if let responseData = data {

        do {

        let json = try
JSONSerialization.jsonObject(with: responseData,
options:
JSONSerialization.ReadingOptions.allowFragments)
```

```swift
        print(json)

    if let dict = json as? Dictionary<String,
AnyObject> {

        if let name = dict["name"] as? String {

            self._cityName = name.capitalized

        }



        if let weather = dict["weather"] as?
[Dictionary<String, AnyObject>] {

        if let main = weather[0]["main"] as? String
{

            self._weatherType = main.capitalized

        }

        }



        if let main = dict["main"] as?
Dictionary<String, AnyObject> {

        if let currentTemperature = main["temp"] as?
Double {

            let kelvinToFarenheitPreDivision =
(currentTemperature * (9/5) - 459.67)

            let kelvinToFarenheit = Double(round(10
* kelvinToFarenheitPreDivision/10))

            self._currentTemp = kelvinToFarenheit

        }

            }

        }

    } catch {

        print("Could not serialize")

    }
```

```
        }

        completed()

    }.resume()

}
```

It's a big one! Now lets go back to our ViewController.swift file and add the final touches. Above the `viewDidLoad` function declare a `currentWeather` variable and instantiate it: `var currentWeather = CurrentWeather()`

And the inside the `locationAuthStatus` function modify as follows:

```
func locationAuthStatus() {

    if CLLocationManager.authorizationStatus()
== .authorizedWhenInUse {

        currentLocation = locationManager.location

        Location.sharedInstance.latitude =
currentLocation.coordinate.latitude

        Location.sharedInstance.longitude =
currentLocation.coordinate.longitude

        currentWeather.downloadWeatherDetails {

            DispatchQueue.main.async {

                self.updateMainUI()

            }

        }

    } else {

locationManager.requestWhenInUseAuthorization()

    }

}
```

We are adding `currentWeather.downloadWeatherDetails` which will then call an async task that will then call a function `updateMainUI` which we will create next. And we don't have to worry about crashes due to trying to assign variables that don't exist, all because of our use of `closures`!

In our `updateMainUI` function, all we are going to do is assign our UI elements IBOutlets to the properties of the custom class. The current weather image is assigned based on the image title, which we cleverly named the same as the weather type returned by the `API` call. So find those images in the resources, and drop them into your Assets folder.

```
func updateMainUI() {

    dateLabel.text = currentWeather.date

    currentTempLabel.text = "\
(currentWeather.currentTemp)"

    currentWeatherTypeLabel.text =
currentWeather.weatherType

    locationLabel.text = currentWeather.cityName

    currentWeatherImage.image = UIImage(named:
currentWeather.weatherType)

}
```

And that seals the deal. Run it, and if you are on the simulator it will probably default to Cupertino. If you are not getting anything, check that there is a location set in the menu `Debug` > `Location` while in the simulator. If you are on device it should give your current location temperature and weather conditions.

Wrapping up

So let's recap what we've learned in this chapter. We have learned a little about how `APIs` work, how to contact them using `URLSession` to make web requests, how to work with `JSON` and how to use CoreLocation. Quite a lot for such a simple app! Now I want to give you a challenge to think of some ways you could expand on this app and make it even more awesome! The OpenWeather `API` has more options for getting a ten day forecast, high and low temperatures, and much much more.

Exercise

Sometimes you don't want to know the weather conditions in your current location, but want to check the weather in a different city. You exercise is to add a button that takes you to a new view controller where you can enter in a city and return the weather details for that city. The weather API we have been dealing with allows you to do this quite easily. You will just need to modify the existing API call slightly. Happy coding!

Chapter 22: Core Data - Dream-Lister App

Learn all about CoreData in this app that will let you make a wish list of all your most coveted items.

What you will learn

- How to use Core Data
- How to use NSFetchedResultsController
- How to sort Core Data results
- How to use PickerViews

Key Terms

- Core Data
- NSFetchedResultsController
- Picker View

Resources

Download here: https://github.com/devslopes/iOS13-book-assets/wiki/iOS13-Book

In this chapter you'll be building the DreamLister app. Figure 22.0 shows what this app will look like. The main goal of this app is to do a deep dive on `CoreData`, learning about when to use it and how to use it.

You'll learn how to use the `NSFetchedResultsController` which facilitates displaying data in a Table View while using `CoreData`. You will also learn how to use `Picker Views`. So let's get started!

Figure 22.0 A & B

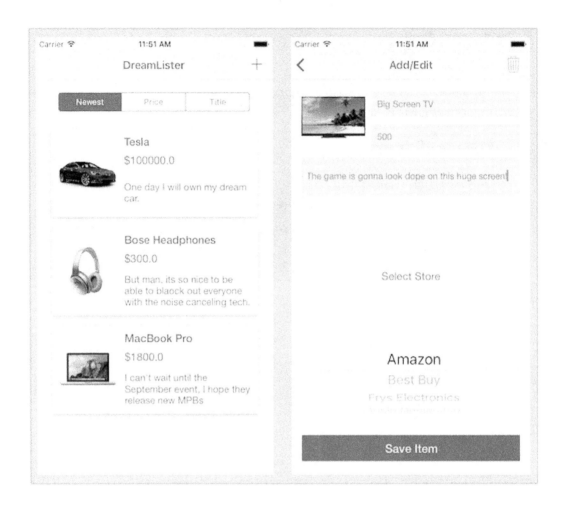

When and Why to Use Core Data

In the `myHood` app we learned about saving data using UserDefaults. The other common way is using `CoreData`. You may have heard how scary and complex `Core Data` is, and it is a little bit complex, which is why many programmers avoid it.

But thanks to the recent changes beginning in iOS 10, it is a little easier than it was before. In this chapter we're going to break it down and simplify it for you.

But first, what is `Core Data` and when would you use it?

`Core Data` is a framework provided by Apple that allows you to persist, or save, complex data to your device so it can be accessed off-line. The keywords here being complex and offline.

If you're just saving simple things like user settings, or login name, then you're totally fine using `UserDefaults`. Or if you don't need data offline, then you may not need `Core Data`.

These days just about everywhere you go you have an internet connection in some form, so these are things you need to think about when deciding whether or not to use `Core Data`.

Just because you need to save something, doesn't always mean `Core Data` is the right option. Another thing to think about is nowadays you have some services like `Firebase/Firestore` that provide both on and offline syncing.

So just to reiterate, you want to use `Core Data` when you have complex data you need to save offline. I should clarify, it's not just for offline use, you can also download data from the Internet, save it to `Core Data`, then fetch it and serve it up locally. This provides for a very fast experience in serving up the data.

So what are some other benefits to using `Core Data`?

`Core Data` is set up to manage a lot of things for you:

- Like Save and Undo functionality, sorting and filtering based on customizable attributes. (Apple claims Core Data typically decreases 50 to 70 percent the amount of code you would write)
- `Core Data` tracks changes for you. Better memory management. (when you have changed or updated objects you don't have to change the entire data set, just the objects being modified)
- Makes it easy to display your data (i.e. `NSFetchResults-Controller`)
- Provides a graphical user interface to manage:
    1. Your entities
    2. Attributes
    3. Relationships and other details related to your model data.

So, now that you know WHEN and WHY to use `Core Data`, lets go over HOW `Core Data` works at a high level.

How Core Data Works

Here, we have a model of the `Core Data` stack based on versions by Apple and the site objc.io. This is the entire `Core Data` stack basically. The whole framework boiled down.

Figure 22.1

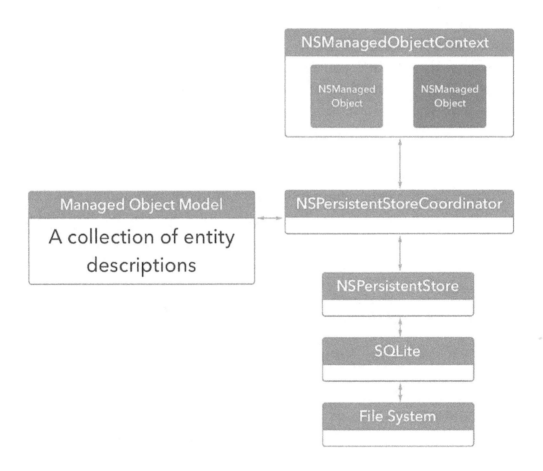

So, lets talk about storage and databases. With `Core Data` or really any storage, you have a database. And the most common one for iOS and `Core Data` is SQLite.

In the past, you had to work with SQLite directly. And thats a huge pain. So `Core Data` was born to help ease data management. It was introduced in April 2005 and has been making improvements ever since.

So how does it work? You're familiar with custom classes by now. In the `myHood` app we worked with a custom `Post` class with properties like *title* and *description*, etc.

With `Core Data` we have entities that have attributes. These entities are `NSManagedSubclasses`, and reside in the `NSManagedContext`.

`Figure 22.2`

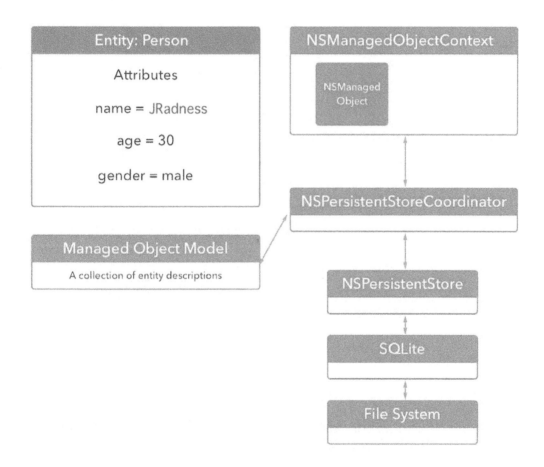

Think of the context like a scratch pad. When you create or insert an entity into the context, it is created in memory. You can modify it and display it, but it is not yet persisted (or saved) to memory.

Once you are ready to save it, the persistent store coordinator and managed object model work to send it down to the persistent store and then to the database, where it is stored. That data is now there permanently, until it is deleted.

With the changes back in iOS 10, `NSManagedObject` context, managed object model and persistent store coordinator that were previously separate functions in the app delegate are all now combined under the `NSPersistentContainer`.

Figure 22.3

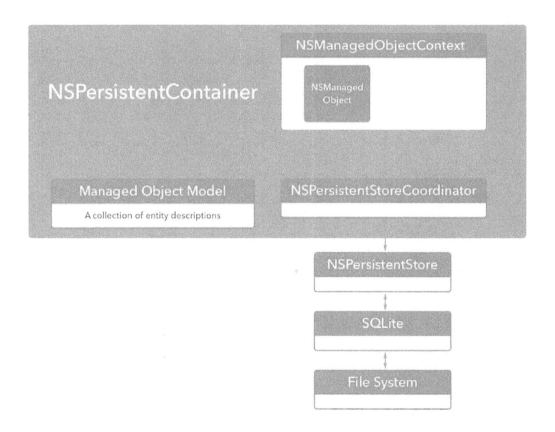

Now the nice thing about `Core Data`, is that you don't actually need to worry about most of this chart. Most of this is handled behind the scenes by `Core Data`.

What you need to understand is how to create `NSManagedObject` entities, define attributes, relationships, and how insert into the context, save, and fetch those results to be used at a later point in time.

That's basically `Core Data` from a very high level. It's really not too bad once it is broken down. So, remember this terminology and the flow chart, because that will really help you get a handle on things quickly.

In fact, once you're done reading this for the first time. Go back and read this a couple times just to get the high level terminology and flow ingrained. Then, we'll be ready to start our project!

Creating an Xcode Project

Let's begin by creating a new project `Single View Application`, set the User Interface to `Storyboard` and call it whatever you'd like. In this case we're calling it `DreamLister`.

`IMPORTANT` - We `DO` need `Core Data` so make sure that is checked! We do not need Unit or UI Tests for this chapter, so you can leave those unchecked.

Exploring a CoreData project

First lets take a look into the `AppDelegate` file. Because we selected to include `Core Data` when we created our project, the app delegate has a few functions specific to this. Check out the functions under the `// MARK: - Core Data stack` and `// MARK: - Core Data Saving support` comments in the code file.

As we saw in Figure 22.3 the `NSPersistenContainer` now includes the `NSManagedObjectContext`, the Managed Object Model, as the `NSPersistentStoreCoordinator`. We will mostly only be working directly with the Context.

Then we have the `saveContext()` function at the bottom.

This is a nice baked in function that we call when we're ready to save an entity to the database.

Next, look in the `Project Navigator` on the left, and you will see a new file we have not yet encountered yet called `DreamLister.xc-datamodelid`.

When you click on it you'll see + buttons at the bottom of the screen for adding an Entity and Attribute. Remember that an `Entity` is equivalent to a custom class, and an `Attribute` is equivalent to a property of a custom class.

So let's think about our app from Figure 22.0 B. We have a Table View that displays some information about an item we want. It has an image, a name, description, and a store we can select from a Picker View.

Let's go ahead and create our first entity. The first entity we create will be for the Item itself. Click on the plus button to **Add Entity**. The "Entity" will then appear in the left column under the **ENTITIES** header. Double click on it to rename it to `Item`.

Then to the right there is a header called `Attributes`. There is a small + sign to add attributes.

Click the + and set the name of the attribute to *title*.

Then there is an option to set the type. The same way we declare the type of a property in a custom class, for example `var name: String!`. Here we also set the type. Since our title is a *String*, go ahead and select `String` as the type. Good job, you just created your first `CoreData` entity with an attribute!

Now add the following attributes to your Item entity.

`details` of type `String`
`created` of type `Date`
`price` of type `Double`
It should end up looking like this:
`Figure 22.4`

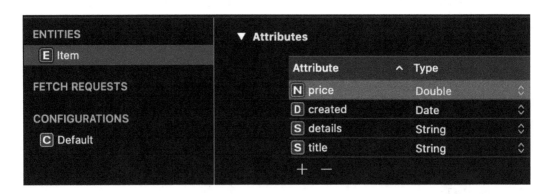

We're going to need three more Entities. Create each Entity just like you did the `Item` entity and add the following Attributes:

1. Image: make an Attribute titled *image* of type `Transformable`.
2. Store: make an Attribute titled *name* of type `String`

3. ItemType: make an Attribute titled *type* of type `String`

Now we want to set the `Codegen` option to `Manual/None` for each entity. To do that, look at the right column, under the `Class` section and you will see a `Codegen` property. Select `Manual/None` from the dropdown. As mentioned before, do this for each of our four Entities we created.

Now you may be wondering, why are we having separate entities for things like Image and ItemType? Couldn't those just be Attributes of the Item entity itself?

Yes, they could be. But, I want to teach you about data relationships as well.

For instance, if we wanted the `Store` to also have an Image, instead of both the `Item` AND the `Store` having *Image* attributes; instead you have them both reference an *Image* entity.

So what are relationships? In life we have relationships. In your family, lets say you have a Mom, brothers, sisters and a house. There's relationships between all of these. Now lets pretend that your Mom is an instance of the entity `Parent`.

You and your siblings are instances of the entity `Child`.

And your house is an instance of the entity `House`.

There's a relationship between you and your Mother. But what kind is it?

For you (a Child entity) it's *one to one*. Meaning that you have one Mother. But for your Mother, who has several children, the relationship of a `Parent` entity to a `Child` entity is *one to many*.

And the relationship of both the `Child` and `Parent` entity to the `House` is *one to one*, while the relationship of the `House` to both `Parent` and `Child` entity is *one to many*.

So looking at our data set of entities, how do we want our relationships to look?

For each *Item* there should be one *Store*.

But for each *Store* there could be many associated *Items*.

For each *Item* there will be one type, but for each type there potentially could be many *Items*.

For each *Item* and *Store* there will be one *Image*, and for each *Image* there will be one *Store* or *Item*.

So lets see how to make this work in Xcode.

Lets start with the *Item* entity.

Below `Attributes`, you'll see a section under `Relationships`.

Let's first create a relationship that goes from the *Item* to the *Image*.

Click the `Item` entity, then click the + button to create a relationship and name that relationship "image". Select the `Destination` as *Image*. At this point we won't add the *Inverse* value.

On the right hand `Utilities Pane`, in the `Data Model Inspector`, you'll see a dropdown menu with a `Type` property. You can choose *To One* or *To Many*. For the `Item` to the `Image` relationship, we want it to be *To One*. So select your *Image* relationship and set it *To One*.

Now add relationships for the remaining entities. We want `Item` to be able to connect as follows (All should have `Type` *To One*):

-   Relationship name -> "itemType" -> Destination -> `ItemType`
-   Relationship name -> "store" -> Destination -> `Store`

Next, lets add the following relationships to the `Image` Entity. (Both should have `Type` *To One*):

-   Relationship name -> "item" -> Destination -> `Item`
-   Relationship name -> "store" -> Destination -> `Store`

Also, now that we have added a relationship from `Image` to `Item`, and we already have a relationship from `Item` to `Image`, we can select the *Inverse* relationship for the *Item* from the dropdown, which is `image`.

You'll notice this won't be available for the `Store` relationship yet.

`Figure 22.5`

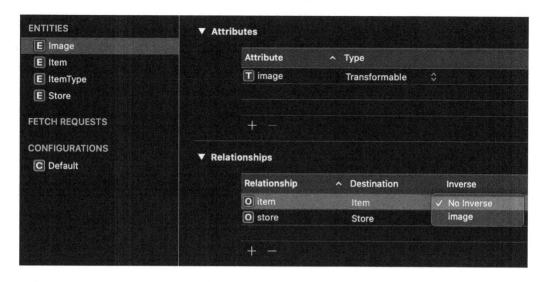

Next add relationships for `Store` Entity.

- Relationship name -> "image" -> Destination -> `Image`
- Relationship name -> "item" -> Destination -> `Item`

We'll create two relationships of title *image* and *item*, supply their Destinations, and at this point the *Inverse* will be available for both.

This time though, for the *Item* relationship type, it will be `To Many`. Then set the *Inverse* to *store* for both the "image" and "item".

This is because we want a `Store` type to be able to be applied to many different types of *Items*. I buy a ton of stuff from Amazon. So Amazon has to have a relationship type of `To Many` to `Items`.

Finally, we need to add the relationships for the `ItemType` Entity.

- Relationship name -> "item" -> Destination -> `Item` -> Inverse -> `itemType`

Set the Type `To Many`.

Again, you could have many `Items` of ItemType: *electronics*, *cars* or whatever you want!

Now that all the relationships have been defined, click through each Entity and make sure the *inverse* values have been set for all relationships.

Now for those of you that are visual learners, there is a graphical representation of the Entities and the Relationships between them that can be seen by clicking in the bottom right and toggling the `Editor Style`.

You may need to drag the Entities around a little the first time you open it, and you'll see the arrows that represent the relationships. The arrows that end with a single arrow represent `To One` relationship. The double arrows represent `To Many` relationships.

Now that we have created our data models, we need to create our `NSManagedObjects` (refer back to Figure 22.1).

Select all 4 of our entities from the left column, then go to `Editor` from Xcode's navbar at the top and select `Create NSManagedObject Subclass` from the dropdown menu.

A window will pop up with the project selected, click `Next`.

Then a second window will pop up with all our entities checked, click `Next`, then click `Create`.

This will create two files for each Entity as shown below:

`Figure 22.6`

Let's clean up our file system a little. Create a `New Group` called `Model`. Within that group create another `New Group` called `Generated`. Then place the four new files that end with `Class` in the `Model` group.

Then select the four new files that end in **Properties** in the Gen-erated folder. Your folder structure should now look like this:

`Figure 22.7`

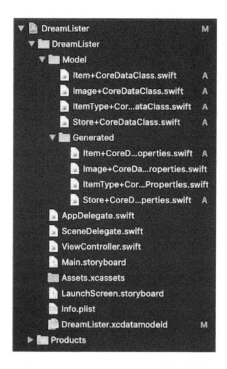

Now lets take a look at these files, and talk about them a little. Click on the file named `Item+CoreDataClass.swift`.

```
import Foundation
import CoreData


@objc(Item)
public class Item: NSManagedObject {


}
```

This is the class for the `Item` entity we created in our `.xcdatamodelid`.

If we need to implement any code for these classes, this is where you would do that. Now let's look at the extension file called `Item+CoreDataProperties.swift`.

```
import Foundation

import CoreData


extension Item {


    @nonobjc public class func fetchRequest() ->
NSFetchRequest<Item> {

        return NSFetchRequest<Item>(entityName: "Item")

    }


    @NSManaged public var title: String?

    @NSManaged public var details: String?

    @NSManaged public var created: Date?

    @NSManaged public var price: Double

    @NSManaged public var itemType: ItemType?

    @NSManaged public var store: Store?

    @NSManaged public var image: Image?


}
```

So this file is an extension of the previous Item class we looked at.

You don't want to change anything here. This is auto generated code that manages the relationships and fetchRequests. If you do need to make a change to the data model, make the change in the .xcdatamodelid file, then re-generate this file.

Now lets go back to the Item+CoreDataClass file and add some custom code. You remember that one of the attributes of the Item entity is created of type 'Date'.

We want to know the time and date that an item is created so that later on, we can add sorting by date added. So we're going to write some code to set the `created` attribute equal to the time the `Item` was created in the Context (or scratchpad).

```
import Foundation

import CoreData


@objc(Item)

public class Item: NSManagedObject {


    public override func awakeFromInsert() {

        super.awakeFromInsert()

        self.created = NSDate()

    }

}
```

So all we're doing here is saying when the `Item` is inserted into the Context, set the `created` attribute equal to the current date and time.

I also want to make a quick change by renaming the `ViewController.swift` file to `MainVC.swift` just to eliminate confusion when I am referencing this file and not a generic ViewController.

Select `ViewController.swift` from the Project Navigator, press `Enter` and rename the file to `MainVC.swift`. Then rename the class, and rename the commented part at the top so everything is consistent with the name change.

Lastly, we need to change the class of the View Controller in the Storyboard to our newly renamed file `MainVC`. Click on `Main.storyboard` and from the bar above the device UI click the first icon (ViewController). Select the Identity Inspector from the right column and rename the "ViewController" to "MainVC" and press `Enter`.

Building the User Interface

Now we're ready to start building the user interface for the `MainVC` screen.

Open the `Main.storyboard` file and select the `View Controller` and go to `Editor` at the top of Xcode's navbar, then `Embed In` and select `Navigation Controller`.

Navigation Controllers basically provide some built in functionality for menu bars, and moving between screens.

Lets start putting our view together. If we go back to Figure 22.0 A, we see we need a Table View, a Segmented Control, a Title, and a + button to add new posts.

Lets start from the top and add that + button. In the Object Library search for `bar button` item and drag it into the top right of your `View Controller` (not the Navigation Controller), and it will snap into place.

Select the button, and open the `Attribute Inspector` set the `System Item` property to `Add`. Change the `Tint` to `Dark Gray Color`.

Then select the `Navigation Item` from the Document Outline and set the `Title` property to "Dream Lister" (Figure 22.8)

Figure 22.8

Next, select the Navigation Bar (located in the `Navigation Controller Scene` in the Document Outline) and set the `Bar Tint` property to `White`, and the `Title Color` property to `Dark Gray Color`.

Now we need to add the segmented control. Search for *segmented control* in the Object Library and drag it to the top of the View Controller, below the navigation bar.

Set the constraints with `Constrain to margins` checked 0 from the left, 20 from the top, and 0 from the right and *check* the height.

Then from the Attributes Inspector, set the `Segments` property to 3.

To change the name of the segment sections, select the drop down menu next to the `Segment` property that you want to change the name for, then just change the `Title` property.

We want segment 0 to be "Newest", segment 1 to be "Price" and segment 2 to be "Title". Then scroll down a little in the Attributes Inspector and change the `Tint`property to `Dark Gray Color`.

Next we need to add our Table View. Search for "Table View" in the Object Library and drag it into the View Controller under the segmented control.

Add constraints with `Constrain to margins` checked, 20 from the top, and 0 from the right, left and bottom0. Click `add constraints`.

Now drag in a Table View Cell, and with the Table View Cell selected, set the Row Height to 150 in the Size Inspector (uncheck "Automatic" if needed).

Then go to the `Attributes Inspectors` and set `Selection` property to `none`.

Next we want to add another view INSIDE the Table View Cell that will contain the information. We do this so that we have separation between the cells.

Search for `uiview` in the Object Library and drag it into the Table View Cell.

Add constraints with `Constrain to margins` checked and set left, top, right, and bottom to 0. And set the height of the inner view to 133.

Next, add a UIImageView on the left side of the inner view we just added.

From the Size Inspector make the image view 100 x 100.Then set constraints 8 from the left.

Set height and width and click `add constraints`.

Then add an alignment constraint `Vertically in Container`.

Now we need to add three labels for the title, price, and description. Drag those three Labels from the Object Library and place them on the UIView and name them accordingly - "Title", "Price" & "Details".

For the "Title" Label, set the constraints to 8 from the top, left and right.

Check height, and click `add constraints`.

For the "Price" Label, add constraints 8 from the top, left, and right.

Check height and click `add constraints`.

For the "Description" Label, set left, top, right, and bottom constraints to 8 and click `add constraints`.

Now select all three labels and change the color to `Dark Gray Color` and change the font to *Helvetica Neue*.

Set the `Style` property for the top Title label to `Medium` (click the 'T' in the `Font` property to find it).

Then change the `Lines` property to 3 for the bottom description label, and in the `Font` property drop the font size to 15.

Now select the `Content View` from the Document Outline and change the `Background` to `Clear Color`. Then do the same thing for the Table View.

Now to make the prototype cell look nicer while we're working on this, I'm going to drag in a test image of a Tesla into the `Assets.xcassets` and set the image view to the file name (you can choose any image you like, or you can go with the Tesla image that can be found in the assets folder) then change the `Content Mode` to `Aspect Fit`.

View Styling

Now that we have the Table View Cell all set up with constraints, we're going to add a little styling to it to make it really pop.

In your Project Navigator, select your project folder, right-click and select `New Group` and name it `View`.

Then right click on that new folder and select `New File`, Select `Cocoa Touch Class` and click `Next`.

Make the subclass inherit from `UIView`, and name it `MaterialView`.

Then go ahead and delete the auto generated comments, and let's get started.

First, change the *class* to an *extension*:

Was:

```
class MaterialView: UIView {
```

Change to:

```
extension UIView {
```

What we're doing here is instead of creating a class that inherits from UIView, we are making an extension of the UIView that will be available to anything that inherits from it.

We'll then be able to toggle the MaterialView properties we add on and off depending on whether we want it to apply. Since pretty much all the UI elements inherit from UIView, this styling will be available to all of them.

Next modify the file as follows:

```
import UIKit


private var materialKey = false


extension UIView {


    @IBInspectable var materialDesign: Bool {


        get {

            return materialKey

        }
        set {

            materialKey = newValue

        }
    }
```

```
}
```

First we define a variable `materialKey` outside the extension and initialize it to `false`. This is the variable that will determine whether the view is using this styling.

Then we create an `IBInspectable`. This is what actually creates the interface to select in Storyboard. Next we create a `getter` and `setter` for the `materialKey`.

Then under the `materialKey = newValue` add this `if` statement.

```
if materialKey {

    self.layer.masksToBounds = false

    self.layer.cornerRadius = 3.0

    self.layer.shadowOpacity = 0.8

    self.layer.shadowRadius = 3.0

    self.layer.shadowOffset = CGSize(width: 0.0, height:
2.0)

    self.layer.shadowColor = UIColor(red: 157/255,
green: 157/255, blue: 157/255, alpha: 1.0).cgColor

} else {

    self.layer.cornerRadius = 0

    self.layer.shadowOpacity = 0

    self.layer.shadowRadius = 0

    self.layer.shadowColor = nil

}
```

All we're doing here is saying, "if the user has selected to use this `MaterialView` styling, then this is the styling we will implement, followed by the corner radius, shadow, shadow color etc. If the user does **NOT** select the `MaterialView` option, then we remove any styling to return it to the default state."

So now, when we head back over to the `Main.storyboard` file and select the inner view of the Table View Cell, we'll see the option for `Material Design`. Set it to `On`.

Figure 22.9

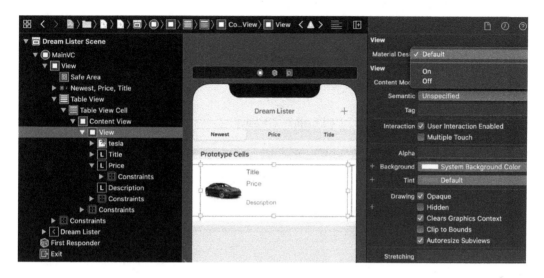

Now that you can see the behavior of the code you wrote, it should make a little more sense. So lets quickly revisit what we did.

The `IBInspectable` is what implements the ability to view a property in the Storyboard. We initialized the default behavior to be `off`, and then checked for the `newValue` that the user enters (on, off). Then we set the styling depending on which is selected.

Creating the Custom Cell

Next up is creating the custom cell. Hopefully you remember how to do this from the `myHood` app.

Right-click on the *View* group and select `New File`, then select `Cocoa Touch Class`. Set the subclass to `UITableViewCell` and name it `ItemCell`. Click `Next` and then `Create`.

We're creating this custom class that inherits from `UITableViewCell` so that we can have outlets that hook up to the UI elements we created in the Table View Cell in the Storyboard.

Replace the contents of the `ItemCell.swift` file with the following:

```
class ItemCell: UITableViewCell {
```

```swift
@IBOutlet weak var thumb: UIImageView!

@IBOutlet weak var title: UILabel!

@IBOutlet weak var price: UILabel!

@IBOutlet weak var details: UILabel!


func configureCell(item: Item) {

    title.text = item.title

    price.text = "$\(item.price)"

    details.text = item.details

}

}
```

Here we have written out our IBOutlets and created our configure-
Cell function. Let's come back to the configureCell function and
hook up our IBOutlets.

Go to the Storyboard and the first thing we need to do is change
the Class to "ItemCell". In the Document Outline, select the Table
View Cell nested within our Tabel View and change the Class to
ItemCell in the Identity Inspector. Then click on the Attributes
Inspector and in the Identifier property write "ItemCell". This allows
us to reference the ItemCell in our code by with it's *Identifier*.

Then right-click on ItemCell in the Document Outline and drag
from the IBOutlet labels to their corresponding UI element:

thumb goes to the Image.

title to the top label.

price to the second label.

details to the bottom label.

Now lets talk a little about the configureCell function.

This function will be used in the MainVC View Controller.

What it does is accept an Item object, then set the attributes of the
Table View Cell to the the corresponding properties of the item that is
passed into the configureCell function. We're not going to worry
about the image at this point.

Next we're going to hook up the Table View to the MainVC.

Open up the `MainVC` file and create an `IBOutlet` for the Table View as follows:

```
@IBOutlet weak var tableView: UITableView!

@IBOutlet weak var segment: UISegmentedControl!
```

and place this above the `viewDidLoad()`.

Then in Storyboard, right-click on the `Dream  Lister` folder from the Document Outline and connect the `tableView` outlet to the table view. Then connect the **segment** outlet to the segmented control.

Lets head back to the `MainVC` file and start implementing the code we will need to work with the Table View. We need to add two protocols, and set the delegates. So add the following code:

```
class MainVC: UIViewController, UITableViewDelegate,
UITableViewDataSource {
```

then in `viewDidLoad()` add:

```
override func viewDidLoad() {

        super.viewDidLoad()

        tableView.delegate = self

        tableView.dataSource = self

    }
```

What we've done here is add the two protocols to our class that will allow us to work with the Table View. We then set the delegate and dataSource to `self`, meaning that this class will handle both of those.

Now you will probably be getting an error that says "Type `MainVC` does not conform to protocol `UITableViewDataSource`".

This means that we have not yet implemented the required Methods that go along with these protocols. For the Table View Protocols, place these methods just below the `viewDidLoad()`:

```
func tableView(_ tableView: UITableView, cellForRowAt
indexPath: IndexPath) -> UITableViewCell {
```

```swift
        return UITableViewCell()

    }


    func tableView(_ tableView: UITableView,
numberOfRowsInSection section: Int) -> Int {

        return 0

    }


    func numberOfSections(in tableView: UITableView) ->
Int {

        return 0

    }


    func tableView(_ tableView: UITableView,
heightForRowAt indexPath: IndexPath) -> CGFloat {

        return 150

    }
```

We're familiar with these Methods. The first one is used to dequeue and fill the cells. The second returns the number of rows. The next one returns the number of sections in our Table View. And the last one sets the height of the row to 150. Right now, it's still pretty boiler plate stuff.

NSFetchedResultsController

We're finally ready to start working with some CoreData code. First thing to do is at the top of the MainVC.swift file, import CoreData.

```swift
import CoreData
```

Next we need to add a new protocol for the NSFetchedResults-Controller.

Lets modify the class declaration as follows:

```
class MainVC: UIViewController, UITableViewDelegate,
UITableViewDataSource,
NSFetchedResultsControllerDelegate
```

So what is an FRC? From the Apple documentation: "You configure an instance of this class using a fetch request that specifies the entity, optionally a filter predicate, and an array containing at least one sort ordering. When you execute the fetch, the instance efficiently collects information about the results without the need to bring all the result objects into memory at the same time.

As you access the results, objects are automatically faulted into memory in batches to match likely access patterns, and objects from previous accessed disposed of. This behavior further serves to keep memory requirements low, so even if you traverse a collection containing tens of thousands of objects, you should never have more than tens of them in memory at the same time."

So basically, it is a handy dandy class Apple has made for us to make it easier to connect the data in CoreData with displaying it in a Table View (or Collection View).

It has built in functionality for things like memory saving, filtering, saving and deleting entries, and more. It's really pretty cool once you get it all set up. So lets keep trucking.

First we'll declare the variable for our FRC right under the IBOutlets in the MainVC.swift file. Add the following:

```
var controller: NSFetchedResultsController<Item>!
```

We're declaring our FRC, but what is important to note here is that we are required to state what Entity we will be working with, so thats why we have <Item>.

Now I gotta warn you, that we're going to be writing a LOT of code here without being able to test anything. So strap in tight!

Next thing I think we will do is head into the AppDelegate file, and at the very bottom, even outside of the last curly brace, add the following:

```
let ad = UIApplication.shared.delegate as! AppDelegate
```

```
let context = ad.persistentContainer.viewContext
```

What we did is created a constant called **ad** that is a path to the app delegate. So for instance, now when we want to access the **saveContext()** function that lives in the **appDelegate**, all we have to do is say **ad.saveContext()**.

We also made it easier to call the context from the app delegate by creating the constant **context**.

Now press **save**, so that these constants will be available in other files.

Now lets go back into **MainVC.swift** file. We're going to add a BIG function called **attemptFetch()**. This can be placed at the bottom of the file, but still inside the class as follows:

```
func attemptFetch() {

        let fetchRequest: NSFetchRequest<Item> =
Item.fetchRequest()

        let dateSort = NSSortDescriptor(key: "created",
ascending: false)

        fetchRequest.sortDescriptors = [dateSort]


        let controller =
NSFetchedResultsController(fetchRequest: fetchRequest,
managedObjectContext: context, sectionNameKeyPath: nil,
cacheName: nil)


        controller.delegate = self

        self.controller = controller

        do {

            try controller.performFetch()

        } catch {

            let error = error as NSError

            print("\(error)")
```

```
        }

    }
```

Lets break this down line by line.

First we create a `fetchRequest`. This is like saying, "hey, go down into the database and see what you can find that's of the type entity, Item"

Then we have a *sort descriptor*. This class allows you to compare attributes of an entity. In this case we have put "created" because we're going to sort on `Newest` as default.

Then we create the controller and pass in the fetch request and the context from the app delegate. We can then put `nil` for the last two parameters.

Next we set the Controller variable we declared at the beginning to the Controller we just instantiated.

Last, we attempt the fetch, using the `do-catch` method.

Next we are going to add a few more methods below the `attemptFetch()` function as follows:

```
func controllerWillChangeContent(_ controller:
NSFetchedResultsController<NSFetchRequestResult>) {

        tableView.beginUpdates()

    }



    func controllerDidChangeContent(_ controller:
NSFetchedResultsController<NSFetchRequestResult>) {

        tableView.endUpdates()

    }
```

What these methods do is listen for when changes are about to be made and when they have been made, respectively.

When they're about to be made, they get ready to update the Table View with the `beginUpdates()` function. This is analogous to the `tableView.reloadData()` you should be familiar with.

Next we have another big function to write. This one you can get to auto generate by typing **didChange** and finding the method autocomplete.

```
func controller(_ controller:
NSFetchedResultsController<NSFetchRequestResult>,
didChange anObject: Any, at indexPath: IndexPath?, for
type: NSFetchedResultsChangeType, newIndexPath:
IndexPath?) {


    }
```

This is another helper method that we get with `CoreData` and the `FRC`. It listens for specific changes and can perform actions based on the type of change. If you **command** click on the `NSFetchedResults-ChangeType` you will see the following types of changes:

`case insert`

`case delete`

`case move`

`case update`

We need to write code to handle each of those cases so lets get to it. Modify the function as follows:

```
func controller(_ controller:
NSFetchedResultsController<NSFetchRequestResult>,
didChange anObject: Any, at indexPath: IndexPath?, for
type: NSFetchedResultsChangeType, newIndexPath:
IndexPath?) {


        switch type {


        case .insert:

            if let indexPath = newIndexPath {
```

```
                tableView.insertRows(at: [indexPath],
with: .fade)
            }
        case .delete:
            if let indexPath = indexPath {
                tableView.deleteRows(at: [indexPath],
with: .fade)
            }
        case .update:
            if let indexPath = indexPath {
            let cell = tableView.cellForRow(at:
indexPath) as! ItemCell
            //come back later
            }
        case .move:
            if let indexPath = indexPath {
                tableView.deleteRows(at: [indexPath],
with: .fade)
            }
            if let indexPath = newIndexPath {
                tableView.insertRows(at: [indexPath],
with: .fade)
            }
        @unknown default:
            default
        }
    }
```

It may seem like a lot, but it is mostly repetitive and self explanatory. We have a switch statement and cases that represent each type of possible changes.

Then for each type, we have the suitable action.

For **insert**, we grab a new index path (since it is new) and insert a new row.

If the case is **delete** we grab the **indexPath** that we want to delete, and delete it!

The **update** case is an interesting one, we'll come back later to it.

Finally we have the case of **move**, where we take the row at one location, delete it, and then insert it at another location.

Next we are ready to start updating some of our Table View methods. Now in the past while working with Table Views, you would usually have an array with data in it and return the **.count** value for number of rows in the section. You would also manually select the number of sections. Since we are working with the FRC, the number of rows and sections depends on what the **FetchRequest** returns. Let's update our two existing functions **numberOfRowsInSection** and **numberOfSections** with the following code:

```
func tableView(_ tableView: UITableView,
numberOfRowsInSection section: Int) -> Int {

        if let sections = controller.sections {

            let sectionInfo = sections[section]

            return sectionInfo.numberOfObjects

        }

        return 0

    }



    func numberOfSections(in tableView: UITableView) ->
    Int {

        if let sections = controller.sections {

            return sections.count

        }

        return 0
```

```
        }
```

Next we want to update the `cellForRowAt` function. We're going to do something a little different than we're used to doing. Remember in our `ItemCell.swift` file, we created a `configureCell` function.

Normally we'd call that directly in the `cellForRowAt` function. But we actually need to use that function twice in the `MainVC` file.

So what we're going to do is create a secondary `configureCell` function inside the `MainVC` file right below the `cellForRowAt` function as follows:

```
func configureCell(cell: ItemCell, indexPath: IndexPath)
{

        let item = controller.object(at: indexPath)

        cell.configureCell(item: item)

    }
```

This function accepts a cell and an index path, then calls the original `configureCell` function in `ItemCell.swift`.

Now we can update the `cellForRowAt` function as follows:

```
func tableView(_ tableView: UITableView, cellForRowAt
indexPath: IndexPath) -> UITableViewCell {

        let cell =
tableView.dequeueReusableCell(withIdentifier:
"ItemCell", for: indexPath) as! ItemCell

        configureCell(cell: cell, indexPath: indexPath)

        return cell

    }
```

Here we are creating a cell from a dequeued cell, then passing that cell into our secondary `configureCell` function, which is then passed to the ItemCell `configureCell` function that actually updates the cell.

And we can also return to our `case.update` function down at the bottom of MainVC that we said we would return to. So go ahead and update it as follows:

```
case.update:

    if let indexPath = indexPath {

        let cell = tableView.cellForRow(at: indexPath)
as! ItemCell

                configureCell(cell: cell, indexPath:
indexPath)

    }
```

When we update a cell, it will grab that cell, and send it to the MainVC configureCell function which then sends it to the ItemCell configureCell function that makes the updates to the modified cell.

With a final addition to our code we will be ready to run it for the first time! In viewDidLoad under the tableView delegate and data source add attemptFetch().

```
override func viewDidLoad() {

        super.viewDidLoad()

        tableView.delegate = self

        tableView.dataSource = self


        attemptFetch()

    }
```

And run it! It won't be very exciting yet because we don't have any data, but it should look something like this.

Figure 22.10

Let's make a quick change to the `TableView` in Storyboard. With the `TableView` selected, go into the `Attributes Inspector` in the right `Utilities` pane, find `Separator` and change it from `Default` to `None`.

Then scroll down to the `Scroll View` section and un-check both the `Scroll Indicators Shows Horizontal Indicator` and `Shows Vertical Indicator`.

Lets go back to our `MainVC` and put in some test data so that we can actually test that our `FRC` is working correctly.

At this point we finally get to save something to the database using CoreData. Create a new function called `generateTestData()` and create it as follows:

```
func generateTestData() {

        let item = Item(context: context)

        item.title = "MacBook Pro"

        item.price = 1800

        item.details = "I can't wait until the September
event, I hope they release new MPBs"


        let item2 = Item(context: context)

        item2.title = "Bose Headphones"

        item2.price = 300

        item2.details = "But man, it's so nice to be
able to block out everyone with the noise canceling
tech."


        let item3 = Item(context: context)

        item3.title = "Tesla Model S"

        item3.price = 110000

        item3.details = "Oh man this is a beautiful car.
And one day, I will own it"


        ad.saveContext()

    }
```

Let's look at one of these items. To create an item in the Context, or our *scratchpad*, all we have to do is `let item = Item(context: context)`.

You create the name of the variable, the type of Entity, then pass in the Context we created the path too in the appDelegate.

Now that entity has been created in the context and we can assign values to its attributes. We did that three times. Last but most important, we add `ad.saveContext()`.

If we did not have the `ad.saveContext()` and then generate the test data, it would still show up in our simulator.

BUT if you stopped the simulator, removed the test data, and ran it again, the Table View would return nothing because the `ad.saveContext()` command was not included. Just because you have an entity created in the context, does not mean it is saved to disc!

Add `generateTestData()` to `viewDidLoad` above the `attemptFetch()`:

```
override func viewDidLoad() {

        super.viewDidLoad()

        tableView.delegate = self

        tableView.dataSource = self


        generateTestData()

        attemptFetch()

    }
```

Press **command + r** to run the simulator.

Ta-da! You should have three items displaying in your simulator as follows:

Figure 22.11

Dream Lister ＋

Newest	Price	Title

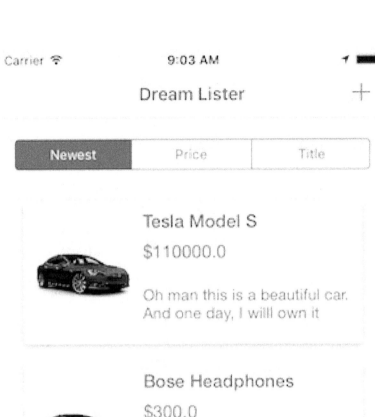

Tesla Model S

$110000.0

Oh man this is a beautiful car.
And one day, I willl own it

Bose Headphones

$300.0

But man, its so nice to be
able to blaock out everyone
with the noise canceling tech.

MacBook Pro

$1800.0

I can't wait until the
September event, I hope they
release new MPBs

If you run it again, you will see there are now 6 entries. This is because each time you run `generateTestData()` it will add three more entries to your database. If you don't want to keep adding entries, you can just comment out the `generateTestData()` function. So go ahead and do that.

Create Second ViewController

In the `Project Navigator` on the left, create a new group by right-clicking on your project and select `New Group` and name it `Controller`.

Then right-click on the group `Controller` and select `New File`, select `Cocoa Touch Class` and click `Next`.

Name the file `ItemDetailsVC` and set the subclass to `UIViewController` then click `Next` and `Create`.

Then head over to Storyboard and drag a new View Controller into the Storyboard next to the initial screen. Now make sure to go to the `Identity Inspector`, and change the class to `ItemDetailsVC`. Don't forget it!

So what do we need? We have a + button on the `MainVC` screen, so we will need a segue from the button to the `ItemDetailsVC` screen.

But we also want to be able to tap a cell that will open a second screen for editing that cell. So we're going to have two segues, one from the '+' button and one from the `MainVC` View Controller to the `ItemDetailsVC` View Controller.

Control click and drag from the + button to the new View Controller and select `show` for the segue type. Click on the arrow with the square that's between the two View Controllers, and from the Attributes Inspector name the identifier `ItemDetailsVCNew`.

Next control click and drag from the initial View Controller icon (on the bar above the device UI) to the new View Controller and select `show` for the segue type. You'll see a second arrow show up between the View Controllers, click it name the identifier `ItemDetailsVC`.

Now lets start adding our UI elements. Below is a mockup reference to our end goal:

`Figure 22.12`

Drag an image view from the Object Library and place it in the top left, and make it 100 x 100 from the Size Inspector, and constraints 8 from the top, 0 from the left and set the width and height with `Constrain to margins` checked. At this point, drag in the `imagePick.png` file to the `Assets.xcassets` folder and set the image to 'imagePick.png'.

Drag a button from the Objects Library over the Image View, and set the same size of 100 x 100 and the same constraints as the image, 0 from the left, and 8 from the top with `Constrain    to    margins` checked.

Next we need to add three text fields. Make sure you're adding `text fields` and not *text views* or *labels*.

Place two `text fields`, to the right of the image/button and one below the image just like the mockup shows us.

For all three text fields remove the border, and set the `Background` to a `Light Gray Color`. Change the height to 40 in the Size Inspector.*

Add placeholder text to *Title*, *Price*, and *Details*. Change the font of all three to *Helvetica Neue* and drop the size to 15.

Add constraints to the *Title* field: 8 from the left, 20 from the top, and 0 from the right, with `Constrain to margins` checked. Set height, click `Add Constraints`.

Add constraints to the *Price* field of 8 from the left, top, and 0 from the right. Set height, and `add constraints`.

Add constraints to the *Details* field of 0 from the left and right, 8 from the top, and set height = 60 and `add constraints`.

The details field is a little taller because it may hold more text.

Next we are going to add a file called `CustomTextField` that's available in the resources, or you can create a new file in the `View` group of `Cocoa Touch Class`, name it `CustomTextField` and set subclass to `UITextField` and paste the following code into it.

```swift
import UIKit

/** extension to UIColor to allow setting the color

 value by hex value */

extension UIColor {

    convenience init(red: Int, green: Int, blue: Int) {

        /** Verify that we have valid values */

        assert(red >= 0 && red <= 255, "Invalid red
component")

        assert(green >= 0 && green <= 255, "Invalid
green component")

        assert(blue >= 0 && blue <= 255, "Invalid blue
component")


        self.init(red: CGFloat(red) / 255.0, green:
CGFloat(green) / 255.0, blue: CGFloat(blue) / 255.0,
alpha: 1.0)

    }


    /** Initializes and sets color by hex value */

    convenience init(netHex:Int) {
```

```swift
        self.init(red:(netHex >> 16) & 0xff, green:
(netHex >> 8) & 0xff, blue:netHex & 0xff)

    }

}


@IBDesignable

class CustomTextField: UITextField {


    // MARK: - IBInspectable

    @IBInspectable var tintCol: UIColor =
UIColor(netHex: 0x707070)

    @IBInspectable var fontCol: UIColor =
UIColor(netHex: 0x707070)

    @IBInspectable var shadowCol: UIColor =
UIColor(netHex: 0x707070)


    // MARK: - Properties

    var textFont = UIFont(name: "Helvetica Neue", size:
14.0)


    override func draw(_ rect: CGRect) {

        self.layer.masksToBounds = false

        self.backgroundColor = UIColor(red: 230, green:
230, blue: 230)

        self.layer.cornerRadius = 3.0

        self.tintColor = tintCol

        self.textColor = fontCol

        self.layer.borderWidth = 1

        self.layer.borderColor = UIColor(red: 255,
green: 255, blue: 255).cgColor
```

```
        if let phText = self.placeholder {

            self.attributedPlaceholder =
NSAttributedString(string: phText, attributes:
[.foregroundColor: UIColor(netHex: 0xB3B3B3)])

        }



        self.font = textFont

    }



    // Placeholder text

    override func textRect(forBounds bounds: CGRect) ->
CGRect {

        return bounds.insetBy(dx: 10, dy: 0)

    }



    // Editable text

    override func editingRect(forBounds bounds: CGRect)
-> CGRect {

        return bounds.insetBy(dx: 10, dy: 0)

    }

}
```

I'm not going to go over this file in detail, simply because it is outside the scope of our purpose in this chapter which is learning `CoreData`. Also, we already went over a styling section in detail for the `Material-View file`. But basically, it just supplies some nice styling to text fields.

So select all three *text fields*, go to the `Identity Inspector`, and change the Class to `CustomTextField`. And then you'll see the Storyboard rebuild, and you'll see some subtle shifts in the text field appearance.

The text is slightly indented, and the corners are slightly rounded.

Now for the bottom half of the screen we need a Label, `picker view`, and a Button. Lets start from the bottom with the Button.

Add the following constraints, 0 from the left, bottom, and right. And set the height to 40. Click `Add constraints`.

Change the font to *Helvetica Neue*, bump up the text size to 20 with style of `Medium`.

Change the font color to `Light Gray Color`, and the background color to `Dark Gray Color`. Change the button title to `Save Item`

Add a `picker view` from the Object Library and place it above the Save Item button. Set constraints with `Constrain to margins` checked, 0 from the right and left, 8 from the bottom and a height of 216 is fine.

Finally, drag on a Label just above the `picker view` and change the text to "Select Store", change the color to `Dark Gray Color`, change the font to *Helvetica Neue*, bump the font size up to 20. Resize the Label box to hug the edges of the Label and click the "center text" icon. Align the label `Horizontally in Container` with the alignment constraint. Pin it 8 for the bottom and set height and width.

Now let's work on the menu. From the Object Library, search for `navigation item` and drag it into the top of the View Controller. Change the title to `Add/Edit`.

Next we need a way to delete entries, so drag in a `Bar Button Item` from the Object Library, change the `System item` to `Trash` and the `Tint` to a `red` color.

Figure 22.13

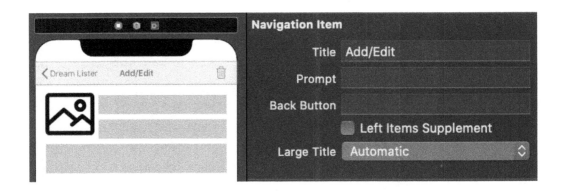

Now go ahead and run it and make sure the segue from the plus button is working to take you to the new screen. The Table View segue wont work yet until we hook it up - but the plus button should.

It's looking pretty good... except I don't like that ugly blue back button with the prior VC title. So lets get rid of that. To fix the blue tint, select the `Navigation Bar` in the Navigation Controller Scene VC and set the `Tint` to `Dark Gray Color`.

Then open the `ItemDetailsVC.swift` file and modify the `viewDidLoad()` function as follows:

```
override func viewDidLoad() {

        super.viewDidLoad()



        if let topItem =
self.navigationController?.navigationBar.topItem {

            topItem.backBarButtonItem =
UIBarButtonItem(title: "", style:
UIBarButtonItem.Style.plain, target: nil, action: nil)

        }

    }
```

All we are doing here, is programmatically changing the title of the existing `backBarButtonItem` to not have a title, leaving just the back arrow.

Now lets hook up all our UI elements to the code. Open the `ItemDetailsVC.swift` file and delete any commented code. Then right below the class declaration add the following code:

```
@IBOutlet weak var storePicker: UIPickerView!

@IBOutlet weak var titleField: CustomTextField!

@IBOutlet weak var priceField: CustomTextField!

@IBOutlet weak var detailsField: CustomTextField!

@IBOutlet weak var thumbImg: UIImageView!
```

Then below the rest of the functions add the `IBAction` for the `Save Post` button, the `Add Picture` button and the `Trash` button.

```
@IBAction func savePressed(_ sender: UIButton) {


}


@IBAction func addImage(_ sender: UIButton) {


}


@IBAction func deletePressed(_ sender: UIBarButtonItem)
{


}
```

Head back to the Storyboard and right-click the `Add/Edit` View Controller from the Document Outline (`hint` it has the yellow circle/square next to the name). Then drag from each `IBOutlet` we created in our code to the UI elements on the View Controller. You'll also hook up the button `@IBActions` (Received Actions section) located at the bottom of this menu. You'll be asked to select a type of *event*, choose `Touch Up Inside`.

Picker View

Now we have everything hooked up to our code, lets get to work on making that `Picker View` work. There's more than one way to work with `CoreData`, you don't have to only use an `NSFetchedResults-Controller`. You can use regular Table Views, or you can simply save data into arrays and display them in a `Picker View` like we are going to do here.

So first off, like Table Views, `Picker View` has protocols and methods we must implement. So modify the class declaration as follows:

```
class ItemDetailsVC: UIViewController,
UIPickerViewDataSource, UIPickerViewDelegate {
```

You'll see an error, we'll take care of that in a moment.

Then just like we do with table views, add the following to view-DidLoad:

```
storePicker.delegate = self

storePicker.dataSource = self
```

And before we forget, go ahead and add import CoreData to your file. Next, we are going to create an array of objects of entity Store eventually, so lets create that variable now, underneath the IBOutlets:

```
var stores = [Store]()
```

Now we need to add the methods to conform with the protocols. Add the following beneath the viewDidLoad():

```
func pickerView(_ pickerView: UIPickerView, titleForRow
row: Int, forComponent component: Int) -> String? {

        let store = stores[row]

        return store.name

    }
```

This function is in charge of displaying the row information. So we create a store from our array of stores that corresponds to the picker row, then display the name of that store at that specific row. And remember, the store.name comes from the attribute that you created in the .xc-datamodelid at the very very beginning.

```
func pickerView(_ pickerView: UIPickerView,
numberOfRowsInComponent component: Int) -> Int {

        return stores.count

    }
```

This method simply counts the number of objects in the stores array and returns that number to be the number of rows in the Picker View.

```
func numberOfComponents(in pickerView: UIPickerView) ->
Int {

        return 1

    }
```

This method determines how many columns there are in the `Picker View`. For instance if you have a date picker, you'll usually have a few columns for month, day, year. In that case you would return 3. Add this method should remove the protocol error we were getting earlier.

Lets create some `stores` so that we can populate the `Picker View`.

Add this function down at the bottom, below your @IBActions:

```
func generateStores() {

    let store = Store(context: context)

    store.name = "Best Buy"

    let store2 = Store(context: context)

    store2.name = "Tesla Dealership"

    let store3 = Store(context: context)

    store3.name = "Frys Electronics"

    let store4 = Store(context: context)

    store4.name = "Target"

    let store5 = Store(context: context)

    store5.name = "Amazon"

    let store6 = Store(context: context)

    store6.name = "K Mart"


    ad.saveContext()

}
```

Just like we did with the test data for the items in **MainVC.swift**, we create store objects of entity `Store`, insert them into the context, then assign values to the **store.name** attribute. Then most importantly, we call the built in **saveContext()** function that is found in the app delegate.

We need a way to fetch those object we just saved to **core data**, so create the following function:

```
func getStores() {

        let fetchRequest: NSFetchRequest<Store> =
Store.fetchRequest()

        do {

            self.stores = try
context.fetch(fetchRequest)

            self.storePicker.reloadAllComponents()

        } catch {

            // handle error

        }

    }
```

This is a little different from what we saw with the **FetchedResults-Controller**, so lets break it down.

We create a **fetchRequest** which we've seen before.

Then since a fetch request *can fail*, we have our **do-catch** block.

We are directly assigning the result of the fetch to the stores array in this line **self.stores = try context.fetch(fetchRequest)**.

Then we tell the store picker to **reloadAllComponents**. This is analogous to the Table View **reloadData** function.

When changes have been made to the **Picker View**, it will reload and show the data. If there is an error, you can write some code to handle it.

Next add those two functions to **viewDidLoad** and run it!

```
generateStores()

getStores()
```

Go ahead and run the project once, then back in the code, comment out the `generateStores()` function in `viewDidLoad` or it will continually add those stores to the `stores` array and you're `Picker View` will be really long!

Saving an Item

We're now ready to implement the `Save Item` button. So let's think about what we need to have happen for that to work.

First we are going to create an item of entity type `Item`.

Then we're going to check to see if there is anything written in each of the text fields.

If there is, we're going to assign the item attributes to those values.

To assign the store for the item, we need to use the relationship to the store, so we say `item.store` is equal to the store that is picked.

At this point we need to clarify something. We're not assigning the name of the store we picked to the item. We're connecting two *independent* entities to each other.

If you wanted to access the name of the store we just associated with the item (which we'll do later), you'd need to say something like `item.store.name`, or in other words, get the name (attribute) of the store (entity) that is associated with this item (entity).

Then we'll save it and segue back to initial screen.

So here it goes, modify the `savePressed` function as follows:

```
@IBAction func savePressed(_ sender: UIButton) {


    let item = Item(context: context)


    if let title = titleField.text {

        item.title = title

    }

    if let price = priceField.text {

        item.price = Double(price)!
```

```
    }
    if let details = detailsField.text {

        item.details = details

    }



    item.store =
stores[storePicker.selectedRow(inComponent: 0)]

    ad.saveContext()
```

```
navigationController?.popViewController(animated: true)

    }
```

Now that should work! Run it! Add an item, save it, and watch it pop up in the Table View!

Edit existing items

We can already add new items. But now we want to make it so we can edit existing items by clicking on them and changing their values.

So what we are going to need is a way to pass the item that was clicked on in the first screen, to pass that item to the second screen for editing. We'll create a function that loads the items information into the second screen.

So first, we're going to create a variable in **ItemDetailsVC** called

var itemToEdit: Item? and place it right under the **stores** array variable.

We're saying it's optional, because a user could create a new item via the + button instead of editing an item.

So we'll do a check in **viewDidLoad()** to see if there's actually an item to edit.

So in **viewDidLoad** add the following:

```
if itemToEdit != nil {

    loadItemData()
```

}

And if you don't remember creating a function called `loadItemData` you would be correct, so lets create it now, beneath the `savePressed` function.

```
func loadItemData() {

    if let item = itemToEdit {

        titleField.text = item.title

        priceField.text = "\(item.price)"

        detailsField.text = item.details


        if let store = item.store {

            var index = 0

            repeat {

                let s = stores[index]

                if s.name == store.name {

                    storePicker.selectRow(index,
inComponent: 0, animated: false)

                    break

                }

                index += 1

            } while (index < stores.count)

        }

    }

}
```

We've checked in `viewDidLoad` to make sure that there's an `itemToEdit`, meaning that we can be sure we have arrived at this screen by selecting an item from the Table View.

So what we want to happen when we call this function, is load into the text fields and set the `picker view` to the data of that item, so they can then be edited as desired.

The text fields are pretty straight forward. All we have to do is retrieve the values of the attributes of the item and set the text fields to those values.

Getting the title of the store is bit trickier.

What we do is create a `repeat while` loop that loops through the stores in our `stores` array, and compares the name of the store of our item with that in the `stores` array. If it matches, it grabs the index and sets the `storePicker` row to that index.

Now we're ready to receive the item in `ItemDetailsVC` from the `MainVC` screen. We start by implementing the `didSelectRowAt` method in `MainVC`.

Be careful when you get this function, many many people accidentally grab the `didDEselectRowAt`. So add the following function under the `cellForRowAt` function:

```
func tableView(_ tableView: UITableView, didSelectRowAt
indexPath: IndexPath) {

        if let objs = controller.fetchedObjects ,
objs.count > 0 {

            let item = objs[indexPath.row]

            performSegue(withIdentifier:
"ItemDetailsVC", sender: item)

        }

    }
```

This method is called whenever the user taps on a cell. So what we're doing is checking first to make sure that there is in fact an object in the `fetchedObjects`. That way we don't get a crash.

Then we're assigning the item object at the row that is connected to the constant `item`. Next we are going to perform the segue, and send `item`.

To actually send **item**, we need to use another function called **prepareForSegue**. Go ahead and place it below our **didSelectRowAt** function:

```
override func prepare(for segue: UIStoryboardSegue,
sender: Any?) {

        if segue.identifier == "ItemDetailsVC" {

            if let destination = segue.destination as?
ItemDetailsVC {

                if let item = sender as? Item {

                    destination.itemToEdit = item

                }

            }

        }

    }
```

So lets break this one down. This function is called in preparation to change screens. So the first thing we do is check which segue we are going to use, then we assign what the destination screen is going to be.

Next we assign what item we are sending is.

And lastly we assign the item we are sending to the variable in the **destination** View Controller that it will be assigned to.

So that inner most assignment is saying, "that variable over in the next screen called **itemToEdit**, we're assigning the **item** we created in this screen to that one."

Let's run it and make sure everything we have written so far is working.

What we should expect to see is that when we click on an item, it will segue to the next screen and fill in the text fields and select the correct store on the **picker** view. You can then edit the text fields and store selection, save it, and it will update the table view accordingly! Pretty cool!

But there is a catch, it didn't **actually** update the existing entry, it simply created a new entry with the updated info, so lets fix that.

What we need to do in the **savePressed** function in our `ItemDe-`
`tailsVC.swft` , is implement another check as to whether we are saving a new item, or saving an edited item. At the top of the function replace `let item = Item(context: context)` with:

```
var item: Item!
```

```
    if itemToEdit == nil {

        item = Item(context: context)

    } else {

        item = itemToEdit

    }
```

Here we're declaring an item of entity type `Item`.

Then we do a check to see if we've received an item from the first
screen to edit. If not, then we continue as before, creating a new item in
the context and saving it.

However, if we have an item to edit, all we do is set the item we declared equal to that item. Then `CoreData` actually knows what to do
with it and will update the cell accordingly when we press save! Pretty
cool right? And that's part of the big `didChangeFunction` in `MainVC`
where we check for `.update` changes.

Deleting an Item

Now that we can add and edit, its time to delete. Make sure you're still
in the `ItemDetailsVC.swft` file and go to the **deletePressed** function and modify it as follows:

```
@IBAction func deletePressed(_ sender: UIBarButtonItem)
{
        if itemToEdit != nil {

            context.delete(itemToEdit!)

            ad.saveContext()

        }
```

345

```
navigationController?.popViewController(animated: true)
```

    }

How easy is that?? All we have to do is check that we have an `itemTo-Delete`.

Then say `context.delete()` and pass in the item to be deleted and save. That is the power of using the `NSFetchedResultsController` with `CoreData`.

Imagine if you had to write all the code to do that yourself.

So try and run it, select an existing item and try to delete it. It should pop you back to the table view and watch it disappear.

Adding Images

Lets get to adding images. Just like we did with the `myHood` app we're going to start out by adding the necessary protocols for working with `UIImagePickers`. So add the following to your class declaration:

```
class ItemDetailsVC: UIViewController,
UIPickerViewDelegate, UIPickerViewDataSource,
UIImagePickerControllerDelegate,
UINavigationControllerDelegate {
```

Then declare a variable for our `imagePicker` just below the `stores` array and `itemToEdit` variable called:

```
var imagePicker: UIImagePickerController!
```

The UIImagePickerController is a class that manages taking pictures and video, and accessing user media. Next in the `viewDidLoad` instantiate the `imagePicker` and set the delegate.

```
imagePicker = UIImagePickerController()

imagePicker.delegate = self
```

Now we need to implement the `imagePickerController` method as follows, you can add this at the bottom of the file:

```
func imagePickerController(_ picker:
UIImagePickerController, didFinishPickingMediaWithInfo
info: [UIImagePickerController.InfoKey : Any]) {

    if let img = info[.originalImage] as? UIImage {

      thumbImg.image = img

    }

    imagePicker.dismiss(animated: true, completion:
nil)

   }
```

This method tells the delegate that the user picked a still image or movie.

Next we grab the picked image and set it equal to the thumbnail image, and then dismiss the picker view.

Now we're ready to present the `imagePickerController` when the `addImage` button is pressed. So modify the `addImage` function as follows:

```
@IBAction func addImage(_ sender: UIButton) {

        present(imagePicker, animated: true, completion:
nil)

   }
```

Last thing we need to do before we can just test that the `imagePicker` is working is provide permissions in the `info.plist`.

Open the `info.plist` from the left hand pane and in the last entry, when you hover over the cell there should be a + sign that pops up. Click on it and type `Privacy`.

You should get some auto completed entries, and we are looking for "Privacy - Photo Library Usage Description". You can click on the up/down arrows to open a list of options. On the right there is space available to enter a message to the user why you would like to access their photos. Say something like "DreamLister needs to access your photos.

Go ahead and run it, and verify that when you click the "Add Pic" button, you are asked to allow access to photos. Then when you click a photo, it returns to the **ItemDetailsVC** and the image you selected is now displayed.

Next, we need to save the image to `CoreData`.

So go to the **savePressed** function and create a new Image entity. Then set the image attribute of that entity equal to the image we just selected.

Add the following under **var item: Item!**

```
let picture = Image(context: context)

picture.image = thumbImg.image
```

So we're creating **picture** of entity `Image` then setting the attribute of **image** to the thumbnail image we picked using our ImagePicker.

Right below we do our check to see whether we're editing or creating a new entity:

```
if itemToEdit == nil {

    item = Item(context: context)

  } else {

    item = itemToEdit

}
```

Just beneath the if/else statement add:

```
item.image = picture
```

And again, just reiterating the fact that here we're associating two independent entities. And when we access the image to load upon editing, we do it as seen in the **loadItemData()** function by adding:

```
titleField.text = item.title

priceField.text = "\(item.price)"

detailsField.text = item.details

thumbImg.image = item.image?.image as? UIImage // <- Add
this
```

When an edited cell is loaded, we simply access the image entity associated with our item, grab the image out of it and set it equal to the thumbnail image.

And finally, to enable the images being set in the Table View, let's modify the `ItemCell.swift configureCell` function as follows, just add:

```
thumb.image = item.image?.image as? UIImage
```

Now if you run it, you will see that any existing test data or entries you had will not have any images in the Table View. That's because there had not been any image associated with the item before. But now you should be able to either edit one of the existing cells, or add a new one and add an image. It should work!

And if you don't add an image, it will use the placeholder image instead.

Sorting

Next up is sorting. Open the `MainVC.swift` file and find your `attemptFetch()` function.

We currently have only one `SortDescriptor`, which compared the `created` attributes.

We want to add a few more in order to sort by price and alphabetically.

So right under the current `SortDescriptor` add these two:

```
let priceSort = NSSortDescriptor(key: "price",
ascending: true)

let titleSort = NSSortDescriptor(key: "title",
ascending: true)
```

Then we need to write some logic to determine which `SortDescriptor` to use when the segmented controller is changed. Replace the `fetchRequest.sortDescriptors = [dateSort]` with:

```
switch segment.selectedSegmentIndex {

    case 0:
```

```
        fetchRequest.sortDescriptors = [dateSort]

    case 1:

        fetchRequest.sortDescriptors = [priceSort]

    case 2:

        fetchRequest.sortDescriptors = [titleSort]

    default:

        break

}
```

All we're doing here is checking which segment is selected, and depending on which one is selected, we'll apply a different `sortDescriptor`.

But the problem is, we don't currently have any way of knowing when a user chooses a different sort method. So we need to add a listener for that.

Add the following `IBAction` below the `attemptFetch` function:

```
@IBAction func segmentChange(_ sender: AnyObject) {

    attemptFetch()

    tableView.reloadData()

}
```

Go into Storyboard. From the Document Outline, right-click the `Dream Lister` View Controller and hook up the segmented control. Remember, when you right-click it, at the bottom of the menu in "Received Actions", drag from the circle on **segmentChange** to our Segment Control on the UI.

When you do, it is going to ask what type of *event* to select, and we want `Value changed`.

What this action does, is it listens for whenever a different segment is selected, then runs the code inside the method. In this case, we're going to run the **attemptFetch** function. This will reload the `CoreData`, then it will reload the `tableView`. Give it a try!

Add some items that are different in price and name, and see how the sorting goes. Play with the `ascending` value in the `SortDescriptor` declaration to learn how it works.

Wrapping up

And that's a wrap for DreamLister! This has been a huge section and we've gone over a LOT. We've learned all about Core Data, NSFetched Results Controller, Picker Views, sorting, and a lot more.

Exercise

I'm going to leave you with a final challenge, and that is to implement `ItemType`. Come up with a way to assign an item type and then sort by item type. Possibly a second Picker View that has item types such as electronics, games, etc. Then like you did with store, you would save that item entity and associate it with a specific item. Happy coding!

Chapter 23: In-App Purchases

Monetizing your apps is a common way to create wealth as a developer. Apple has made it easy to do this by integrating In-App Purchases.

What you will learn

- How to create a Collection View
- Navigating App Store Connect for IAP's
- Registering a App Id for IAP's
- Creating multiple IAP tiers
- Sandbox testing IAP's

Key Terms

- IAP (in-app purchase)
- UICollectionView
- UICollectionCell
- SKPayment
- Non-Consumable
- Restore Purchases
- Sandbox

Resources

`Download here:` https://github.com/devslopes/iOS13-book-assets/wiki/iOS13-Book

Setting up `in-app purchases` is easier than you'd think. I'll take you through it step by step.

First, we need to make products in App Store Connect * *This requires a paid developer account.*

Once we have them set up we need to request those products to see if they are available. Once we know they are available we can display the product info. Then the purchase can be made by creating an `SKPayment` and add that to the queue.

We'll set up a system to handle all the responses we get from Apple, such as successful or declined. Once a payment is successful, we provide the user with the purchase. We are going to make a simple Collection View with custom cells and a purchase **restore** button. That will recover all your purchases if you ever delete the app or get a new device.

Your **IAP** iOS App (Figure 23.0) will have a **UICollectionView**, five **UICollectionViewCells** and one UIButton.

Figure 23.0

Creating an Xcode Project

To begin, open up Xcode and double-click **Single View Application** to create a new project. Name it whatever you'd like and save it anywhere.

Okay, so we are going to get straight to the purchase screen.

Click on **Main.Storyboard** and lets place a **UICollectionView** on it. Let's leave some space on the bottom for our restore purchase button.

Now `pin` it to the margins 0 to the `top`, 0 `left` and `right` and 40 from the `bottom`.

Because this is not a tutorial on how to set up a `UICollection-View` or constraints, I'm going to go through it pretty quickly and just explain what we did.

Okay, so I made the cell `160 x 160 points` big. I added a UIView to the cell and constrained it to the margins (so I can round the corners and add a shadow later on to make it prettier).

Second, I added a UIImage view and a label inside the view that was just added and pinned them 8 points all the way around and 4 points from the label (we can always adjust these as needed once we have real images in them).

Lastly, I added the restore button under the Collection View and pinned it to the corner.

Lets add the assets now.

I added *Arcade Time Background*, *Arcade-1*, *Arcade-2*, *Arcade-3*, *Arcade-4*, and *Bear-1*.

We can now add an image placeholder for the cell we created and also set up a UIImageView for a background.

First select the UIImageView inside the cell.

Then select the **Attributes inspector**, where it says Image select the **dropdown menu** and select *Arcade-1*.

Then for Content Mode select the **dropdown menu** and select **Aspect Fit**.

Drag a UIImageView from the **Object Library** to the View Controller Scene tree hierarchy and place it above our Collection View, this will ensure that the background image will be behind the Collection View.

Once its there and still selected lets `pin` it right away.

Uncheck **Constrain to margins** and lets put 0 from the `top`, `left`, `right` and bottom.

The Collection View needs to be clear so we can see our background when we set an image to it.

Select your *Collection View* on the left side. Then select the **Attributes inspector** on the right and set the background color to `clear`.

Select the UIImageView on the left side that we placed above our Collection View.

Select `Attributes inspector` again and where it says *Image*, select the `dropdown menu` and select *Arcade Time Background*.

Then for Content Mode select the `dropdown menu` and select `Scale To Fill`.

Our Storyboard should now resemble something like this (Figure 3.3.1). We will get our Collection View functioning so we can see it in the simulator before we beautify it like Figure 23.1.

Figure 23.1

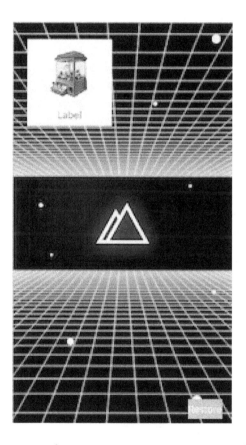

Now, before we can get the `UICollectionView` all set up and have the ViewController inherit from the `UICollectionView` Data source and delegate, we need to make a *UICollectionViewCell* file to customize the cell.

Right click the *InAppPurchases* folder and select `New file`.

Make sure you select iOS, then select **Cocoa Touch Class** and click **Next**.

Make sure the subclass selected is **UICollectionViewCell** and name the class *PurchaseCell*, click **Next**.

Make sure your project is selected on the next screen and click **Create**.

We'll come back to this file later to add more to it, this is good for now.

Now back in the storyboard, you need to click on the **Identity inspector** on the right side and select the **PurchaseCell** class for the Collection View cell.

We need to give this cell a reusable identifier as well.

Click on the **Attributes inspector** and type *purchaseCell* in the identifier text field.

We are now ready to set up our **ViewController** and connect all of our IBOutlets.

Let's add the UICollectionViewDelegate and UICollectionViewData-Source to our **ViewController**.

We also need to set the delegate and data source and add the required methods to allow the UICollectionView protocols to work.

These are `numberOfItemsInSection`, `cellForItemAt indexPath`, and `didSelectItemAt indexPath`.

For sizing purposes so our *Collection View* cells look nice on all screen sizes, lets inherit from one more protocol, add UICollectionView-DelegateFlowLayout next to UICollectionViewDelagate and DataSource at the top.

Then add one more method to our class called *collectionViewLay-out*.

```
import UIKit



class ViewController: UIViewController,
UICollectionViewDelegate, UICollectionViewDataSource,
UICollectionViewDelegateFlowLayout {


    @IBOutlet weak var collectionView: UICollectionView!
```

```swift
override func viewDidLoad() {

    super.viewDidLoad()

    collectionView.delegate = self

    collectionView.dataSource = self

}



func collectionView(_ collectionView:
UICollectionView, numberOfItemsInSection section: Int)
-> Int {

    //This is a temporary value, just to show us
some cells

    return 6

}



func collectionView(_ collectionView:
UICollectionView, cellForItemAt indexPath: IndexPath) ->
UICollectionViewCell {

    if let cell =
collectionView.dequeueReusableCell(withReuseIdentifier:
"purchaseCell", for: indexPath) as? PurchaseCell {

        return cell

    } else {

        return PurchaseCell()

    }

}



func collectionView(_ collectionView:
UICollectionView, layout collectionViewLayout:
UICollectionViewLayout, sizeForItemAt indexPath:
IndexPath) -> CGSize {

    //This is so the cells look good on any screen
size
```

```
        return CGSize(width:
self.collectionView.bounds.size.width/2 - 20, height:
160)

    }



    func collectionView(_ collectionView:
UICollectionView, didSelectItemAt indexPath: IndexPath)
{

        //This gets called when cell is tapped

        //We will add to this later

    }

}
```

Lets connect our Collection View `IBOutlet` to our Storyboard.

Open `Assistant Editor` and click the + next to the `IBOutlet` and drag it to the *Collection View*.

Now, that this is finished we can test and run our app. We should see 6 cells with our claw machine image.

We need to configure the cell with data so we can change the image and also update the image and label.

So first, at the top of `ViewController.swift`, right under the `CollectionView IBOutlet`; declare an array of strings called *products* with the proper purchase item names you want to use.

```
let products = ["tier1","tier2","tier3","tier4","tier5"]
```

Select the `PurchaseCell.swift` file we created earlier, it is now time to add a configuration method and IBOutlets.

We need two *IBOutlets*. One we will call *purchaseImage* of type UI-ImageView and the second one is *purchaseLbl* of type UILabel.

Lastly, lets create a function called *configureCell* and pass in a variable called *imageName* of type String for now.

We'll use a *switch case* and manually set the label name and image for now.

We'll come back and refactor this code to work with our `IAP` stuff later.

This is enough to get everything set up and tested to make sure all our images work and look good.

```swift
import UIKit


class PurchaseCell: UICollectionViewCell {


    @IBOutlet weak var purchaseImage: UIImageView!
    @IBOutlet weak var purchaseLbl: UILabel!


    func configureCell(imageName: String){
        switch imageName {
        case "tier1":
            purchaseImage.image = UIImage(named:
"Arcade-1")
            purchaseLbl.text = "$2,500"
        case "tier2":
            purchaseImage.image = UIImage(named:
"Arcade-2")
            purchaseLbl.text = "$5,000"
        case "tier3":
            purchaseImage.image = UIImage(named:
"Arcade-3")
            purchaseLbl.text = "$10,000"
        case "tier4":
            purchaseImage.image = UIImage(named:
"Arcade-4")
            purchaseLbl.text = "$25,000"
        case "tier5":
```

```
            purchaseImage.image = UIImage(named:
"Bear-1")

            purchaseLbl.text = "$50,000"

        default:

            break

        }

    }

}
```

Time to connect those *IBOutlets* to our Storyboard.

Open `Assistant Editor` and click the + next to the *IBOutlet* and drag *purchaseLbl* to the Label in the cell, and *purchaseImage* to the *UIImageView*.

Alright, we are almost ready to test this to see if we have 5 different cells.

We need to refactor our `ViewController.swift` file a little, so select that.

Lets change the `return  6` in the `numberOfItemsInSection` to the count of our **products** array.

```
func collectionView(_ collectionView: UICollectionView,
numberOfItemsInSection section: Int) -> Int {

        return products.count

}
```

One more code addition, we have to call our new *configureCell* method we created in our cell view and pass in one of our String values in our **products** array.

```
func collectionView(_ collectionView: UICollectionView,
cellForItemAt indexPath: IndexPath) ->
UICollectionViewCell {

        if let cell =
collectionView.dequeueReusableCell(withReuseIdentifier:
"purchaseCell", for: indexPath) as? PurchaseCell {
```

```
            cell.configureCell(imageName:
products[indexPath.row])

            return cell

        } else {

            return PurchaseCell()

    }

}
```

Okay, lets run this in our simulator and we should have something that looks like this. (Figure 23.2)

Figure 23.2

The cells are really boring and just don't look great.
Lets create a custom view that will round the corners and put a shadow around the edge.

Right click the *InAppPurchases* folder and select `new   file` -> select `iOS`, then select `Cocoa  touch  class` and click `Next`.

Make sure the subclass selected is `UIView` and name the class *CustomView*.

Click `Next`.

Make sure your project is selected on the next screen and click `Create`.

Add the code shown below to this new swift file.

```swift
import UIKit



class CustomView: UIView {


    override func awakeFromNib() {

        layer.cornerRadius = 2.0

        layer.shadowColor = UIColor(red: 157.0 / 255.0,
green: 157.0 / 255.0, blue: 157.0 / 255.0, alpha:
0.5).cgColor

        layer.shadowOpacity = 0.8

        layer.shadowRadius = 5.0

        layer.shadowOffset = CGSize(width: 0.0, height:
2.0)

    }

}
```

We need to add another *UIView* to our cell, so lets go to the Storyboard and drag a UIView right above our view that contains our UIImageView and UILabel.

```
- PurchaseCell

    --> add UIView here <--

    - UIView

        - Purchase Image
```

362

- Purchase Label

Once thats there, select the new view and `pin` the view to the `leading`, `trailing`, `top` and `bottom` edges of the view thats already there.

With the new view we placed in the cell, go to your `Identity  inspector` and select `CustomView` for the class.

Now head over to your `Attributes  inspector` and change the alpha to *0.6*.

Select the UIView that contains our UIImageView and UILabel and set the background to `clear`.

Lastly, select the `Restore` button and change the font to anything you like and make sure you change the background color to `clear`.

Now build and run your project and your cells will have slightly rounded corners and a little bit of a shadow (it is hard to see since the background is so dark).

It should look just like figure 3.3.0 at the beginning of this section.

Time to setup In App Purchases!

First, we need to go to our App Store Connect page and Click on `My Apps`.

Then click the + symbol on the left side and select `New  App`.

We then need to create a bundle ID for our app if you haven't already done so. Just click on the `developer  portal` link.

On the left side of the page under `Identifiers` select the `App IDs` link.

Now you just need to name your app, in our case I named it *InApp-Purchases*.

Then create a bundle identifier, ours is *com.devslopes.inAppPur-chaseExample*.

This should use your own custom domain, it can only be used once.

Click `continue`, you will notice that `in-app  purchases` is selected by default. Once you are on the next page just click `register`.

Now we can go back and refresh our App Store Connect account and our bundle ID should be available.

Once you see your bundle ID, fill everything else out. (note: the name of the app needs to be unique and if it's already taken you'll have to rename it). Click **Create**.

Select **Features** at the top and then press the + next to **In-App Purchases** to begin adding them.

Select **non-consumable** for the type for this exercise. If you'd like to know what the other types are, the descriptions are very clear. We are working with non-consumables because we can demonstrate the **restore** purchases feature this way.

We now need to name this **in-app purchase** and give it a unique product ID and select a pricing tier.

I wont be going through this process for every tier (5), so for the other items we'll have in our app, I will be naming them *tier1* through *tier5* and copying the pricing tier to match their name.

We need to have a language selected. For now, just add English and name the item whatever you'd like with a short description. Then press **save**.

Now click **save** to finish entering the first item, and repeat this for tiers 2 through 5.

When you finish adding all 5 items, your **In-App Purchases** should look like this. (Figure 23.3)

Figure 23.3

In-App Purchases (5) ⊕   Q Search   View Shared Secret

Reference Name ^	Type	Product ID	Status
tier1	Non-Consumable	com.devslopes.InAppPurchases.tier1	● Waiting for Screenshot
tier2	Non-Consumable	com.devslopes.InAppPurchases.tier2	● Waiting for Screenshot
tier3	Non-Consumable	com.devslopes.InAppPurchases.tier3	● Waiting for Screenshot
tier4	Non-Consumable	com.devslopes.InAppPurchases.tier4	● Waiting for Screenshot
tier5	Non-Consumable	com.devslopes.InAppPurchases.tier5	● Waiting for Screenshot

Request Available Products

Now that all of our products are entered into App Store Connect, we now need to request our products from Apple to make sure they are available to buy.

First, we need to `import` `StoreKit` in our class and also inherit `SKProductsRequestDelegate`.

Once we do that, we need to create a *requestProducts function*. Inside this function we need a Set of strings with the bundle ID's for all the products we added to App Store Connect and then do a `SKProductsRequest` and wait for a response and hope we're told they're ready.

```
import UIKit

import StoreKit


class ViewController: UIViewController,
UICollectionViewDelegate, UICollectionViewDataSource,
UICollectionViewDelegateFlowLayout,
SKProductsRequestDelegate {


    @IBOutlet weak var collectionView: UICollectionView!


    var products =
["tier1","tier2","tier3","tier4","tier5"]


    override func viewDidLoad() {

        super.viewDidLoad()

        collectionView.delegate = self

        collectionView.dataSource = self

        requestProducts()

    }
```

```
func requestProducts() {

    let ids: Set<String> =
["com.devslopes.InAppPurchases.tier1","com.devslopes.InA
ppPurchases.tier2","com.devslopes.InAppPurchases.tier3",
"com.devslopes.InAppPurchases.tier4","com.devslopes.InAp
pPurchases.tier5"]

    let productsRequest =
SKProductsRequest(productIdentifiers: ids)

    productsRequest.delegate = self

    productsRequest.start()

}
```

Above, you see that we set the SKProductsRequest delegate. Now we need to add a required function called *productsRequest did-Receive response*. This is where we know if our products are available to sell or not.

```
func productsRequest(_ request: SKProductsRequest,
didReceive response: SKProductsResponse) {

    print("Products ready: \
(response.products.count)")

    print("Products not ready: \
(response.invalidProductIdentifiers.count)")

}
```

Build and run your project. If your *products ready* doesn't show all the items you've added, make sure your bundle ID's on your project match the ones on App Store Connect.

Okay, now that we are receiving products ready to sell from the App Store, let's create a new array of SKProduct type. Replace the **products** array.

```
var products = [SKProduct]()
```

Then, inside our **productRequest** function we can set the **products** array equal to our **response.products** array with the items that are ready to sell.

Be sure to reload the Collection View after this and also update the array name.

```
func productsRequest(_ request: SKProductsRequest,
didReceive response: SKProductsResponse) {

    print("Products ready: \
(response.products.count)")

    print("Products not ready: \
(response.invalidProductIdentifiers.count)")

    products = response.products


    for product in response.products {

        print(product.productIdentifier)

    }


    DispatchQueue.main.async {

        self.collectionView.reloadData()

    }

}
```

Alright, we are almost done with this. We need to inherit one more protocol in our class, called `SKPaymentTransactionObserver`.

Place this next to the `SKProductsRequestDelegate` at top, next to the class name.

We will need to add the *paymentQueue function* to abide by this protocol and also set the observer.

Inside the *paymentQueue function* we will add a switch statement that takes care of all the cases that can be returned from Apple.

These are *purchased, failed, restored, purchasing* and *deferred.*

- *Purchased* gets called when the item is successfully processed.
- *Failed* is called if payment transaction fails.
- *Purchasing* is called when the payment is being processed, this is called before the purchase is successful or not.

- *Restored* is an option for non-consumable products like our products, that will restore all purchases automatically if you delete the app or get a new device.
- *Deferred* means something happened and it will be tried again at a later time.

```
func paymentQueue(_ queue: SKPaymentQueue,
updatedTransactions transactions:
[SKPaymentTransaction]) {

        for transaction in transactions {

            switch transaction.transactionState {

            case .purchased:

                print("purchased")


SKPaymentQueue.default().finishTransaction(transaction)

            case .failed:

                print("failed")

                let errorMsg =
transaction.error?.localizedDescription

                showErrorAlert(title: "Oops! Something
went wrong.", msg: "Unable to make purchase.  Reason: \
(String(describing: errorMsg)).")


SKPaymentQueue.default().finishTransaction(transaction)

            case .restored:

                print("restored")

                showErrorAlert(title: "Purchases
Restored.", msg: "Your purchases have been restored.")


SKPaymentQueue.default().finishTransaction(transaction)

            case .purchasing:

                print("purchasing")
```

```
    case .deferred:

        print("deferred")

    @unknown default:

        break

    }

  }

}
```

Also, add a *UIAlert function* that can be called so the user knows what is happening.

```
func showErrorAlert(title: String, msg: String) {

    let alert = UIAlertController(title: title,
message: msg, preferredStyle: .alert)

    let action = UIAlertAction(title: "Ok",
style: .default, handler: nil)

    alert.addAction(action)

    present(alert, animated: true, completion:nil)

}
```

We need to update our **configureCell** method in our **Purchase-Cell.swift** file.

The image name we pass in is going to be the **Product** ID we created for our IAP's in App Store Connect.

We'll also want to pass in the price, because we can now get this from Apple and this allows us to use the correct price associated with the *tier* that was selected.

```
func configureCell(imageName: String, price: String){

    switch imageName {

    case "com.devslopes.InAppPurchases.tier1":

        purchaseImage.image = UIImage(named:
"Arcade-1")
```

```
            purchaseLbl.text = price

        case "com.devslopes.InAppPurchases.tier2":

            purchaseImage.image = UIImage(named:
"Arcade-2")

            purchaseLbl.text = price

        case "com.devslopes.InAppPurchases.tier3":

            purchaseImage.image = UIImage(named:
"Arcade-3")

            purchaseLbl.text = price

        case "com.devslopes.InAppPurchases.tier4":

            purchaseImage.image = UIImage(named:
"Arcade-4")

            purchaseLbl.text = price

        case "com.devslopes.InAppPurchases.tier5":

            purchaseImage.image = UIImage(named:
"Bear-1")

            purchaseLbl.text = price

        default:

            break

        }

}
```

Okay, so because we added another parameter `price` of type String to our `configureCell` method we'll need to get our price from our `products` array.

We are going to format the number to currency and also use a nifty built in tool that will change the currency displayed to whatever country the user is in.

Then we'll convert it to a String and send it into our `configure-Cell` method.

```swift
func collectionView(_ collectionView: UICollectionView,
cellForItemAt indexPath: IndexPath) ->
UICollectionViewCell {

        var cellPrice = ""

        if let cell =
collectionView.dequeueReusableCell(withReuseIdentifier:
"purchaseCell", for: indexPath) as? PurchaseCell {

            let product = products[indexPath.row]

            let formatter = NumberFormatter()

            formatter.numberStyle =
NumberFormatter.Style.currency

            formatter.locale = product.priceLocale

            if let price = formatter.string(from:
product.price) {

                cellPrice = price

            }


            cell.configureCell(imageName:
products[indexPath.row].productIdentifier, price:
cellPrice)

            return cell

        } else {

            return PurchaseCell()

        }

}
```

Let's make our Collection View cells selectable now, we'll need to add an *observer* here, and also send the payment to the queue.

```swift
func collectionView(_ collectionView: UICollectionView,
didSelectItemAt indexPath: IndexPath) {

        SKPaymentQueue.default().add(self)
```

```
    let payment = SKMutablePayment(product:
products[indexPath.row])

    payment.simulatesAskToBuyInSandbox = true

    SKPaymentQueue.default().add(payment)

}
```

One thing you need to remember is that we can't test `in-app purchases` without using our device. You will also need to create a `Sandbox` tester in your App Store Connect account. This cannot be your apple ID you already use.

Select `Users and Roles` and then select `Sandbox Testers` and add a tester.

Next, you need to log out of your apple ID in your `General` settings on your iPhone. Do not log in to your `Sandbox` account here, you will need to do this from inside the app when it prompts you. You are now ready to test your `in-app purchases`!

One last thing to do is connect an *IBAction* to your restore button and add one line of code to it and that's it! All your purchases will be restored.

```
@IBAction func restoreBtnPressed(_ sender: AnyObject) {

SKPaymentQueue.default().restoreCompletedTransactions()

    }
```

Congratulations!

That's all you need to do, to set up `in-app purchases`. Obviously, wherever I printed *purchase* and called a *UIAlert* view, you can add more code to maintain and change your data whether you are using Firebase or core data to keep track of purchases.

Wrapping up

That is all it takes to make in-app purchases. We covered a lot in this section. First we learned how to navigate through App Store Connect and register our app ID for in-app purchases. Then we got multiple tiers set up and connected the app store with our app. Lastly, we learned how to create a sandbox user to test our in-app purchases so we don't actually get charged in our testing phases.

Exercise

I am going to leave you with a final challenge. Implement in-app purchases into one of your apps. Make it possible to track users' purchases and start making money with your apps!

Chapter 24: Submitting to the App Store

There is nothing more exciting than taking your project which has taken your sleep, sweat, and tears and uploading it to the App Store to be seen by the masses. Let's learn how to submit an app to the App Store.

What you will learn

- Overview of Provisioning
- Adding your development account
- Creating & installing Development Certificates/Profiles
- Creating & installing Production Certificates/Profiles
- Adding an App to App Store Connect
- Archiving a release build
- Submitting an App to the App Store

Key Terms

- Certificate
- App ID
- Provisioning Profile

Congratulations! You've finally made it to the point in your development career when you're ready to show the world what you've done. It's time to change the world with your killer app! Let's learn how to upload it to the App Store and release it to the masses.

First let's begin with a flyover of the provisioning process and I will explain what some new terms and concepts mean.

Overview of Provisioning

Provisioning is simply a way of providing something (ie. your app) or making something available to a group of people. The process of making our app available to others via provisioning can cause some headaches. But thankfully Apple has done lots of great work to make this process easier than ever before. The amount of steps needed to get your app on the App Store may seem overwhelming at first, but don't worry - we'll take it step by step.

Checking Out Our Apple Developer Account

First, go to developer.apple.com and click 'Account' on the top right.

Log in with your Apple ID and if you haven't already bought an Apple Developer subscription ($99/yr.) now would be the time to do so because what I will show you in this chapter requires you to have a paid Apple Developer account.

Once you are signed in, click on 'Certificates, Identifiers, & Profiles' and on the following screen you will see several sections. On the left, there is a menu with the major sections Certificates, Identifiers, Devices, Profiles, Keys, and More. Within each section are more specific options that we won't go over until that section is covered in more detail later on in this chapter.

We will now talk about some of the main components inside these sections.

Certificates

A certificate is basically a security measure that allows you to develop and deploy apps. A certificate is provided by Apple and it links your specific computer to your developer account. Any app that you create on your computer gets signed with your certificate (Figure 24.0).

Figure 24.0

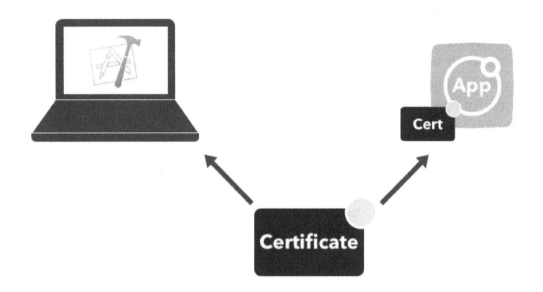

App IDs

An App ID is a unique identifier that helps to set your app apart from any other app. When you submit your app to the App Store, Apple requires it to have this identifier so that it can be separate from all other apps in it's marketplace.

The `App ID` we use in Xcode will need to be the same as the one we use in our Apple Developer account when trying to submit it to the App Store.

An App ID also informs Apple of what features your app uses (i.e. Push Notifications, Apple Pay, SiriKit, etc.).

When you go to create one in your Apple Developer account, you can tick boxes to enable these features. More on that later.

Devices

This section is for your test devices. The ones you can register in your Apple Developer account for development purposes. You may be wondering, "Do I need to register my iPhone or iPad to test my own apps?" The answer, thankfully, is no.

You actually don't even need a paid developer account to test apps on a local device via Lightning cable, but that is beside the point! If you want to build an app over the Internet to many test devices (i.e. beta testing via TestFlight) or via Ad-Hoc, the devices must be registered here.

Profiles

A `provisioning profile` has two main types - Development and Distribution.

A Development `provisioning profile` allows for us to code-sign an app so that it can be installed and tested on various devices via TestFlight or via an Ad-Hoc server. A Distribution `provisioning profile` allows for an app to be submitted to the App Store.

When we create a `provisioning profile`, it will contain our app and allow us to either work towards development or towards distribution.

We will create a profile like this in our Apple Developer account. It will pass through the certificate we created for verification and then will be usable by Xcode. For uploading to the App Store, it works similarly but in reverse. We can use a production `provisioning profile` to send our project from Xcode through our certificate, then through our `provisioning profile`, and to Apple.

This section has served as a very general overview of what we can do in our Apple Developer account. In following the sections, we will go into specific details about each section and how it applies to us as a developer.

Setting Up A Project

Creating A New Xcode Project

First, open Xcode if you haven't already and click `Create New Project` > `Single View App` > `Next`. Give your project a name like *ProvisioningDemo*. Click `Next`. Choose somewhere to save this project file and click `Create` to save it.

We will use this project for the duration of this chapter to help us in installing certificates, provisioning profiles, and submitting to the App Store.

Adding Your Developer Account

Now that we have a project set up, we need to add a development account via our Apple ID so that we can connect Xcode to our developer account. Go to `Xcode` > `Preferences` > `Accounts` and click the + button at the bottom left-hand side of the window. Select `Apple ID` > `Continue` and log in to your Apple ID connected with your Apple Developer account.

After logging in, you should see your Apple ID show up in the `Apple IDs` section on the left. If you click on it, you will see your role under that account. Most likely, you will see `Admin` or `Member` depending if you're working alone or with a team.

If we go back into our Xcode project settings, we can see that under `Signing & Capabilities` > `Signing` there is a new drop-down menu called `Team` where you can select a development team (Figure 24.1):

Figure 24.1

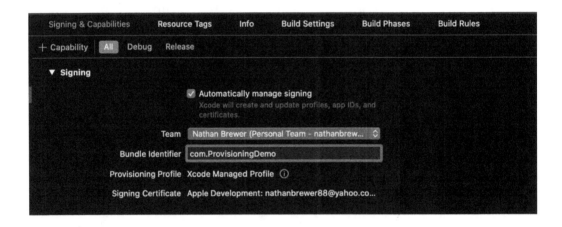

Installing Development Certificates & Provisioning Profiles

Let's set up our project to be available to developers on our team or to beta testers with a Development `provisioning profile`.

Setting Up

First, while in the `Signing` settings notice that there is a check box selected which says, "Automatically manage signing".

Beneath it, there is a message - "Xcode will create and update profiles, app IDs, and certificates." This means that Xcode can and will manage everything we need to do in this chapter, but as it can be a bit buggy, we can't always trust that it will work perfectly. You are learning the manual method to provisioning in case the automatic method doesn't work properly.

Now, look up at the `General` > `Identity` section and notice that our app has a field for `Display Name`, `Bundle Identifier`, `Version`, and `Build` (Figure 24.2). We want to pay attention to the `Bundle Identifier` because that is what we will actually paste into our Apple Developer account in a moment so that we can link our app to our Apple Developer account.

Figure 24.2

Copy the `Bundle Identifier` from Xcode. We will use it in a moment.

Creating an App ID

Go to developer.apple.com and click `Account` at the top. Sign in to your Apple Developer account if you haven't already.

Click on `Certificates, Identifiers, and Profiles` just as we did before. Go to the `Identifiers` section, then click the + sign nexct to the `Identifiers` header. You will see the screen as shown in Figure 24.3:

379

Figure 24.3

On the following page be sure **App IDs** is selected and click **Continue**. Next let's add to the **Description** field. This will be the app name as you'd like it to appear. For our app, we will enter in "Provisioning Demo".

The next field is **Bundle ID**, we need to select the **Explicit** button under the **App ID Prefix** section.

This is where you get to paste in that **Bundle Identifier** you copied from Xcode - get excited!

Figure 24.4

Next, if you want an app to use any of the services listed below in **Capabilities**, you need to tick those boxes. As you can see, I went ahead and ticked **Push Notifications** as that is a commonly used service in mobile apps. Note: You can always edit your App ID later on and add/remove services.

After you've filled out the **Name** and **Bundle ID** fields and have ticked the boxes for the services that you want, click the **Continue** button at the top right.

The page that follows simply is a confirmation of your choices. Look it over carefully and make sure that you've entered everything as you have planned. If you need to change something, there is an `Back` button at the top right of the page. Note that `Game Center` and `In-App Purchases` are always enabled and ready for use (with the proper configuration) and `Push Notifications` are shown as configurable by default. If everything is good to go, click `Register` to create and save your App ID.

Creating A Development Certificate

Now that we have a unique identifier set up for our app, we need to create a certificate which will allow us to securely send our app to other developers within our team or deploy it to beta testers.

We need to create what is called a Development certificate. You should see the menu containing the `Certificates, Identifiers, & Profiles`. Within the `Certificates` section, click the + button.

Make sure you tick the box `iOS App Development` that is listed in the `Software` section.

Click `Continue` and on the next screen you will see that you need to create a `CSR` file. CSR stands for "Certificate Signing Request" and we can create one using an app already on our Mac.

To do so, press ⌘ + `Space` to use Spotlight Search and search for `Keychain Access`. You can also find it by going to `Applications` > `Utilities` > `Keychain Access`.

Creating a CSR File

The whole point of creating a development certificate is to link our physical machine to our Apple Developer account, so we need to request that our certificate be signed by the `Certificate Authority`.

To do this, click `Keychain Access` > `Certificate Assistant` > `Request a Certificate From a Certificate Authority...` (Figure 24.5):

Figure 24.5

On the following screen (Figure 24.6), fill in your User Email Address with your Apple ID email and tick the box entitled Saved to disk. Click Continue. Choose a place to save this file (I chose the Desktop), and click Save.

Figure 24.6

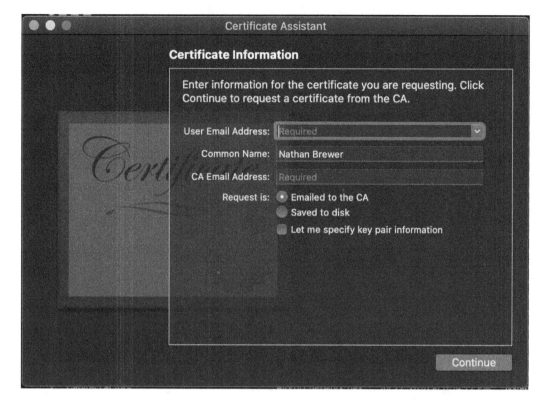

Back in your web browser, click `Choose File` and upload the file we just created called `CertificateSigningRequest.certSigningRequest`.

Click `Continue` to finish making your Development certificate.

Downloading and Installing a Development Certificate

You should now see the certificate you just created and a `Download` button at the top right. Click it to download the certificate, then double-click the downloaded file to install it into Xcode.

Creating a Development Provisioning Profile

Now that we have a certificate linking our physical computer to our Apple Developer account, we need to create a `provisioning profile` so that we can actually send our project to a development test device.

Go back into your Apple Developer account, go out of the `Certificates` section and into the `Profiles` section, and click on + icon, same as we have done in the last two sections.

Select `iOS App Development` and click `Continue`. Next, we need to select the App ID we created earlier for our *Provisioning Demo* project. Select it from the drop-down menu if it isn't selected already (Figure 24.7):

Figure 24.7

‹ All Profiles

Generate a Provisioning Profile

Select Type   ›   Configure   ›   Generate   ›   Download

Select an App ID
If you plan to use services such as Game Center, In-App Purchase, and Push Notifications, or want a Bundle ID unique to a single app, use an explicit App ID. If you want to create one provisioning profile for multiple apps or don't need a specific Bundle ID, select a wildcard App ID. Wildcard App IDs use an asterisk (*) as the last digit in the Bundle ID field.

App ID:

Provisioning Demo (4P43JC4PE2.com.nathan.provisioningDen ˅

Click `Continue` and on the following screen select the appropriate development certificate for your device which we made earlier. Click `Continue` to move on.

The following screen prompts you to select devices which you want your project to be able to be built to. If you want to register team members devices, you can do that back in the `Devices` section on the main screen of your Apple Developer account. Select any or all devices that you'd like and click `Continue`.

Lastly, we need to give a name to our profile which will be seen in the main menu. I named mine `ProvisioningDemoProfileDev` to be specific and clear about the type of profile that it is (Figure 24.8):

Figure 24.8

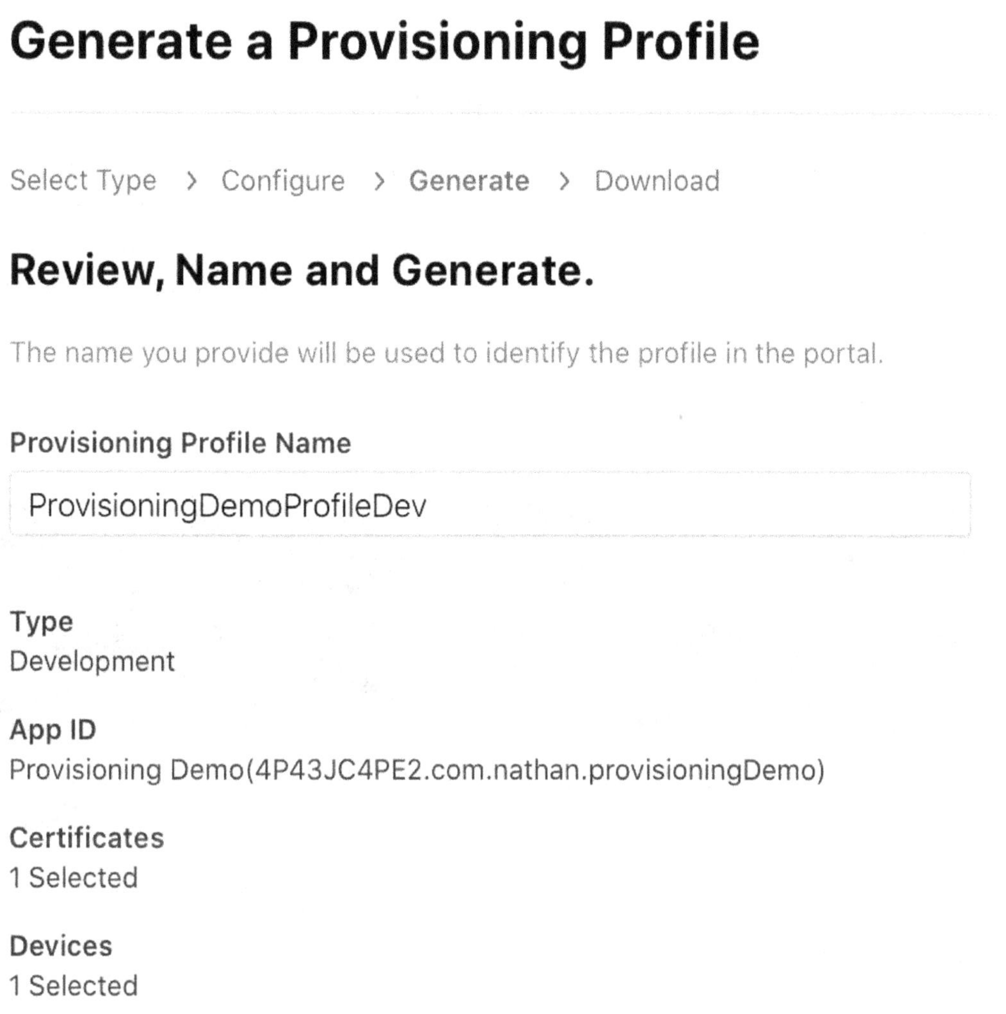

Generate a Provisioning Profile

Select Type > Configure > **Generate** > Download

Review, Name and Generate.

The name you provide will be used to identify the profile in the portal.

Provisioning Profile Name

ProvisioningDemoProfileDev

Type
Development

App ID
Provisioning Demo(4P43JC4PE2.com.nathan.provisioningDemo)

Certificates
1 Selected

Devices
1 Selected

Click `Continue` again and you will be brought to a page where you can download your development `provisioning    profile`. So, click `Download` and double-click the file to install it into Xcode.

Checking Build Settings

Now that our profile is installed, we need to check our build settings in Xcode to make sure that it's configured properly for development. With the `ProvisioningDemo` project open, navigate to your project's settings and in the menu select `Build  Settings`, then scroll down and find the `Signing` section. Expand the `Code Signing Identity` option. Notice that for `Debug` and `Release`, the option `Don't Code Sign` is selected. This may or may not be the case for your project, but what it means is that Xcode can only work with development devices.

You can't submit an app to the App Store without code-signing and we can't even send the build to other developers this way, because code-signing is a way to ensure that our project is being accessed by only those whom we've given access. It is best practice to select either the generic `iOS Developer` profile or our explicit development profile like the one we just created. In Figure 24.9 below, I selected `iOS Developer` under the `Debug` menu for development:

Figure 24.9

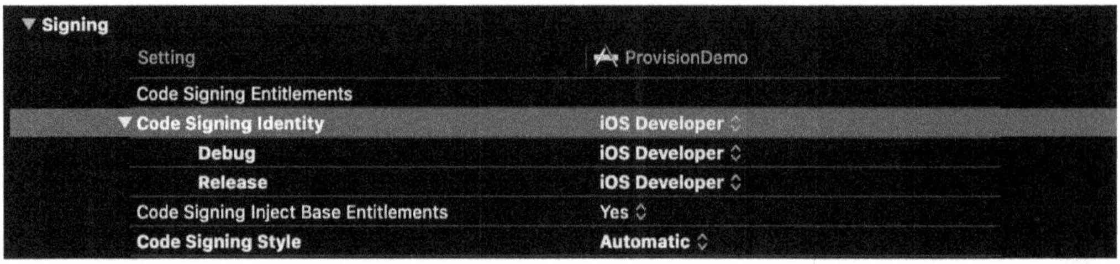

Installing Production Certificates & Provisioning Profiles

A Production certificate and production provisioning profiles are what allow us to submit our app to the App Store for the world to download and enjoy!

To create one, we need to start back at the Apple Developer portal like before. The process to create certificates and provisioning profiles for *Production* is basically the same as making one for development with a few key differences.

In the `Certificates` menu, click the + sign at the top to create a new production certificate. On the screen that follows, select `iOS Distribution (App Store and Ad Hoc)` under the `Software` category. This is so we can connect our project to the App Store or to beta testers via *TestFlight* or an *Ad Hoc* network later on.

Click `Continue` to move on.

Now we need to create a `CSR` request just like before. If you'd like, you can actually use the same `.certSigningRequest` file you saved before. Click `Choose File...` and select the same `.certSigning-Request` file from earlier. Click `Continue` to upload that file and finish making our `Production` certificate.

Now we can download that certificate just like before by clicking on the `Download` button at the top right. Double-click the downloaded file to install the certificate.

Now that we have a certificate in place, we need to create a `provisioning profile` for the distribution of our app. In the Apple Developer portal, leave the `Certificates` section and go into `Profile`. Click the + button to create a new `provisioning profile`.

On the page that follows, tick the box `App Store` under the `Distribution` section.

Then click `Continue`. Next, select the App ID for the app you want to submit (i.e. ProvisioningDemo) and click `Continue` once more.

Select the appropriate `iOS Distribution` certificate on the next page. You should be able to see the one you just made in the last section.

Click `Continue` and give your profile a name. I named mine `ProvisioningDemoDistribution` which is specific to our app and describes the type of profile.

Click `Continue` one last time and click the `Download` button to download your distribution `provisioning profile`. Double-click the downloaded file to install it.

Checking Build Settings

We are now going to modify the build settings in our Xcode project. Earlier, we set up our project's build settings for Development and now we're going to set it up for Production.

In your Xcode project, navigate back to the project settings and click on `Build Settings`, then find the `Signing` section. In the expanded `Code Signing Identity`, under the `Release` section, select `iOS Distribution` from both the `Release` and `Any iOS SDK` dropdown menus (Figure24.10):

Figure 24.10

Signing	
Setting	⚏ ProvisionDemo
Code Signing Entitlements	
▼ Code Signing Identity	<Multiple values> ◇
Debug	iOS Developer ◇
Any SDK ◇	iOS Developer ◇
Release	⊕ iOS Distribution ◇
Any SDK ◇	iOS Distribution ◇
Code Signing Inject Base Entitlements	Yes ◇

At this point, we have set up Xcode as far as we need to. Let's move on.

Using App Store Connect to Create An App Project

To submit our app to the App Store, we must first create an app project on a website called `App Store Connect`.

This site is linked with your Apple ID already, so we don't need to create a new account or anything.

Go to https://appstoreconnect.apple.com in your web browser and log in with your Apple ID. Click `My Apps`, click the + sign in the top left-hand side of the window, then click `New App` (Figure 24.11):

Figure 24.11

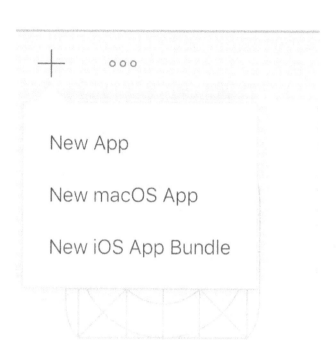

You should see a pop-up appear asking for information regarding this new app. Ensure that the `iOS` box is ticked and then look at the text fields beneath it. You must enter the `Name`, `Primary Language`, `Bundle ID`, and `SKU` fields.

For the `Name` enter the app name that you would like to appear in the App Store. Bear in mind that your app name has the **most** significance to your app being discovered. This is why when you go to download an app like `YouTube`, the actual title of the `YouTube` app at the moment is "YouTube: Watch, Listen, Stream".

This is because the `YouTube` team knows that most people search for those kinds of terms when they are looking for an app like `YouTube`. It actually has the most weight out of anything else that you do to optimize your app, so use your app name to your advantage.

Choose the `Primary Language` your app will use. Our `Bundle ID` is the one we made earlier. If you're following this example, it will be called `ProvisioningDemo`.

The `SKU` of an app is a unique identifier which sets your app apart. Think of it like a bar-code for your app. I chose `ProvisioningDemo-FunTimes` just to have a little fun with it.

After all the required information is entered, click `Create`. The screen that follows is where you need to enter in any relevant information about your app.

First, ensure that the name is correct and that the Bundle ID matches the one you created earlier. It should, but it's best to be safe here. The `Privacy Policy URL` field is where you need to link to your app's Privay Policy. If you don't yet have one, do some research on how to write one and throw it up on a website. You can either buy a domain and design a website for your app (probably a good idea in the long run), or just create a free website using something like Google Sites or Wix.

The reason for needing a Privacy Policy is stated by Apple on this page:

> *A URL that links to your organization's privacy policy. Privacy policies are required for apps that are Made for Kids or offer auto-renewable or free subscriptions. They are also required for apps with account registration, apps that access a user's existing account, or as otherwise required by law. Privacy policies are recommended for apps that collect user- or device-related data.*

So if your app is described in any way by the following statement, you need a Privacy Policy.

Next, you should select a `Category` for your app. Click on the `Primary` drop down (this one is required) and select the category that best fits your app. If you'd like, select a secondary category as well. Click `Save` at the top to save your progress thus far.

Setting Up Our App's Price

Click on `Pricing and Availability` on the left-hand side of the window and you will see the following page appear:

Click on the drop-down menu that says `Choose...` to select a pricing tier. If you want your app to be free, simply select `USD 0 (Free)` as you'd expect. If you'd like to set a fixed price, do so by clicking on the price in the drop-down menu.

Once you've saved your changes, you can even set up price staggering which allows you to set a launch promo price or even schedule a discounted price for your app.

Now we need to add some super critical stuff to our app project - `metadata`!

Adding App Metadata

On the left-hand side, click on `1.0 Prepare for Submission` (Figure 24.12) and you should see this screen appear (Figure 24.13):

Figure 24.12

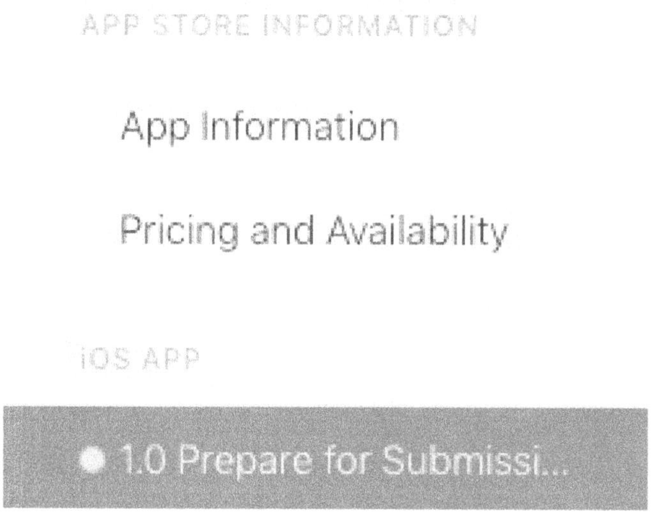

APP STORE INFORMATION

App Information

Pricing and Availability

iOS APP

● 1.0 Prepare for Submissi...

Figure 24.13

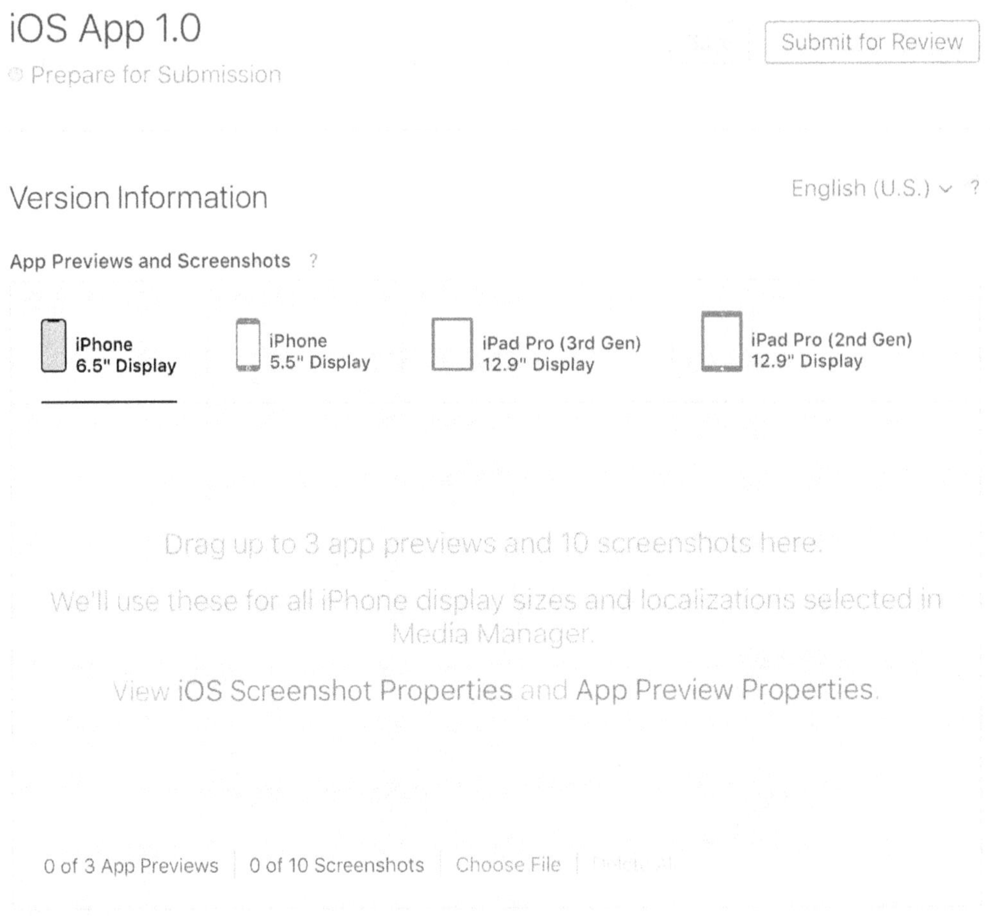

iOS App 1.0   Submit for Review
Prepare for Submission

Version Information   English (U.S.) ∨ ?

App Previews and Screenshots   ?

iPhone   iPhone   iPad Pro (3rd Gen)   iPad Pro (2nd Gen)
6.5" Display   5.5" Display   12.9" Display   12.9" Display

Drag up to 3 app previews and 10 screenshots here.

We'll use these for all iPhone display sizes and localizations selected in
Media Manager.

View iOS Screenshot Properties and App Preview Properties.

0 of 3 App Previews | 0 of 10 Screenshots | Choose File |

Apple requires that you include an app preview video and up to 10
screenshots of your app.

If you look at the most successful apps on the App Store, they are
doing an amazing job at utilizing this space.

Helpful Hint:

*An app preview video can easily be created by using Quick-
Time's Movie Recording feature. Connect your iPhone via Lightning cable and change cameras from your Mac's FaceTime camera to your iPhone! You can then record input from your iPhone
and save it as a video file for editing later on.*

Apple requires App Store screenshots at each device resolution (6.5-inch device, 5.5-inch device). These screenshots will scale down for smaller devices. Whenever your screenshots are created, upload them to `App Store Connect` by dragging them on the grey rectangle in Figure 24.13.

Scroll down and we can add our app *description*, *keywords*, *support URL*, and *marketing URL*.

Your app description is important and I suggest that you research what the big guys are doing and seek to emulate them. Find an app on the App Store like Uber, Instagram, Snapchat, etc. and see how they've formatted and written their app description.

Your keywords are also important as they are used to show your app when a person searches for certain keywords. Your keywords should be specific and relevant to your app. Think of what your prospective user would search for to find your app. Your support URL can be a website you own or a free website as long as it is a legitimate website where users can find more information about your app. The marketing URL is optional but if you have a URL with marketing information about your app (perhaps a press kit, etc.) you should include it here.

Once that's all squared away and filled out nicely, we need to keep scrolling down the page. Scroll past `Build` for now and move on to `General Information` (Figure 24.14):

Figure 24.14

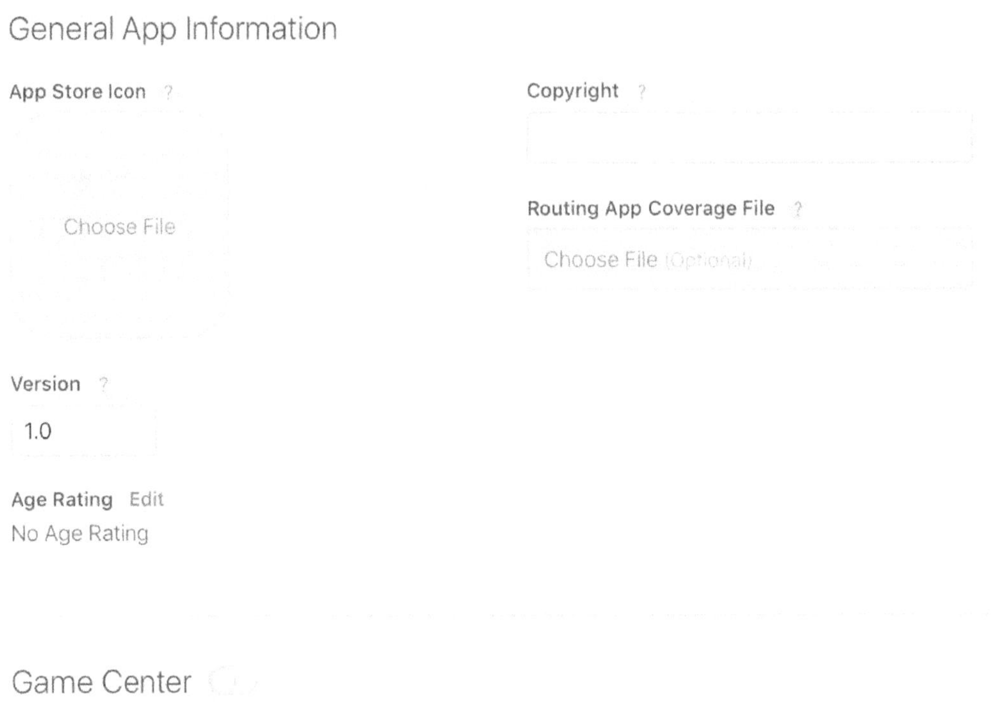

General App Information

App Store Icon ?   Copyright ?

                                           Routing App Coverage File ?

Choose File   Choose File (Optional)

Version ?

1.0

Age Rating   Edit
No Age Rating

Game Center

This is where you need to enter in all relevant information for your app like copyright information. You also need to upload an app icon with these requirements:

> *This icon will be used on the App Store. For apps built with Xcode 9 or later, add this icon in the build. For apps built with earlier versions of Xcode, add the icon here. It must not contain layers or rounded corners.*

You also need to choose a version number. This number needs to match the version number in your project settings in Xcode. If you aren't sure what to put here, go to your Xcode app project and open the project settings.

The version number is in a text field directly beneath the `Bundle Identifier` field. Make sure that this number matches what is in `App Store Connect`.

After uploading and entering in all required data, scroll down to the `App Review Information` section.

You need to give Apple your *name*, *phone number*, *email address*, and a demo account (should your app require any type of authentication). There is also a field for notes which, according to Apple, is meant for:

Additional information about your app that can help during the review process. Include information that may be needed to test your app, such as app-specific settings.

Once you've entered that, we have finally reached the bottom of the page. We need to decide when to release.

The options are shown in Figure 24.15. As you can see, `Automatically release this version` is selected by default:

Figure 24.15

Alright, phew! We made it! Almost there... Click `Save` at the top of the page because now it's time to upload a build to `App Store Connect` so that we can submit it once and for all! Woohoo!

Archiving and Submitting a Release Build to the App Store

Now that we have our certificates and profiles installed as well as our app metadata entered in App Store Connect, we are finally ready to submit our app to the App Store! Yes!

Switch on over to Xcode and open `ProvisioningDemo.xcode-proj` if it isn't already open. Make sure that you are in the project settings then click on `Signing & Capabilities`. Here you can have Xcode Automatically manage signing or if you would prefer to manage selecting the specific profile, you can uncheck that box. Once you do, under the `Provisioning Profile` option, select the Distribution provisioning profile we created earlier in this chapter called `ProvisioningDemoDistribution`.

You will see the `Signing Certificate` fill in automatically with the certificate attached to the profile. You can continue with the manual settings, or allow Xcode to manage signing. It should look similar to Figure 24.16:

Figure 24.16

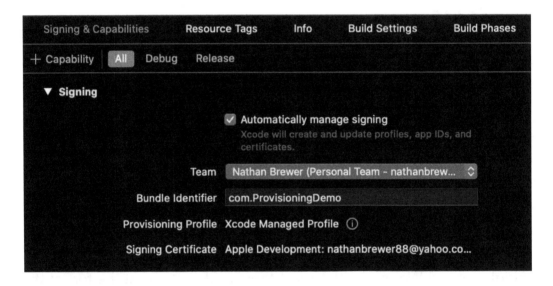

Bear in mind, this will disable you from building your project to a device or the Simulator until you switch this setting back to your development profile.

Changing Our Build Scheme

In the top-left of your Xcode window, click on your project name and click `Edit Scheme` (Figure 24.17):

Figure 24.17

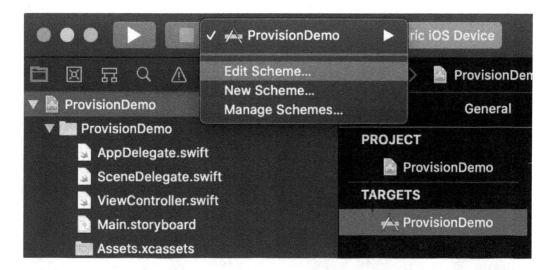

On the screen that pops up you need to click on `Archive` from the menu on the left-hand side.

When submitting a build of our app to the App Store, we need to archive it. Imagine that you're sealing off this build of your project so that it is uploaded to `App Store Connect`, just the way it is.

On the `Archive` screen, we need to verify that `Release` is selected from the `Build Configuration` drop-down menu. Then give the archive a name. Afterward, click `Close` to close out and change our Build Scheme.

Archiving A Release

Next, at the top-left of the Xcode window, we need to switch from a Simulator device to either:

(1) Our actual device plugged via Lightning cable.

(2) `Generic iOS Device`.

Choose one of those options and click to select it.

Here comes the exciting part! In the menu bar at the top of Xcode, click `Product > Archive` and allow for Xcode to do it's thing. It will appear as if it's building as normal, but when it's finished it will open up a new application called `Organizer`. It can take quite a while for your app to successfully archive and copy into `Organizer`, so give it some time.

Once `Organizer` has opened, you will see the following screen (Figure 24.18):

Figure 24.18

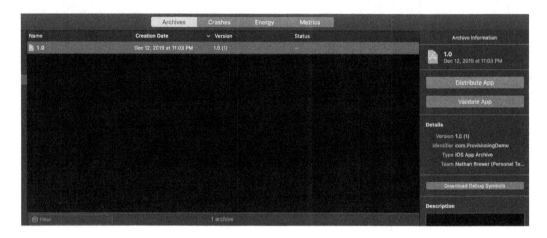

Before we do anything, we should validate our app. This will basically run our app through an automated version of some of Apple's tests they run on our app to make sure it's good to go to the App Store.

This is a huge time-saver because in the good ol' days, you had to submit your app to Apple and wait 7 days just to tell you that you needed to fix some really minor things. Being able to validate it ourselves means that we don't have to waste our time.

Click the `Validate...` button and on the pop-up that follows, you need to select the appropriate development team.

Choose the one you've been using, then click `Continue`.

The pop-up will show the progress of the preparation of our archive. After the archive is ready to be validated, you will see a confirmation screen.

When you're ready to validate your project, click `Validate` and Xcode will do it's thing. After a while, your archive will be uploaded. Should there be any warnings or errors, they will be displayed afterwards. Move by forward by clicking `Done`.

Believe it or not, our build has been uploaded to `App Store Connect`. Go back into your `App Store Connect` account and open up the app project we started earlier. Click `1.0 Prepare for Submission`.

If you scroll to the `Build` section, you should now see the build we just validated and uploaded. It should have a status of `Processing` at the moment.

To officially submit your build to the App Store, ensure that all of the information from above is completed in full. Click `Save` to save all changes then click `Submit for Review` and your app will be sent to Apple for review!

`WOOHOO!`

You finally did it. You've uploaded your first app to the App Store! You will need to wait a few days to hear back from Apple and to be honest, expect that your app won't be approved at first.

Apple is very picky about the apps on their App Store. It is how they ensure they have a top-of-the-line marketplace.

Of course, make sure you refer to Apple's documentation and guidelines for uploading to the App Store which can be found in their developer documentation online. Remember, Google is your friend.

Wrapping up

Wow! As you can see there are quite a few steps to get your app onto the App Store. Apple has helped with a lot of this actually by enabling automatic signing, app ID, and certificate creation, but you now know the entire process.

You can now upload apps to the App Store manually if the automatic features aren't working. As a developer, it is good to learn how these things work behind the scenes.

Pat yourself on the back. Amazing work!

Chapter 25: iOS 13 Features

In this chapter we're going to learn how to work with some amazing new features found in iOS 13. We'll break this chapter up into three parts.

Dark Mode

Learn how to support the new Dark Mode in your apps to stay current with latest iOS design guidelines.

Haptic Feedback Generator

Add engaging interactions to your app while also providing accessibility and usability to a wide range of users.

SF Symbols

iOS 13 brings more than 1500 built-in icons that you can use in your apps. Learn how to use and customize SF Symbols to bring quick visuals into your apps.

Part 1: Dark Mode

What you will learn

- Design apps to support Dark Mode

Resources

`Download here:` https://github.com/devslopes/iOS13-book-assets/wiki/iOS13-Book

In this chapter we'll be building UI for a simple login screen that can toggle between light and dark mode. We will explore how to use Apple's system colors and how to create your own color themes that will support the new Dark Mode.

Here is an example of the finished login screen with both light and dark mode active.

Figure 25.0

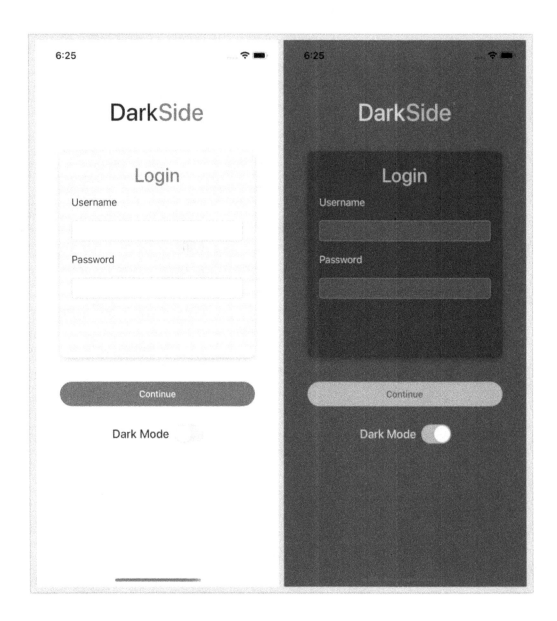

Creating an Xcode Project

Begin by opening Xcode, select `File -> New -> Project`. Be sure you have `iOS` selected, then choose `Single View App`, and then click `Next`. Give your project a name. I named mine `DarkSide`. Use `Swift` for the language and `Storyboard` for the user interface. For this project you can *uncheck* `Core Data`, `UI Tests` and `Unit Tests`, and then click Next. Save the project wherever you would like and click Create.

Testing Dark Mode

Before we begin the project, let's go over a few different ways to toggle between light and dark mode. Also, be sure you are running Xcode 11+. Go ahead and run your newly created project in the simulator. You should see a white screen at this point. With the simulator still running, go back into Xcode and you will see a new symbol on the Degub Options bar. Click the Environment Overrides button, then in the pop up menu toggle the Interface Style to On and select your light and dark mode options like shown in (Figure 25.1).

Figure 25.1

Switch between the Dark and Light options and then look back at the simulator. You should see it change from the white to the black background. Now, go ahead and stop the running app in Xcode. Then go back to the Simulator. While on the Simulator, navigate to the Settings app and scroll down until you see the Developer option. Click Developer and you will see a toggle titled Dark Appearance.

These are a few methods for testing between light and dark mode. You can use these on any of your existing apps to see how they may look when iOS 13 users switch their phones to dark mode.

Prepare for Dark Mode

Apple has provided a series of system colors that will automatically adjust for Dark Mode. If you don't have a full time designer giving you custom theme colors, you will probably be best off using what apple provides. Here is an example of how some of Apple's colors adjust to Dark Mode.

Figure 25.2

Light	Dark	Name	API
R 0 G 64 B 221	R 64 G 156 B 255	Blue	systemBlue
R 36 G 138 B 61	R 48 G 219 B 91	Green	systemGreen
R 54 G 52 B 163	R 125 G 122 B 255	Indigo	systemIndigo
R 201 G 52 B 0	R 255 G 179 B 64	Orange	systemOrange

A full list can be found in the `Color` options in the Attributes Inspector.

For our project, I will show you how to create your own custom colors that adjust for light and dark mode. In Xcode's `Project Navigator`, select the `Assets.xcassets` file. At the bottom of the assets column, you will hit the + symbol and select `New Color Set` as shown in (Figure 25.6)

Figure 25.3

With the new color set selected:

1. Rename the color set to `primaryBackground`
2. Change **Appearances** to `Any, Dark`.
3. Selecting the `Any Appearance` color set, change the `Color -> Input Method` to `8-bit Hexadecimal`
4. Change the **Hex** value to `#FFFFFF`

Select the `Dark Appearance` color set, change to `8-bit Hexadecimal` and assign the **Hex** value to `#3D3D43`

Figure 25.4

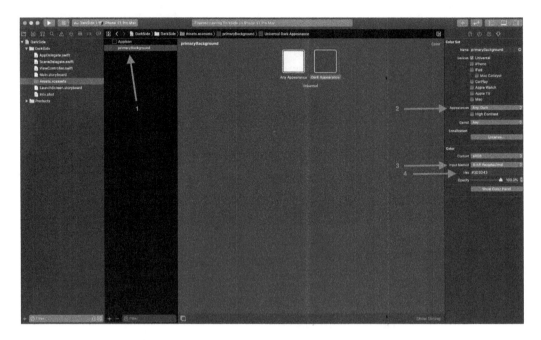

We will be creating 4 total custom color sets. Repeat the steps above, but with the following attributes:

Name	Any Appearance	Dark Appearance
secondaryBackground	#EDF0F5	#2B2A2F
primaryText	#0A152C	#CFCFCF
primaryButton	#5557A9	#9FA3F8

You should now have 4 custom color sets, each with a value for Any Appearance(Light Mode) and Dark Appearance(Dark Mode)

Building the UI

Now, let's go to our `Main.storyboard` file and start laying out the UI. You can use (Figure 25.0) as a reference at any point. First, select the ViewController's view. Go to the `Attributes  Inspector` and click the dropdown menu next to `Background`. This will open up all the system colors, recently used colors, and near the top you should see a new section called `Named Colors`. You should see the 4 custom color sets we just created, so for this view select the `primaryBackground` color.

As a side note, if you want to use any of your custom colors programmatically, you can assign them by initializing a `UIColor` with the `UIColor(named:)` initializer like this:

```
var someView.backgroundColor = UIColor(named:
"yourCustomColorName")
```

If you need backwards compatibility for older iOS versions, but want iOS 13 users to enjoy Dark Mode, your code might look like this:

```
if #available(iOS 13.0, *) {

    someView.backgroundColor = UIColor(named:
"yourCustomColorName")

} else {

    // Fallback on earlier versions

}
```

We will layout our UI starting from the top. The title `DarkSide` is actually two UILabels inside a Stack View. From the `Object Library` drag two labels onto the Storyboard canvas.

The first label will have the following attributes

- Text: `Dark`
- Color: `primaryText`
- Font: `System`
- Style: `Medium`
- Size: `40`

The second label will be the same, except with the following changes:
- Text: `Side`

- Color: `primaryButton`

Select both labels and hit the `Embed in` button on the bottom-right of the editor screen then select Stack View.

The Stack View attributes will be:

- Axis: `Horizontal`

407

- Alignment: `Fill`
- Distribution: `Fill`
- Spacing: `0`

Pin the StackView `top` constraint `40` from the superview and align `Horizontally in container`.

For the LoginCardView (we will actually name this later), drag a UIView below the title and from the **Add New Constraints** button, pin the `leading`, `top`, and `trailing` edges `40` from the superview. Then check the `Aspect Ratio` box. We want to make sure the aspect ratio is `1:1`. If it doesn't default to that, with the view selected go to the `Size Inspector` tab. Scroll down until you see the `Aspect Ratio` section. Click `Edit` on the constraint shown in that section, then in the `Multiplier` dropdown select the `1:1` Preset. Lastly, give this view a background color of **secondaryBackground**.

Drag a label inside the LoginCardView and add the following attributes:

- Text: `Login`
- Color: `primaryButton`
- Font: `System`
- Style: `Medium`
- Size: `32`

Pin the label `top` constraint `20` from the top of the LoginCardView and align `Horizontally in container`.

The login inputs will be two labels and two text fields. Drag them inside the LoginCardView in their proper order. Select the 4 objects and click the **Embed in** button and select Stack View.

The Stack View attributes will be:

- Axis: `Vertical`
- Alignment: `Fill`
- Distribution: `Fill Equally`
- Spacing: `10`

Pin the StackView `top`, `leading`, and `trailing` constraints `20` from the superview. Do *not* add a bottom constraint, this will allow the StackView to resize based on its contents.

The labels here will have the following attributes:

- Text: `Username` or `Password`
- Color: `primaryText`
- Font: `System`
- Style: `Regular`
- Size: `17`

For both of the text fields, go to the **Attributes Inspector** and change the text field `text` color to `primaryText` and the background color to `primaryBackground`.

We are almost done with the UI. Next, we will drag a UIButton underneath the LoginCardView and pin its `leading` and `trailing` edges `40` from the superview. Pin the button `top` constraint `40` from the bottom of the LoginCardView. Add a `height` of `40` as well. Change the button title to `Continue`, the text color to `primaryBackground` and the background color to `primaryButton`.

The last piece of UI will be a toggle used for switching between the light and dark color themes. Drag a label under the button and add the following attributes:

- Text: `Dark Mode`
- Color: `primaryText`
- Font: `System`
- Style: `Medium`
- Size: `20`

Next to the label, drag on a UISwitch. With the switch selected, in the **Attributes Inspector** change the `State` to `off`, and the `On Tint` to `primaryButton`. Select both the label and switch, click the `Embed In` button, click stack view. The stack view attributes should be:

- Axis: `Horizontal`
- Alignment: `Fill`
- Distribution: `Fill`
- Spacing: `8`

Pin the StackView `top` constraint `30` from the `bottom` of our button and align `Horizontally in container`.

Whew! That should be all for the UI. While we are still in the story-board let's connect some IBOutlets and an IBAction for our switch. Open the Assistant Editor (the hot key for this is Ctrl + Optn + Cmnd + return).

Select the LoginCardView and click + control drag into the text editor to make an IBOutlet and name it loginCardView. Select the button and make an IBOutlet named loginButton. We will use these outlets strictly for some design techniques in a moment. Now select the UISwitch and click + control drag to the text editor. Change the Connection to Action and Type to UISwitch and name it toggleDarkMode.

Your ViewController.swift file should look like this:

```
class ViewController: UIViewController {


    @IBOutlet weak var loginCardView: UIView!

    @IBOutlet weak var loginButton: UIButton!


    override func viewDidLoad() {
        super.viewDidLoad()
    }


    @IBAction func toggleDarkMode(_ sender: UISwitch) {
        //TO DO
    }
}
```

We will add a shadow and rounded corners to the loginCardView and loginButton using the didSet method. Change your @IBOutlets as follows:

```
@IBOutlet weak var loginCardView: UIView! {
```

```
        didSet {

            loginCardView.layer.cornerRadius = 10

            loginCardView.layer.shadowColor =
UIColor.black.cgColor

            loginCardView.layer.shadowRadius = 5

            loginCardView.layer.shadowOpacity = 0.3

            loginCardView.layer.shadowOffset = CGSize(width:
0, height: 3)

        }

}

@IBOutlet weak var loginButton: UIButton! {

    didSet {

        loginButton.layer.cornerRadius = 20

    }

}
```

Last but not least, we will add one line of code inside the `toggleDark-Mode` method to alternate between our color themes.

```
@IBAction func toggleDarkMode(_ sender: UISwitch) {

    overrideUserInterfaceStyle =
sender.isOn ? .dark : .light

}
```

Let's talk about the code above. The property `overrideUserInterfaceStyle` is the programmatic way to force select Dark Mode, regardless of the users phone settings. Depending on the state of the UISwitch, we toggle from `.light` to `.dark`

Go ahead and run the project and enjoy the hard work. Dark Mode is new, but soon users will begin to expect their apps to adjust according to this setting so be sure to design your apps with Dark Mode in mind!

Part 2: Haptic Feedback Generator

What you will learn

- How to customize Haptic Feedback

Key Terms

- Core Haptics
- Transient Events
- Continuous Events

What is Haptic Feedback?

Haptics are used to engage a user's sense of touch to signal a notification or an interaction with the screen's interface. These small vibrations are created with a linear actuator, opposed to the older rotating motors used in early iPhone models. Linear actuators are controlled by small magnets and coils, allowing it to deliver precise vibrations, or oscillate continuously. You may be familiar with some haptic events that Apple uses in standard UI elements such as `sliders`, `switches`, and `pickers`.

Core Haptics

With the release of iOS 13, Apple introduced `Core Haptics`, which is supported on iPhone 8 and newer. This framework allows us to customize a variety of vibrations with incredible precision using the iPhone's Taptic Engine.

There are two main types of haptic events that we can adjust when creating our own haptics. They are `Transient` and `Continuous`.

- `Transient` events could be described as similar to a click — small, brief, and distinct. They are typically used to signal a single event.

- `Continuous` events are vibrations, output by a sophisticated motor.

Within these two events, there are parameters that can be adjusted as well. The main ones being `sharpness` and `intensity`. Sharpness can be described as either a dull, or precise tap. Intensity is the relative strength of the vibration. It is easier to *demonstrate* the differences of these parameters than try to put them into words, so lets begin with a new project!

Building Our Project

Open up Xcode > `File` > `New` > `Project...`. Choose `Single View App` > `Next` and give it a name. I named my project `HappyHaptics` and saved it to my `Desktop`. In this project we are going to layout a simple UI. It is really a single button in the middle of the screen that when tapped ,will trigger a custom haptic event.

    Let's start first in the code. Head over to your `ViewController.swift` file. Underneath the `import UIKit` at the top, import the Core Haptics framework like this:

```
import CoreHaptics
```

Next, we will make a variable that will store an instance of the Core Haptics Engine. Now remember, not every phone can support Core Haptics, so we can't initialize our variable right away. Inside your class create your variable like this:

```
var engine: CHHapticEngine?
```

Start Your Engine

We can check if haptics are supported on the current device with the `CHHapticEngine.capabilitiesForHardware().supportsHaptics` method. Let's save this result to a variable to make it faster and easier to use in the future. Add the following code below your `engine` variable:

```
var supportsHaptics =
CHHapticEngine.capabilitiesForHardware().supportsHaptics
```

The result of this is a `Bool` and in our `viewDidLoad()` method we can check if haptics are supported. If they are, we will attempt to initialize and start our haptics engine.

```
override func viewDidLoad() {

  super.viewDidLoad()


  if supportsHaptics {

    do {

      engine = try CHHapticEngine()

      try engine?.start()

    } catch {

      // Handle error here

    }

  }

}
```

Initializing the `CHHapticEngine` can `throw` an error. So it requires a `do, catch` block, which will catch any errors if it fails to create the engine. If you were going to add any handlers to recover from a failed haptic, or if the engine stopped, then you would create them `before` you `start()` the engine. Go ahead and modify the `viewDidLoad()` method as follows:

```
override func viewDidLoad() {

  super.viewDidLoad()


  if supportsHaptics {

    do {
```

```
    engine = try CHHapticEngine()


    // stop handler
    engine?.stoppedHandler = { reason in
       print("haptic engine stopped:", reason)
    }


    //reset handler
    engine?.resetHandler = {
       do {
         try self.engine?.start()
       } catch {
         print("Unable to restart engine")
       }
    }


    try engine?.start()
  } catch {
    // Handle error here
    }
  }
}
```

When the app loads the haptic engine will be started, but we are not quite ready to play a custom haptic. The next piece is to create our haptic, which is known as a **CHHapticEvent**. A haptic event represents a single haptic. The event will be added to a **CHHapticPattern** object. Patterns can consist of a single simple event or multiple complex events. Once the pattern is ready we will pass it to an instance of **CHHaptic-**

`PatternPlayer` which will ultimately call it's `start(atTime:)` method. So let's build our first event!

Events, Patterns, and Players Oh My!

Let's build our first event inside a new function. Below the `viewDid-Load()` method create a function called `intenseAndDullHaptic()`. Now first thing we need to do when this gets called is check that the current device supports haptics. Even though we did this in `viewDid-Load()`, its good practice to ensure haptics are supported before we attempt to create any instance of a `CHHapticPattern` or `CHHaptic-PatternPlayer`. Inside the new function add a `guard` statement to ensure haptics are available, and if not we will `return` out of the function.

```
func intenseAndDullHaptic() {

  guard supportsHaptics else { return }


}
```

The `CHHapticEvent` takes three arguments. The `EventType` is either the `transient` or `continuous` type we described earlier. The `parameters` is an array of event parameters that define the haptics behavior. `relativeTime` specifies when the event begins in relation to when it is first called. Let's create two event parameters below our `guard` statement, then supply them to a `CHHapticEvent`:

```
func intenseAndDullpHaptic() {

  guard supportsHaptics else { return }


  let param1 =
CHHapticEventParameter(parameterID: .hapticIntensity,
value: 1)

  let param2 =
CHHapticEventParameter(parameterID: .hapticSharpness,
value: 0.1)
```

```
let event = CHHapticEvent(eventType: .hapticTransient,
parameters: [param1, param2], relativeTime: 0)

}
```

Both the .hapticIntensity and .hapticSharpness can have an adjusted value between 0.0, being the weakest, and 1.0 being the strongest. We selected the .hapticTransient in the event type to create a small, distinct, and intensely dull haptic. Creating the pattern and player will be performed in a similar fashion as creating the engine, using a do, catch block. Add the following below your event:

```
do {

    let pattern = try CHHapticPattern(events: [event],
parameters: [])

    let player = try engine?.makePlayer(with: pattern)

    try player?.start(atTime: 0)

  } catch {

    print("Unable to play pattern")

  }
```

Like we discussed, we have made a series of events, passed them into a pattern, asked the engine to make a player object with that pattern, then attempted to start those events in the player. We are so close to being able to test this, now we just need a way to call the function. Let's make an IBAction that will call our intenseAndDullHaptic() . Then we will connect it to a button on the Storyboard in a moment.

```
@IBAction func playHaptic(_ sender: UIButton) {

        intenseAndDullHaptic()

  }
```

Head over to your Main.storyboard and from the Object Library drag on a button to the center of the screen. Hit the Align button to center the button Horizontally and Vertically in container. To connect this button to your IBAction, right click the View Con-

troller in the `Document Outline`. The popup should have a **Received Actions** section at the bottom with our `playHaptic` method. Hover over the circle to the right until you see a **+**, then click and drag over to your button on the screen to connect. Select the **Touch Up Inside** event then go ahead and run your project! Be sure you are running it on an actual device, not the simulator. When you tap the button you should feel our custom haptic event!

Ramping Up

That was cool, but lets turn things up a notch. Lets customize a **continuous** event type now. Make a function called `highScore()`, which is what this haptic makes me think of, and put in the `supportsHaptic` check.

```
func highScore() {

  guard supportsHaptics else { return }



}
```

For this event we want to increment the `intensity` and `sharpness` over the duration of 1 second. Lets use a **for in** loop to accomplish this. Place the following inside our `highScore()` function:

```
  var events = [CHHapticEvent]()


  for i in 0...10 {

    let value = Double(i) / Double(10)



    let param1 =
CHHapticEventParameter(parameterID: .hapticIntensity,
value: Float(value))

    let param2 =
CHHapticEventParameter(parameterID: .hapticSharpness,
value: Float(value))
```

```
    let event =
CHHapticEvent(eventType: .hapticContinuous, parameters:
[param1, param2], relativeTime: value, duration: 0.2)

    events.append(event)

  }
```

Since the haptic parameter values range from 0.0 to 1.0, we want to increment by 0.1 on each iteration. the `let value = Double(i) / Double(10)` will give us that decimal value we want.

We have an **events** variable that will add each event to an array and later pass into the **CHHapticPattern**. You will notice on the event we have an extra argument called **duration**. This is simply how long each event will last, we specify 0.2 so the events will slightly overlap each other to make it feel like a more continuous and gradual pattern.

We can initialize the pattern and player the same way we did on our **intenseAndDullHaptic()** function. Your **highScore()** method should look like this:

```
func highScore() {

  var events = [CHHapticEvent]()


  for i in 0...10 {

    let value = Double(i) / Double(10)


    let param1 =
CHHapticEventParameter(parameterID: .hapticIntensity,
value: Float(value))

    let param2 =
CHHapticEventParameter(parameterID: .hapticSharpness,
value: Float(value))

    let event =
CHHapticEvent(eventType: .hapticContinuous, parameters:
[param1, param2], relativeTime: value, duration: 0.2)

    events.append(event)

  }
```

```
do {

    let pattern = try CHHapticPattern(events: events,
parameters: [])

    let player = try engine?.makePlayer(with: pattern)

    try player?.start(atTime: 0)

} catch {

    print("Unable to play pattern")

}

}
```

replace the `intenseAndDullHaptic()` function in the `IBAction` with our new `highScore()` function and launch the project. Do you feel like you just got a high score?!

Wrapping Up

We've covered an introduction to `Core Haptics` and even made two of our own events. You should continue to explore adding events, and altering values and make some of your own haptics for your apps.

Part 3 - SF Symbols

What you will learn

- How to use the new catalog of SF Symbols
- How to configure symbols size, weight, and colors

What Are SF Symbols?

Have you ever wished you could use some basic icons without having to hire a designer or take the time to make your own? Well, thanks to the release of `SF Symbols` in iOS 13, you now have access to over `1,500` highly configurable symbols! Apple has designed these to work seamlessly with the San Francisco system font. This means that each symbol's height and weight will be consistent with the sizes and weights of the fonts in your app.

How do we use SF Symbols?

Apple has built a convenient Mac App called `SF Symbols` that is a catalog for all 1,500+ symbols available. I highly recommend downloading it from the App Store and browsing through them. A screenshot of the Mac App can be seen in (Figure 25.5)

Figure 25.5

Symbols can be exported from the app, but that's not necessary in order to use them inside Xcode. Lets take a look at how we can access and configure them in the code.

Swift now provides us with a `UIImage(systemName:)` initializer, where `systemName` is the name of the symbol you want to use. That's why having the SF Symbols app is so convenient so you can browse through your options and know what names to call. An example would look like this:

```
let symbol = UIImage(systemName: "square.and.arrow.up")
```

There is also the `fill` version:

```
let symbolFill = UIImage(systemName:
"square.and.arrow.up.fill")
```

These would produce symbols that look like (Figure 25.6)

Figure 25.6

If you're browsing through the SF Symbols Mac app and you find a symbol you want to use, select the symbol and you can go to `Edit` > `Copy Name`. Or use the keyboard shortcut shift + command + C. Provide the name to the `UIImage(systemName:)` initializer and you can use the image on any `UIImageView` or `UIButton`.

We demonstrated how to initialize an image with the symbol's name, and the options of `regular` or `fill`. Now, let's look at how to change the weight of the symbol.

UIImage contains a property called `SymbolConfiguration` that can take a variety of arguments. We are going to use the `weight` argument and change the symbol to `bold`. First make a variable to hold the configuration, then when we initialize the symbol image we will pass in our configuration.

```
let config = UIImage.SymbolConfiguration(weight: .bold)

let symbol = UIImage(systemName: "square.and.arrow.up",
withConfiguration: config)
```

When we create `symbol`, we pick the initializer with the `systemName:` and `withConfiguration:` arguments. Pretty easy right? But what if we want more than one option in our configuration?

We can use the `applying` method on our `config` variable to combine multiple configurations. Let's make a `large semibold` symbol using the `applying` method.

```
  let largeConfig =
UIImage.SymbolConfiguration(scale: .large)

  let semiboldConfig =
UIImage.SymbolConfiguration(weight: .semibold)

  let joinedConfig =
largeConfig.applying(semiboldConfig)
```

```
let symbol = UIImage(systemName:
"square.and.arrow.up", withConfiguration: joinedConfig)
```

One thing to keep in mind is that any configuration you apply to another will override the original value if they contain the same argument. So a `boldWeightConfig.applying(thinWeightConfig)` would end up with just the `thinWeightConfig` since they are both modifying the `weight` argument.

Coloring Your Symbols

The color of the symbols will inherit the `tintColor` of the UIImageView or UIButton that holds the symbol. If you want to guarantee its color, you can use the `withTintColor` method on the symbol.

```
let redHeart = UIImage(systemName:
"heart.fill")?.withTintColor(.systemRed,
renderingMode: .alwaysOriginal)
```

Figure 25.7

Symbols In iOS 12 and Below

Unfortunately you can't use the `UIImage(systemName:)` initializer in anything below iOS 13. In order to use symbols, you simply need to download them from the SF Symbols Mac app and add them to your projects `.xcassets` file.

SF Symbols will greatly speed up any project's design and development time with their variety of options and configurations. Browse the app and look no further for pixel perfect symbols.